THE
COMPLETE WORKS
IN
VERSE AND PROSE
OF
SAMUEL DANIEL.
VOL. I.

Samuel Daniel

Engraved by W. J. Alais from the original by Cookson.

THE
COMPLETE WORKS

IN

VERSE AND PROSE

OF

SAMUEL DANIEL.

*EDITED, WITH MEMORIAL-INTRODUCTION AND A GLOSSARIAL
INDEX EMBRACING NOTES AND ILLUSTRATIONS.*

BY THE

REV. ALEXANDER B. GROSART,

D.D., LL.D. (EDIN.), F.S.A. (SCOT.),

St. George's, Blackburn, Lancashire;

IN FIVE VOLUMES.

VOL. I.

87

New York

RUSSELL & RUSSELL

1963

First Published in 1885 and
Reissued in 1963 by Russell & Russell, Inc.,
in an Edition Limited to 400 Sets
L. C. Catalog Card No: 63–15155

PRINTED IN THE UNITED STATES OF AMERICA

TO

LEWIS MORRIS, Esq.,

The Poet of

"Songs of Two Worlds," "Epic of Hades," "Songs Unsung,"
etc., etc., etc.

I dedicate this first collective and critical edition of the Works of Samuel Daniel.

SEER AND SAGE—SAMUEL AND DANIEL—
  UNITED IN HIS NAME WHOSE WORKS I BRING,
  MORRIS, TO THEE. SO WITS OF OLD WOULD RING
QUAINT CHANGES ON A NAME THEY LOVED FULL WELL.
NOR LESS OWN WE TO-DAY THE DULCET SPELL
  LAID ON US BY HIS OLD-WORLD CAROLLING:
  THOUGHT-LADEN, YET OF SINGER THAT DOES SING;
HALF O' THE EARTH, HALF O' THE SKY,—AS BELL
  IN CHURCH-TOWER HEARD FAINT ACROSS MOOR OR MERE.
I LOVE THIS GENTLE SPIRIT, MAN AND BARD;
  I WOULD NOT HAVE HIS WREATH GROW DIM OR SERE:
TRUE POET OF OUR AGE, LET THY REGARD
    SANCTION MY WORK OF LOVE, AS WITH STOOP'D KNEE
    I HONOUR HIM, AND SEEK TO HONOUR THEE.

Alexander B. Grosart.

CONTENTS.

ILLUSTRATIONS IN VOL. I.

PREFATORY NOTE.

MY rule in reproducing the WORKS of SAMUEL DANIEL has been, as throughout, to furnish the unmutilated, untampered-with text of the Author. I hold with deepened conviction that modernisations, improvements (so called), and arbitrary accommodation to modern syntax, orthography, punctuation, and the like, vitiate any classic, and render it impossible to trace the growth and gradual enrichment of our national Literature. I simply correct self-evidencing misprints—*e.g.*, p. 264, st. 3, l. 7, 'sparkling' for 'sprakling'; p. 265, st. 7, l. 4, 'veines' for 'weaues'; st. 8, l. 7, 'ouer-sowne' for 'ouer-swone'; and occasionally (,) comma for (.) period in middle of an unfinished sentence, and (;) semicolon for (,) comma—nothing more. Prefixed or affixed in their several places, the sources of the successive poems, etc., will be found recorded. I have also taken pains in noting 'various readings' wherever they occur. The value and interest of these are specially illustrated in the 'Delia' Sonnets.

As with SPENSER, 'Notes and Illustrations' are reserved for the Glossarial - Index in the closing volume. Toward them I have the pleasure and satisfaction of promised aid from various capable and sympathetic fellow-workers on our elder Poets and Dramatists. In the same volume, the ' Memorial-Introduction II.—Critical ' will be given, with the completed text before the reader for reference. Therein tributes paid to " well-languaged Daniel," earlier and recent, may be looked for ; also evidence of his influence from SHAKESPEARE to WORDSWORTH and COLERIDGE. Meantime, if the ' Memorial-Introduction I.— Biographical '—though fuller than any hitherto —is far from being so matterful as I should have wished, it has not been from lack of search or research, or willing helpers. It is infinitely pathetic to find how very little the world knows of its most elect spirits.

It is with no ordinary satisfaction I furnish a dainty reproduction (by Alais) of the portrait of our Worthy—after that in the quarto of 1623— in all the four forms ; and underneath it a fac simile of his autograph from the Letter given in fac-simile (in the largest paper only) from H.M. Public Record Office. I owe thanks to the authorities there for facilitating the fac-simile being taken.

I am not without a hope of adding to our knowledge of Daniel as the Works proceed, as various friends are following up lines of inquiry.

ALEXANDER B. GROSART.

ST. GEORGE'S VESTRY, BLACKBURN, LANCASHIRE,
    26th March, 1885.

MEMORIAL-INTRODUCTION I.—
BIOGRAPHICAL.

DANIEL and Daniell, Danyel and Danyell (and other variants) is a not infrequent surname in England, earlier and later. But there is a tantalizing absence of connecting links, as of anything in any way notable: *e.g.*, the Calendars of State Papers, somewhat preceding and contemporary with our "sweet Singer," bring up a contentious John Daniel and his wife in weary iteration of complaint and appeal*—all long since passed into silence—together with others of the name, but without recognisable relationship between them. Certain Cornwall Daniels appear to have migrated from the "Low Countries," albeit it is just possible that originally they had passed as Merchant-adventurers to 'Middleburg' from Cornwall.† Others are met with in Cheshire and several southern English counties.

The various authorities—Anthony à-Wood to Nightingale and Collinson—unite in describing our Poet as

* 'Calendars,' 1566 to 1618, *et alibi*.

† In *Gentleman's Magazine*, 1826 (vol. xcvi., P. i., pp. 130-2), is an interesting account of Daniels at Penzance in the reign of James I. His father was 'Depute-Governor' at Middleborough (Brabant) in 1613, and the Diarist of this paper notifies that he himself had been born there in 1599.

son of a JOHN DANIEL, a 'music-master'; and upon
this Thomas Fuller writes—"his harmonious mind made
an impression on his son's genius, who proved an
exquisite poet," and again characteristically on Christian
and surname—"He carried in his Christian and surname
two holy prophets, his monitors, so to qualify his
raptures that he abhorred all profaneness" (*Worthies :*
by Nuttall [1840], iii. 104). No one appears to have
traced a 'musical' John Daniel, except the brother of
the name. I am inclined to query whether the fraternal
John Daniel has not been split into two John Daniels.
Certes, the brother, has left tangible evidence that he
was a 'music-master,'* whilst of the father as such
nothing has been transmitted. Anthony à-Wood
(*Athenæ Oxoniensis,* by Bliss, *s.n.*) has designated Samuel
as sprung of "a wealthy family." 'Wealth' was unlikely
to belong to a 'music-master.' Unfortunately the
County Historians in all their big books yield no speck
of light on this or aught else—merely perfunctorily
repeating after Wood, Fuller, Biographia Britannica
(Kippis), Chalmers' Biographical Dictionary, etc., etc.

There is a shadow of uncertainty on his birth-place.
According to Anthony à-Wood he was born at Beckington, near Philip's Norton (Somerset) ; but the
historian apparently confused his burial-place with his
birth-place. The Parish Register of Beckington goes back
to 1559; but there is no recorded baptism of any Daniel
there until 1567 (as onward). This is decisive on Wood's

---

* Dr. Rimbault, in *Notes and Queries* (1853), No. 179,
records John Daniel's *Songs for the Lute, Viol, and Voice,*
1606, and that his name occurs among the Musicians for the
Lutes and Voices in a Privy Seal of Dec. 20, 1625.

mistake (Rev. J. L. Sainsbury, M.A., rector of Beckington, to me). Le Neve* assigns it to "Wilmington, in
Wiltshire, neare the Plaine of Salisburie." Unfortunately
the earliest-dated Parish-register entry at Wilmington is
1688. Dr. Thomas Fuller, with an express note that he
had been 'certified' of this by "some of his acquaintance,"
states that he was born "not far from Taunton (Somerset-
shire)." The 'acquaintance' cannot have been very
intimate, as they were unable to inform him of either
the date or place of his death. Again, unluckily, the
Parish Registers of St. James's, Taunton (which at the
period might have been accurately described as 'near'
or 'nigh' Taunton), commence only in 1610. That of
St. Mary's, Taunton, commencing before our Daniel's
period, has no Daniel entry whatever.†

As his contemporaries have celebrated him as a
'Somerset' man,‡ we may safely assume that Le Neve
was misinformed about Wilmington having been his
birth-place, and that Fuller was correct in assigning it
to "not far from Taunton." Surely some Somerset
antiquary will 'take trouble' and elucidate the point.
Ad interim, I judge not Taunton itself but (probably)
some near-adjoining hamlet was the birth-place ; per-
chance in Taunton Dean, "a parcel of ground round
about Taunton," renowned in a still current proverb.§

* Lansdowne MSS. 983 f. 343.
† The Rev. Samuel Wilkinson, and Arthur Kinglake, Esq.,
J.P., Taunton, did their utmost to get at *data*; in vain thus far,
save above.
‡ See 'Memorial-Introduction II. — Critical' for various
notices.
§ "Where should I be born else than in Taunton Dean—
with soil so rich that zun (= sun) and zoil (= soil) are all
needed?"—*i.e.* no manure.

Somewhat somnolent Somerset has the distinction of
having produced earlier, Hooper the martyr-bishop and
Sir James Dyer, Lord Chief Justice, Sir John Harington
and Blake and Pym; and later, Bishop Bull, Ralph
Cudworth, John Locke, and Henry Fielding; but no
recognised Poet except Samuel Daniel (Thomas Coryat
not in the running). It is about time Somerset erected
some memorial of "well-languaged Daniel"?

The year birth-date was 1562 or 1563. This is arrived
at from his entry as 'commoner' in Magdalen Hall,
Oxford. This was in 1579, when he was in his seventeenth
year; which carries us back to 1562-3. He was thus
about a decade of years younger than Spenser (1553)
and Sir Philip Sidney (1554), two or three years or
thereby younger than Robert Greene ('about 1560'), and
a little older than Shakespeare (1564), and Thomas Nashe
(1564), and nearly contemporaneous with Michael
Drayton (1563).

Of his preparatory education nothing whatever is
known. He is alleged to have had an 'excellent tutor'
at famous Magdalen. But according to Anthony à-Wood
his 'geny' having inclined him rather to lighter studies, he
remained under academic training for only "three years,"
and finally left the University—as did Philip Massinger
—"without a degree" (Wood, as before). This brings
us to 1582 or 1583. Wood's full account is :—

"He continued about three years, and improved himself much
in academical learning, by the benefit of an excellent tutor.
But his geny being more prone to easier and smoother studies,
than in pecking and hewing at logic, he left the university
without the honour of a degree, and exercised it much in
English history and poetry, of which he then gave several
ingenious specimens" (*Ath. Oxon.*, by Bliss, ii. 268).

But though he thus left Oxford, he must have continued his scholarly studies and bookish habits, seeing that in 1584-5 there was published the following considerable book : —

The

Worthy tract of

Paulus Iouius, contayning a

Difcourfe of rare inuentions, both

Militarie and Amorous

called Imprefe.

Whereunto is added a Preface contay-
ning the Arte of compofing them, with
many other notable deuifes.
By Samuel Daniell, late Student
in Oxenforde.

At London,
Printed for Simon Waterfon.
1585.

In succession to the Translator's own Epistle-dedicatory of the 'Worthy Tract' to "The right worshipful, Sir Edward Dimmock, Champion to her Maiestie," is a lengthy Epistle "To his good friend Samvel Daniel" by an (unknown) N. W. from 'Oxenforde,' wherein many well-turned compliments are paid to the young scholar, closing thus:—

"Thus am I bold to animate and encourage you to your credite, which if I haue done to long, so vppon occasion did Tullio, Plato, Seneca : if rudely, ascribe it to simplicitie : if slightly, to the rarenes of your arte : if to copiously, to too feruent desire : for seeing that *in verbis est aliquod prœmium*, I had rather shewe myself to prodigall to my friends then a snudge : which when you haue read, fier it."

In his "Defence of Rhyme," which was addressed to Philip Herbert, Earl of Pembroke, we get a pleasant glimpse of his position from (probably) 1585 onward·

He is defending his love of 'rhyme' in verse against
Campion's heresy of hexameters, and thus acknowledges
his obligations to his patron's mother—

> " Sidney's sister, Pembroke's mother ":—

> " Hauing been first encouraged and framed thereunto by
> your most worthy and honourable mother, and receiud the
> first notion for the formal ordering of these compositions, at
> Wilton, which I must euer acknowledge to haue been my best
> school, and thereof always am to hold a feeling and a grateful
> memory.   Afterwards, drawn farther on by the well-liking and
> approbation of my worthy lord, the fosterer of me and my muse,
> I adventured to bestow all my powers therein, perceiuing it
> agreed so well both with the complexion of the times, and my
> own constitution, as I found not wherein I might better
> employ me."

This seems to warrant us in concluding that upon
leaving Oxford he was introduced to the 'charmed
circle' of Wilton ; albeit John Morris (in his Biographical Introduction to his " Selections " from Daniel)
thus put it :—

> " This may have been the case ; but a closer examination
> will perhaps show his meaning to be, that in the first place he
> felt a grateful obligation to the Countess of Pembroke, for his
> having, through her kindness and encouragement, gained his
> earliest acquaintance with the delights of literature at Wilton,
> *his best school* ; and that, in the next place, under the patronage
> of the Earl, he was *drawn further on*, or enabled to prosecute
> higher studies at the University.   If this be his meaning, then
> it will appear that, while yet *young*, he had obtained the notice,
> and was favoured with the patronage, of Sidney's sister, the
> excellent Countess of Pembroke " (p. xiv).

The thing cannot be dogmatically pronounced upon
under our dim light, but in my judgment he is con-
trasting the after-delights at Wilton as his ' best school '

with the (to him) dry-as-dust studies of Oxford that he had escaped from. This later date of residence at Wilton seems further strengthened by the headings of two of the 'Delia' Sonnets which inform us that he went to Italy; and it has been the unvarying tradition that he went thither with a Herbert. Besides, it is in relation to the same Sonnets and kindred poems—from 1590-1 onward—that he pays glowing homage to the illustrious Mary, Countess of Pembroke.* It is pleasant even at this late day to indulge the Pleasures of Imagination in a vision of young Samuel Daniel pursuing his poetical and other cultured studies at Wilton, while Sir Philip Sidney's death was still a recent memory (1586).

It was in 1591 that Samuel Daniel first came before the world as a Poet. This he did by the semi-furtive publication of twenty-seven of his Love-sonnets by Thomas Nashe in his famous edition of Sidney's *Astrophel* and *Stella*, 'edited' by this fiery Free-lance of our Literature (see 'Note' before 'Delia'). This led to his own publication of the series of Sonnets addressed (mainly) to 'Delia' in 1592. This first (authoritative) edition was followed by a second in the same year. A third appeared in 1594.

I do not suppose it is likely now that we shall ever know who 'Delia' was. But I for one recognize in these Sonnets a human passion, and not mere 'sportive wit' or 'idle play.' The grief grows o'times monotonous and even grotesque, but ever and anon there comes the genuine 'cry' of a man's heart in suspensive anguish. He is by no means a strong man—contrariwise reveals

---

* See Glossarial-Index, *s.n.*, for full notices of all the 'fair women' and 'brave men' celebrated by Daniel.

a good deal of valetudinarian sentimentalism; yet is there reality of 'love,' and not simply rhyme-craft.

Elsewhere (viz., in Note before 'Delia' and beneath the successive Sonnets) I record the variations of the several editions of 'Delia.' *At this point* it seems expedient to notice one Sonnet that is found in the first edition alone of 1592. It opens the series. It is headed simply 'To M. P.' John Morris (as before), as have others, explains, "the initials evidently stand for *Mary*, Countess of *Pembroke*" (p. 1). But this cannot be. For (*a*) How should he have used initials only in 1592, and given the name in full in 1594 ('Delia')? (*b*) Can we conceive such a liberty as a dependant thus using the simple initials M. P.? (*c*) It has been overlooked that in N. W.'s Epistle before 'Paulus Jovius' (1585) an unmistakable reference is made to 'M. P.' as a common friend and a MAN, thus :—

"A frend of mine whom you know, M. P., climing for an *Egles* nest but defeated by the mallalent of fortune, limned in *his* studie a *Pine* tree striken with lightning, carying this mot, Il mio sperar . . . . Yet in despight of fortune *he* deuised a Pinnace or small Barke, tossed with tempestuous stormes, and on the saile was written *expectanda dies*, hoping as I think for one sunne shine day to recompence so many gloomy and winter monethes."

Who this M. P. was it is vain to conjecture; but the tone of the opening Sonnet of the 1592 volume utters personal disappointment and "want" and "care."

His 'journeying' to Italy being celebrated in the 'Delia' of 1592 dates it prior to that year. We know not how long or short before. The 47th Sonnet of 1594 is headed "At the Authors going into Italie," and the 48th "This Sonnet was made at the Authors being in

Italy "* (see present vol., pp. 71, 72). More interesting
still—and hitherto strangely overlooked—his Verses on
the translation of 'Pastor Fido' (see 'Occasional Poems'
in the present volume) seem to make a personal reference
to a conversation with Guarini, wherein the Italian
depreciated the "English tongue." 'Pastor Fido' first
appeared in 1590. This fact will require fuller after-
notice (in 'Memorial-Introduction II.—Critical'). The
publication of the Sonnets to 'Delia' made him 'famous'
at a bound. He was in all men's mouths. He was a
new voice in the heaven of English Song. Surrey and
Wyatt had now an 'heir.' If thinner in substance,
these Sonnets have finer literary form than theirs. His
'Verses commendatory'—as given in 'IX. Occasional
Poems' in the present volume—testify that speedily his
word went a long way to win public notice.

His 'Complaint of Rosamond' accompanied the
'Delia' Sonnets from the outset, and contained a
memorable reference to his 'lady-love.' Between 1591-2
and 1600—wherever located—he must have burned the
midnight oil over his Verse. The 1594 'Delia' was
accompanied by 'Cleopatra,' a tragedy. In 1595
appeared the 'First Foure Bookes of the Ciuill Wars.'
In 1599 was issued 'The Poeticall Essayes of Sam.
Danyell, newly corrected and augmented.' This added
a fifth Book to the 'Ciuil Wars.' In 1600-1 he prepared his folio of the 'Works of Samuel Daniel, newly
augmented.' This fine volume was primarily printed
for gift-copies or private circulation. Some copies have
special dedicatory poems prefixed (see pp. 4—9 of the

* To Mr. J. Payne Collier belongs the praise of having first
observed these headings.

present volume). In 1600 he was engaged as tutor to
the (afterwards) renowned Lady Ann Clifford, then in
her eleventh year.   Dr. Whitaker in his 'Craven' (by
Morant, vol. i., pp. 386-7), thus writes :—

   "Among the papers at Skipton Castle I met with an original
book of accounts, filled with memoranda, relating to this lady's
education from 1600 to 1602.   In the beginning is the following prayer, intended, I suppose, to be used on entering the
church—

   'O Lord, increase o'r fayth, and make us euermore attentyve hearers,
true conceiuers, and diligent fulfillers, of thy heauenly will.'

And after—

> 'To wish and will it is my part,
> To you, good lady, from my hart,
> The yeares of Nestor God you send,
> With hapynes to your life's end !'

These lines are, I think, in the handwriting of Samuel Daniel,
her tutor ; and when compared with the future history and
long life of this young lady, then only eleven years old, it
cannot be denied that their prayer was heard.   She actually
saw ninety years wanting only three, and the 'happiness' of
the last thirty had no abatement to her 'life's end.'"

A still more noteworthy memorial of this tutorship is
extant in his verse-address to his fair and precocious
pupil.   It is after the type of his friend Fulk Greville,
Lord Brooke's philosophic poetry, more thought-laden
than wrought.   He must have had a prescient discern-
ment of the strength and intellectual capacity of young
'Lady Anne' (see present vol., p. 213).   Doubtless his
post at Appleby and Skipton had its pleasantnesses,
and the Lady through life held her tutor in grateful
memory—as witness his being introduced into a great
family picture (still preserved), and his 'Whole Works
in Verse' being placed along with Spenser's on

bookshelves introduced into the background, and his monument at Beckington. None the less his Letter to the Lord Chancellor Egerton has these unsatisfied words—

"Such hath been my misery, that whilst I should have written the actions of *men*, I haue been constrayned to liue with *children*, and contrary to myne owne spirit, putt out of that scene which nature had made my parte" (the present vol., p. 10).

From this memorandum it would seem that Daniel relinquished his tutorship in 1602, in which year first appeared Book VI. of the 'Civil Wars.' He had been 'at Court' toward the close of the foregoing century. There is a kind of vague tradition that Elizabeth appointed him 'Laureate' on the death of Spenser (in 1599). I find no evidence of this. But his 'Panegyrike' to King James must have been composed off-hand and as speedily printed (privately)—seeing that copies are found bound up in the folio of 1601—though it does not appear to have been formally or publicly delivered until 1603 in Rutlandshire, as the heading bears (present vol., p. 141). He is most uncourtlily plain-spoken in his 'Panegyrike'; and the King and Queen (Ann) deserve all credit for not taking offence. With all his faults and failings, the new king was in sympathy (in the beginning at any rate), with learning and genius. Equally manly was his splendid verse-epistle to Henry, Earl of Southampton. The Queen must have 'taken' to him right cordially. Whether his office was 'at pleasure' or by a verbal understanding, he was called upon from time to time to prepare 'Masks' and quasi-theatrical entertainments—as his 'Dramatic' productions show, *e.g.*, "Tethys' Festival" and the "Vision of the Twelve

Goddesses," and "Hymen's Triumph" and "Queen's
Arcadia." He must have been frequently at Court,
and in intimate association with the royal family and
nobility. Latterly he was eclipsed by "rare Ben" (who
was surly and malignant toward him), and in his
melancholy wrote "bitter things" against himself. His
self-depreciation, if it be painful, is not without touch
of grotesquerie. He grew weary of 'high life,' and
secluded himself. Thomas Fuller quaintly describes
his periodic retreats thus :—

"As the tortoise burieth himself all the winter in the ground,
so Mr. Daniel would be hid at his garden house in Old Street,
near London, for some months together (the more retiredly to
enjoy the company of the Muses); and then would appear in
public to converse with his friends, whereof Dr. Cowel and
Mr. Camden were principal" (*Worthies*, as before).

Spite of these retirements, he was a keen observer from
his "loophole of retreat," and could express himself
incisively. Thus his Tragedy of " Philotas " had been
misapplied to the brilliant but unfortunate Earl of
Essex. Thereupon the Author added a spirited ' Vin-
dication ' to the play—'spirited,' yet after all we had
rather have had it unwritten. And not only so, but it
having reached him that his patron-friend, the Earl of
Devonshire (' Stella's ' lord), was displeased with his use
of his name, he addressed to this nobleman (in 1604) a
striking Letter, as follows : *—

    " My Lorde,
        "Vnderstanding yoᵣ lo: is displeased wᵗ mee, it hath
more shaken my harte then I did thinke any fortune could

---

* See fac-simile from the original in H.M. Public Record
Office, in post 4to copies of the present volume, in this place.

have donne in respect I have not deservd it, nor donne or
spoken any thing in this matter of Philotas vnworthy of yo^u
or mee. And now having fully satisfyde my L. of Cranborne,
I crave to vnburthen me of this imputation w^t yor ho: and it is
the last suite I will euer make. And therefore I beseach yo^u
to vnderstand all this great erro^r I have cōmitted.

"first I tolde the Lordes I had written 3 Acts of this
tragedie the Christmas before my L. of Essex troubles, as
diuers in the cittie could witnes. I saide the maister of the
Revells had p'vsed it. I said I had read some parte of it to yor
ho: and this I said having none els of powre to grace mee now
in Corte & hoping y^t yo^u out of yo^{r}knowledg of bookes, or
fauo^r of letters & mee, might answere that there is nothing in
it disagreeing nor any thing, as I protest there is not, but out
of the vniuersall notions of ambition and envie, the p'petuail
argum^{ts} of bookes or tragedies. I did not say yo^u incouraged
me vnto the p'senting of it; yf I should I had beene a villayne,
for y^t when I shewd it to yor hono^r I was not resolud to haue
had it acted, nor should it haue bene had not my necessities
ouermaistred mee. And therefore I beseach yo^u let not now
an Earle of Devonsh^r ouerthrow what a L. Mountioy hath
donne, who hath donne me good and I haue donne him
hono^r : the world must, or shall know myne innocencie whilst
I haue a pen to shew it, and for y^t I know I shall liue inter
historiam temporis as well as greater men, I must not be such
an abiect vnto my self as to neglect my reputation, and having
bene knowne throughout all England for my virtue, I will not
leave a stayne of villanie vppon my name whatsoeuer erro^r els
might skape me vnfortunately thorow myne indiscreation, &
misvnderstanding the tyme : wherein good my L. mistake not
my harte that hath bene & is a syncere honorer of yo^u and
seekes yo^u now for no other end but to cleare it self, and to be
held as I ame (though I neuer more come nere yo^u)

"Yo^r hono^{rs}

"pore follower & faithfull Servant,

"SAMUEL DANYEL."

He was early in 1603-4 given charge in some way of
the Theatre in connection with the licensing of 'Plays':

e.g., in the Calendars of State Papers under "January 31, 1604," we read :—

"Grant to Edward Kirkham, Alexander Hawkins, Thos. Kendall and Robert Payne, of license to train up children, to be called 'Children of the Reuels to the Queen,' and to exercise them in playing within the Blackfriars in London, or elsewhere; *all plays to be allowed by Sam. Danyell*" (p. 72).

This must have been a permanent function and post, for under "July 10, 1615," we find the following :—

"Sir Geo. Buck to John Packer, Secretary to the Lord Chamberlain Somerset. The King has been pleased at the mediation of the Queen *on behalf of Sam. Danyell*, to appoint a company of youths to perform comedies and tragedies at Bristol, under the name of the Youths of Her Majesty's Royal Chamber of Bristol. Has consented to it as being without prejudice to the rights of his office " (p. 294).

The late Mr. J. Payne Collier and Peter Cunningham have other entries and notes ; but the forgeries of the former, and the unreliableness of the latter, compel me to leave them unutilized. The biographic fact to be accentuated is that he had (in Fuller's words) "a fair salary " from Queen Ann as "servant in ordinary."   His own language is unmistakable in his verse-address " To her sacred Maiestie "—

" I who by that most blessed hand sustain'd,
    In quietnes, do eate the bread of rest :
    And by that all-reuiuing powre obtain'd
    That comfort which my Muse and me hath blest."
                              (Present vol., p. 9.)

Later (1618) his theatrical office must have passed to his brother, John Daniel (Calendars, *s.n.*).

When he was married, and to whom, still remain unknown.   It has been stated—on the usual loose acceptance of inferential statements—that JOHN FLORIO married a sister of Daniel. But he had no sister, so far as appears.* The Poet's use of 'brother' in his Verses to him was as 'brother' scholar or writer, not as relative. Only the Christian name—a foreign-like one, as if brought from Italy—Justina, has come down to us. They had no issue.

Equally untraced has been the date of his withdrawal from town to the country. The fact of such withdrawal is thus put by Fuller :—

"In his old age he turned husbandman, and rented a farm in Wiltshire near to Devizes. I can give no account how he thrived thereupon; for though he was well versed in Virgil, his fellow-husbandman-poet, yet there is more required to make a good farmer than only to say the Georgics by heart ; and I question whether his Italian will fit on English husbandry. Besides, I suspect that Mr. Daniel's fancy was too fine and sublimated to be wrought down to his private profit. However, he had neither a *bank* of *wealth* nor a *bank of want*; being in a competent condition " (*Worthies*, as before).

Up to 1618—and so probably to the end—he was designated a Groom of the Privy Chamber to the Queen, as is seen in the royal licence then issued, which granted him the privilege of printing for his personal benefit his ' History of England.' In this licence he is described as "our well-beloued seruant Samuel Daniell, one of the Groomes of the Priuy Chamber, to our

* See our edition of Spenser, vol. iii., pp. lxxxviii—cii, "Who were Rosalinde and Menalcas ? " : also Bolton Corney's paper in *Notes and Queries*, 3rd S., viii., pp. 4, 35, etc. Though mistaken as to Bacon, Corney is certainly right as to Florio and Daniel. I am not aware that Florio had a sister whom Daniel might have married. In his Will there is no mention of a ' Justina ' by Florio.

deerest wife the Queen" (Rymer's *Fœdera*, vol. xvii., p. 22).

His 'farm' was near Beckington (Somerset)—where Daniels are found to have been resident *—and was named 'Ridge.' It is within hail of Bath—on the highway from Bath to Salisbury—and is still in a pleasant country. Here most probably he wrote his 'History.' Our final glimpse of him is in his Will, as follows : †—

"WILL OF SAMUEL DANIEL, THE POET.

"From the original in the Will Office of the Prerogative Court of Canterbury.

"I, Samuelis } In the name of God, Amen. I, Samuel Danyel, Danyell } sick in bodie but well in mynde, make heer my last will and testament.

"First, I comitt my soule unto God, trusting to be saved by the pretious blood and deathe of my Redeemer, Jesus Christe; and my body to the earth, to be interred in the parish church where I dye.

"Item, I bequeathe to my sister, Susan Bowre, one feather bed, and wth the furniture thearto belonging, and such lynnen as I shall leave at my house at Ridge.

"Item, I bequeathe to Samuel Bowre x^{li}.

"Item, to Joane Bowre x^{li}.

"Item, to Susan Bowre x^{li}.

"Item, to Mary Bowre x^{li}.

"For the disposing of all other things, I referre them to my faithfull brother, John Danyel, whome I here ordaine my sole executor, to whose care and conscience I comitt the performance thereof.

"And I likewise appoynt and ordayne my loving friend Mr. Simon Waterson, and my brother in lawe John Phillipps, to be

---

* The Parish Register, which begins in 1559, has a Thomas Daniell baptized in 1567, and an Editha Daniell in 1574.

† Shakspere Society Papers, iv., 156-8.

overseers of this my last will and testament, whereunto I have set my hand and seal. Dated the 4th daye of September 1619.

"SAMUEL DANYEL.

"Witnesses of this my last will and testament."
Umphery X Aldenes mark.
William X Wheatlyes mark.

The Will is written on one side of a sheet of foolscap paper, and signed by the poet himself in a neat but rather tremulous hand. The words "Witnesses of this my last will and testament," are also autograph.

He 'sleeps well' at Beckington. His 'pupil,' the Lady Anne, years after placed a mural monument within the Church. It still bears the following inscription :—

HERE LYES' EXPECTINGE THE SECOND COMMING OF OUR LORD & SAUIOUR JESUS CHRIST Y^E DEAD BODY OF SAMUELL DANYELL ESQ THAT EXCELLENT POETT AND HISTORIAN WHO WAS TUTOR TO THE LADY ANNE CLIFFORD IN HER YOUTH SHE THAT WAS SOLE DAUGHTER AND HEIRE TO GEORGE CLIFFORD ÆARLE OF CŪBERLAND WHO IN GRATITUDE TO HIM ERECTED THIS MONUMENT IN HIS MEMORY A LONG TIME AFTER WHEN SHE WAS COUNTESSE DOWAGER OF PEMBROKE DORSETT & MOŪTGOMERY. HE DYED IN OCTOBER 1619.

Such is the brief story of Samuel Daniel's 'Life.' *
The impression left on one, after pondering the facts, is that he was an infirm, over-sensitive man, physically

---

* Langbaine, *s.n.*, in his 'Lives and Characters of the *English Dramatick* Poets . . . . (1691)' blunders throughout in his account of Daniel—*e.g.*, he represents him as "weary of the world" and as "living . . . . till he was near eighty years old"!! (really 57). Wood's Ashmolean MSS. (quoted in Bliss's edition

and intellectually, though (as to Spenser) he led observers to conclude that he was capable of far greater things than ever he wrote. But for a ' Critical ' estimate of his work the Reader is respectfully asked to wait until our closing volume.

ALEXANDER B. GROSART.

of *Ath. Oxon.*, ii. 26) furnishes this singular note—" Sam. Daniel being for the most part *in animo* Catholicus, was at length desired to be openly a Roman Catholic ; but he denied, because that when he died he should not be buried in Westminster Abbey, and lie interred there like a Roman Catholic " —oracular and improbable. See 'Memorial-Introduction II.— Critical,' in our closing volume.

I.

INEDITED POEMS, ETC.

INTRODUCTORY TO THE

WORKS OF SAMUEL DANIEL.

FROM VARIOUS SOURCES.

1595—1623.

NOTE.

Examination of the successive issues (private or semi-private and published) of his Poems, reveals that Samuel Daniel was wont to insert special Dedications and Addresses in gift-copies of his books ; none of which are found in the Quarto of 1623, or known to Bibliographers or Editors : *e.g.*, in the 'Poeticall Essayes' of 1599 (but incorporating the first 'Foure Bookes' of the 'Ciuill Wars,' dated on title-page 1595) there is an overlooked Sonnet to Lord Mountjoy ; and again in successive exemplars of the 1601 folio of his 'Works' as 'newly augmented' there occur the following : (*a*) In the beautiful presentation-copy in the Bodleian there is prefixed a long and characteristic poem on its being deposited in the renowned library. (*b*) In the British Museum copy (C. 39, h. 23) there is a verse-dedication 'to her sacred Majestie' (= Anne, consort of James I.), which takes the place of the one in the Bodleian, neither having the other. (*c*) In the Bridgewater copy is an autograph letter to the 'Lord Keeper Egerton,' first published in *Censura Literaria* (vol. vi. 291-3) and later by the late Mr. J. Payne Collier. On this and another Letter printed by the latter, see our Memorial-Introduction. Further, in the little volume of 'Certaine Small Workes' of 1607 (not of 1611, as stated by the late Rev. Thomas Corser, M.A., 'Anglo-Poetica,' *s.n.*) is an extremely noticeable verse-address 'To the Reader,' which was revised for the re-issue of the same volume in 1611—the latter supplying a line that had been inadvertently dropped in 1607. Finally, John Daniel introduces the Quarto of 1623 with an Epistle-dedicatory to Charles I. Though some of these have mainly reference to the 'Ciuill Wars' poems, yet as being so placed as to be introductory to the Works, it has been deemed expedient to bring them together here. Accordingly the whole will be found in their places. Other inserted and withdrawn Poems—equally unknown with these—are also given in their places, and indicated in relative footnotes (IX. Occasional Poems in the present volume). It is just possible that other gift-copies, more especially of the 1601 folio, may yield other special Poems.

A. B. G.

I. TO THE RIGHT HONORABLE, SIR
Charles Blunt Knight, Lord *Mountioy*,
and Knight of the moſt Noble
order of the Garter, and his
moſt worthy Lord.[1]

DO not plant thy great reſpeeted name
    Here in this front, to th' end thou
       ſhouldſt proteet
    Theſe my endeuors from contempt
       or blame,
    Which none but their owne forces
       muſt effeet :
Nor do I ſeeke to win thy more reſpeet,   10
    Moſt learned Lord, by theſe Eſſaies of mine,
    Since that cleere iudgement that did firſt eleet
    To fauor me, will alwaies keepe me thine :
Nor do I this more honour to aſſigne,
    Vnto thy worth, that is not more hereby,
    Since th' offrings made vnto the powers deuine,
    Enrich not them, but ſhew mens pietie:
But this I do to th' end if deſtinie
    Shall any monument reſerue of me,
    Thoſe times ſhould ſee my loue, how willing I   20
    That liu'd by thee, would haue thee liue with me.
                           S. D.

[1] From "The Poeticall Eſſayes of Sam. Danyel. Newly corrected and
augmented. Aetas prima canat veneres, postrema tumultus. At London.
Printed by P. Short for Simon Waterson, 1599" (4°). "First Foure Bookes
of the Ciuill Wars," title-page 1595.

II.   S. D.
         TO HIS BOOKE,
In the Dedicating thereof to the Li-
    brarie in Oxford, erected by
         Sir Thomas Bodley
             Knight.[1]

Eere in this goodly Magazine of
    witte,
This Storehoufe of the choifeft
    furniture
The world doth yeelde, heer in this
    exquifite,
And moft rare monument, that
    dooth immure   10
The glorious reliques of the beft of men ;
Thou part imperfect worke, voutfafed art
A little roome, by him whofe care hath beene
To gather all what euer might impart
Delight or Profite to Pofteritie ;
Whofe hofpitable bountie heere receiues
Vnder this roofe powers of Diuinitie,
Inlodg'd in thefe transformed fhape of leaues.
For which good Worke his Memorie heere liues,
As th' holy guardian of this reuerent place,   20
Sacred to Woorth, being fit that hee which giues
Honour to others, fhould himfelfe haue grace.

¹ From the 'Works of Samuel Daniel newly augmented,' 1601 (folio), in the Bodleian.

And charitable BODLEY that hath thus
Done for the good of thefe, and other times,
Muft liue with them, and haue his fame with vs.
For well wee fee our groueling fortune climes
Vp to that fphere of glory, to be feene
From farre, by no courfe elfe, but by this way
Of dooing publique good ; this is the meane
To fhew we were, how fram'd, of what good clay.   30
For well we fee how priuate heapes (which care
And / greedy toyle prouides for her owne endes)
Doe fpeede with her fucceeders, and what fhare
Is left of all that ftore, for which it fpendes
It felfe, not hauing what it hath in vfe,
And no good t' others nor it felfe conferres :
As if that Fortune mocking our abufe
Would teach vs that it is not ours, but hers
That which we leaue : and if we make it not
The good of many, fhe will take that paine,   40
And re-difpers th' inclofed parcelles got
From many hands, t' in-common them againe.
Which might aduife vs, that our felues fhould doe
That worke with iudgement, which her blindneffe will,
And paffe a State which fhe cannot vndoe,
And haue th' affurance in our owne name ftill.
    For this is to communicate with men
That good the world gaue by focietie,
And not like beafts of prey, draw all to' our Den
T'inglut our felues, and our owne progenie.   50
This is to make our giftes immortall giftes,
And thankes to laft, whilft men, and bookes fhall laft ;
This heritage of glory neuer fhiftes
Nor changes Maifters ; what thou leau'ft thou haft.

The grounds, the lands, which now thou calleſt
    thine,
Haue had a thouſand lords that term'd them
    theirs,
And will be ſoone againe pent from thy line,
By ſome concuſſion, change, or waſtefull heires.
We can no perpetuitie collate
Vpon our race that euer will endure ;   60
It is the worlds demaines, whereof no ſtate
Can be by any cunning made ſo ſure,
But at the change of Lordes for all our paine,
It will returne vnto the world againe.
    And therefore did diſcreet Antiquitie,
Heere / (ſeeing how ill mens priuate cares did
    ſpeede),
Erect an euerlaſt[ing] Granery
Of Artes, the vniuerſall State to feede,
And made the worlde their heire, whereby their
    name
Holdes ſtill a firme poſſeſſion in the ſame.   70
O well giuen landes, wherein all the whole land
Hath an eternall ſhare ! where euery childe
Borne vnto Letters, may be bolde to ſtand
And claime his portion, and not be beguilde.
Happy erected walles whoſe reuerent piles
Harbour all commers, feede the multitude :
Not like the prowd-built pallace that beguiles
The hungry ſoule with empty ſolitude ;
Or onely raiſde for priuate luxurie
Stands as an open marke for Enuies view,   80
And being the purchaſe of felicitie
Is Fortunes in remainder, as her due.

But you, bleft you, the happy monuments
Of Charitie and Zeale, ftand and beholde
Thofe vaine expences, and are documents
To fhew what glory hath the fureft holde.
You tell thefe times, wherein kind Pietie
Is dead inteftate, and true noble Worth
Hath left no heire, that all things with vs die,   89
Saue what is for the common good brought forth.
   Which this iudicious Knight did truely note,
And therefore heere hath happily begunne
To fhew this age, that had almoft forgot
This way of glory, and thereby hath wonne
So much of Time, as that his memorie
Will get beyond it, and will neuer die.   96

III. To her sacred Maieſtie.[1]

EERE ſacred Soueraigne, glorious
    Queen of Peace,
    The tumults of diſordred times I
    ſing,
    To glorifie thy Raigne, and to in-
    creaſe
    The wonder of thoſe bleſſings thou
    dooſt bring
Vpon thy land, which ioyes th' intire releaſe
From bloud and ſorrowes by thy gouerning,
That through affliction we may ſee our ioyes
And bleſſe the glorie of Elizaes dayes.

Happier then all thy great Progenitors   10
That euer ſate vpon that powrefull Throne ;
Or all thy mightieſt neighbour-Gouernors,
Which wonder at the bleſſings of thy Crowne,
Whoſe Peace more glorious farre than all their
    warres,
Haue greater powres of admiration ſhowne ;
Receiue theſe humble fruites of mine increaſe,
Offered on th' Altare of thy ſacred Peace.

[1] From 1601 folio in British Museum.

I, who by that moſt bleſſed hand ſuſtain'd,
In quietnes, do eate the bread of reſt :
And by that all-reuiuing powre obtain'd   20
That comfort which my Muſe and me hath bleſt,
Bring here this worke of Warre, whereby was gain'd
This bleſſed Vnion which theſe wounds redreſt,
That ſacred Concord which prepar'd the way
Of glory for thee onely to enioy.

Whereto if theſe my Labors ſhall attaine,
And which, if Fortune giue me leaue to end,
It will not be the leaſt worke of thy Raigne,
Nor that which leaſt thy glory ſhall commend,
Nor ſhall I hereby vainely entertaine   30
Thy Land, with ydle ſhadowes to no end,
But by thy Peace, teach what thy bleſſings are,
The more t' abhorre this execrable warre.

IV. AN ORIGINAL LETTER OF SAMUEL
Danyel fent to Lord Keeper Egerton with
a prefent of his Works newly augmented, 1601, extant in the
Bridgewater Library.[1]

IGHT HONOURABLE,

Amongſt all the great workes
of your Worthynes, it will not be the
leaſt that you haue done for me in
the preferment of my brother, with 10
whome yet now fometimes I may
eat, whilſt I write, and ſo go on with
the worke I haue in hand which God knowes had long
fince been ended, and your Honour had had that
which in my haſte I haue prepared for you, could I
haue but fuſtayned myſelf, and made truce within, and
peace with the world.

But ſuch hath been my miſery, that whilſt I ſhould
haue written the actions of *men*, I haue been con-
ſtrayned to liue with *children*, and contrary to myne 20
owne ſpirit, putt out of that ſcene, which nature had
made my parte; for could I but liue to bring this
labour of mine to the Union of Henry, I ſhould haue
the end of all my ambition in this life, and the utmoſt
of my deſires; for therein, if wordes can work any

[1] From 'Censura Literaria,' vi., 291-3.

thing vppon the affections of men, I will labour to giue the beſt hand I can to the perpetuall cloſing vp of theſe woundes, and to my keeping them ſo, that our land may lothe to look ouer thoſe bleſſed boundes, which the prouidence of God hath ſet us, into the 30 horror and confuſion of further and former clymes: and though I know the greatnes of the worke require a greater ſpirit than myne, yet we ſee that in theas frames of motions, little wheels moue the greater, and ſo by degrees turne about the whole; and God knowes what ſo poore a muſe as myne may worke upon the affections of men.

But howeuer I ſhall herein ſhew my zeal to my country, and to do that which my ſoule tells me is fit; and to this end do I propoſe to retyre me to my pore 40 home, and not again to ſee you till I haue paid your Honor my voues; and will only pray that England, which ſo much needes you, may long enjoy the treaſure of your counſell, and that it be not driuen to complayne with that good Roman: *Videmus quibus extinctis jurisperitis, quam in paucis nunc ſpes, quam in paucioribus facultas, quam in multis audacia.*

And for this comfort I haue receiued from your goodness, I muſt and euer will remayne your Honour's in all &c.
50

I am, &c.,

SAMUEL DANYEL.

To the Rt. Hon. Sir Thomas Egerton,
    Knt., Lord Keeper of the Great
        Seale of England.

V. *To the Reaaer.*[1]

EHOLD once more with ferious labor here
Haue I refurnifht out this little frame,
Repaird fome parts defectiue here and there,
And paffages new added to the fame :
Some rooms inlargd, made fome les thē they were
Like to the curious builder who this yeare
Puls downe, and alters what he did the laft,
As if the thing in doing were more deere
Then being done, & nothing likes thats paft.   10
    For that we euer make the latter day
The fcholler of the former, and we find
Something is ftill amiffe that muft delay
Our bufines, and leaue worke for vs behinde,
As if there were no faboath of the minde.
And howfoeuer be it, well or ill
What I haue done, it is mine owne, I may
Do whatfoeuer therewithall I will.

[1] From "Certaine Small Workes Heretofore Divulged by *Samvel Daniel,* one of the Groomes of the *Queenes Maiefties Priuie Cham*-ber, & now againe by him *corrected and augmented.* Ætas prima canat veneres poftrema tumultus. At London. Printed by I. W. for *Simon Waterfon.* 1607." (12°).

I may pull downe, raife, and reedifie :
It is the building of my life, the fee   20
Of Nature, all th' inheritance that I
Shall leaue to thofe which muft come after me ;
And all the care I haue is but to fee
Thofe lodgings of m' affections neatly dreft,
Wherein fo many noble friends there be
Whofe memories with mine muft therein reft.
And glad I am that I haue liud to fee
This edifice renewd, who doo but long
To liue t' amend.   For man is a tree
That hath his fruite late ripe, and it is long   30
Before he come t' his tafte ; there doth belong
So much t' experience, and fo infinite
The faces of things are, as hardly we
Difcerne which lookes the likeft vnto right.

Befides thefe curious times, ftuf'd with the ftore
Of cōpofitions in this kind, to driue
Me to examine my defects the more,
And oft would make me not my felf belieue,
Did I not know the world wherein I liue :
Which neither is fo wife, as that would feeme   40
Nor certaine iudgement of thofe things doth giue
That it difliks, nor that it doth efteeme.

I know no work from man yet euer came
But had his marke, and by fome error fhewd
That it was his, and yet what in the fame
Was rare, and worthy, euermore allowd
Safe cōuoy for the reft : the good thats fow'd
Though rarely paies our coft, & who fo lookt
T' haue all thinges in perfection, & in frame
In mens inuentions, neuer muft read books.   50

And howfoeuer here detraction may
Difvalew this my labour, yet I know
There will be foūd therein, that which wil pay
The reckning for the errors which I owe,
And likewife will fufficiently allow
T' an vndiftafted iudgement fit delight,
And let prefumptuous felfe-opinion fay
The woorft it can, I know I fhall haue right.

I know I fhalbe read among the reft   60
So long as men fpeake englifh, and fo long
As verfe and vertue fhal be in requeft,
Or grace to honeft induftry belong :
And England fince I vfe thy prefent tongue,
Thy forme of fpeech, thou muft be my defēce
If to new eares it feemes not well expreft ;
For though I hold not accent I hold fence.

And fince the meafures of our tong we fee
Confirmd, by no edict of power doth reft
But onely vnderneath the regencie   70
Of vfe and fafhion, which may be the beft
Is not for my poore forces to conteft :
But as the Peacock, feeing himfelfe to weake,
Confeft the Eagle fairer farre to be,
And yet not in his feathers but his beake ;
Authoritie of powerfull cenfure may
Preiudicate the forme wherein we mould
This matter of our fpirite, but if it pay
The eare with fubftance, we haue what wee wold,
For that is all which muft our credit hold.   80
The reft (how euer gay, or feeming rich
It be in fafhion wife men will not wey),
The ftamp will not allowe it but the touch.[1]

[1] This line only in 1611 edition—dropped inadvertently in 1607.

And would to God that nothing falty were
But only that poore accent in my verfe,
Or that I could all other recknings cleere
Wherwith my heart ſtands charg'd, or might
　　reverſe
The errors of my iudgmēt paſſed here,
Or els where, in my bookes, and vnrehearce
What I haue vainely faid, or haue addreſt
Vnto neglect, miſtaken in the reſt. 90

Which I do hope to liue yet to retract
And craue that England neuer will take note
That it was mine.　Ile difauow mine act,
And wifh it may for euer be forgot.
I truſt the world will not of me exact
Againſt my will, that hath all els I wrote.
I will afke nothing therein for my paine
But onely to haue in mine owne againe. 99

TO THE HIGH AND MOST IL-
luſtrious Prince CHARLES *His Excellence.*[1]

SIR :

Reſents to gods were offered by the hands of graces ; and why not thoſe of great Princes, by thoſe of the Muſes ?   To you therefore Great Prince of Honor, and Honor of Princes ;   I ioyntly preſent Poeſie and Muſicke : in the one the ſeruice 10 *of my defunćt Brother, in the other, the duty of my ſelfe liuing, in both the deuotion of two Brothers, your High-nes Humble ſeruants.   Your Excellence then who is of ſuch recommendable fame, with all Nations, for the curioſity of your rare Spirit to vnderſtand, and ability of Knowledge to iudge of all things, I humbly inuite ; leauing the Songs of his Muſe, who liuing ſo ſweetly chanted the glory of your High Name : Sacred is the fame of Poets, Sacred the name of Princes ; To which*

Humbly bowes, and vowes   20
Himſelf, euer your
Highneſſe Seruant,
Iohn Daniel.

[1] From the ' Works ' of 1623 (4°).

THE
WHOLE
VVORKES OF

S AMVEL D ANIEL Eſquire
in Poetrie.

LONDON,
Printed by N ICHOLAS O KES , for
S IMON W ATERSON , and are to be
ſold at his ſhoppe in *Paules* Church-
yard, at the Signe of the Crowne.
1623.

☞ The title-page of the Quarto of 1623 is given on other side, as it is our foundation-text.   See Prefatory Note and Memorial-Introduction.—G.

II.

SONNETS TO DELIA.

1592.

NOTE.

The 'Sonnets to Delia' and 'Complaint of Rosamond,' as having been the Poet's first verse-publication, as well as perhaps his most abiding proofs of his faculty, take inevitably the foremost places in any critical reproduction of his Poems. The publication of the Sonnets was in a manner forced, if we are to credit the Author's statement in his preface to the first edition (1592). The reference is to the quasi-surreptitious edition of Sir Philip Sidney's 'Astrophel and Stella' of 1591, the "rascally bookseller" being Thomas Newman, and the editor no less than Thomas Nashe. To this now very rare volume were "added sundry other rare Sonnets of diuers Noblemen and Gentlemen." The larger proportion consists of twenty-seven of Daniel's Sonnets to Delia. Full details of these in the sequel of this Note.

The following is the original title-page, which is within a pretty wood-cut border :—

Delia.
Contayning certayne
Sonnets : with the
complaint of
Rofamond.
(∴)
§☞ *Aetas prima canat veneres*
poftrema tumultus.

AT LONDON.
Printed by I. C. for Si-
mon Waterfon, dwelling in
Paules Church-yard at
the figne of the Crowne.
1592.

On verso is this Note :—

To the Reader.

Gentle Reader, I pray thee correct thefe faultes
efcaped in the printing, finding them as they
are noted heere following.

    Sonnet 5. moſt unkindeſt, read ſweete unkindeſt.
    Sonnet 14. Yer leaſt, read Yet leaſt.
    Sonnet 20. deſires, read deſiers.
    Sonnet 36. yee, read yce
    Sonnet 41. her brow, read her troubled brow.
    Sonnet 44. tunres, read turnes.

The second edition was issued in the same year, though not so marked.
As the above errata are found corrected in it, we are guided to distinguish
it from the other, as second, not first. The following is its title-page, which is
within a somewhat poor architectural design, with two tiny miniatures in
top corners (a man and a woman), and flowers in the bottom corners. The
dove, = Hòly Spirit, is above in arch, and the legend Διος, etc. :—

ΔΙΟΣ ΑΙΓΙΟΧΙΟΝ
DELIA.

Containing
certaine Son-
nets : with the
complaynt of Ro-
ſamond.

Ætas prima ca-
nat veneres poſtre-
ma tumul-
tus.

———

1592
AT LONDON
Printed by J. C. for S.
Waterſonne.

Mr. W. Carew Hazlitt, in his " Bibliography of Old English Literature'
(*s.n.*), describes a third edition, also of 1592. There was none such. He
has confounded the actual first edition with the second, and mis-entered
the first, and made a third out of the second. He and others also prove to
be mistaken in asserting that an exemplar of the first edition (entered by
Hazlitt as second) is at Chatsworth. His Grace the Duke of Devonshire

informs me that no such book appears ever to have been in his library. Fortunately a perfect copy of the first and an only slightly imperfect copy of the second edition, exist in the Bodleian (Malone and Tanner books). A third edition, in a very charming little volume (18mo), was published in 1594. Its title-page, within a miniature copy of the title-page of 1592, second edition, is as follows :

DELIA
and
ROSAMOND
augmented.

CLEOPATRA.

———

By
Samuel Daniel.

———

*Ætas prima ca-
nat veneres poſtre-
ma tumul-
tus.*

———

1594.
Printed at London for *Simon Waterſon*, and
are to be ſold in Paules Church-yarde at the
ſigne of the Crowne.

On verso of Sonnet to Countess of Pembroke :—

Gentle Reader correct theſe
faultes eſcaped in the
printing.

Sonnet 18. lyne 3. for error, reade terror.
G 1. page 2. for Condemning, read Conducting,
In L. page 16. Marke the Speaker, and read thus

The iuſtice of the heauens reuenging thus,
Doth onely ſatiſſie it ſelfe, not vs.

In the laſt chorus, for care, reade cure.

A careful collation shows that these three editions were all Daniel himself supervised throughout. Later texts give a few isolated and verbal changes, but the little volume of 1594 was evidently meant to be the ultimate text. Accordingly, at the bottom of each page of our edition of the 'Sonnets to Delia,' there are furnished the various readings and other alterations of these three editions, respectively designated [1], [2], [3];

and also such as occur in the folios of the 'Works' of 1601 and 1602 (quite distinct), these again being designated respectively ⁴, ⁵. It is to be understood that wherever ⁴, ⁵ are not adduced they agree with our own foundation-text of 1623. It has been my anxious endeavour to record everything in any way noticeable, not however noting all mere orthographic changes or minor punctuations. The following table gives the contents and varying arrangement of the five editions named :—

1592—FIRST EDITION.

I. Title and errata (verso).
II. Prose-epistle to Countess of Pembroke.

Sonnet 1. Vnto... so 1594, 1601, and 1602.
    2. Goe...   ,,   ,,
    3. If...   ,,   ,,
    4. Thefe...   ,,   ,,
    5. Whilft...   ,,   ,,
    6. Faire...   ,,   ,,
    7. O had fhe...   ,,   ,,
    8. Thou poore...   ,,   ,,
    9. If thus...   ,,   ,,
    10. O then...   ,,   ,,
    11. Teares...   ,,   ,,
    12. My fpottes...   ,,   ,,
    13. Behold...   ,,   ,,
    14. Thofe amber...   ,,   ,,
    15. If that...   ,,   ,,
    16. Happie...   ,,   ,,   [and 17 is 18.
    17. Since... in 1594 and 1601-2, 17 Why fhould I fing,
    18. Reftore... in 1594 is 19   19 and 20 in ⁴, ⁵ What, etc.
    19. If Beautie...   ,,   20   21 in ⁴, ⁵.
    20. Come death...   ,,   21   22   ,,
    21. Thofe forrowing...   ,,   22   24   ,,
    22. Falfe hope...   ,,   23   25   ,,
    23. Looke...   ,,   24   26   ,,
    24. If I in vaine...   ,,   28—not in ⁴, ⁵.
    25. Raigne...   ,,   25   27 in ⁴, ⁵.
    26. Whilft...   ,,   26   27 is 27 of ², and 28 in ⁴, ⁵.
    27. The ftarre...   ,,   29   31 in ⁴, ⁵.
    28. Rayfing...   ,,   30 And yet... 28 is 31, and in ⁴, ⁵
    29. O why...   ,,   32   34 in ⁴, ⁵.   [is 33.
    30. I once...   ,,   33   35   ,,

Sonnet 31. Looke...   in 1594 is 34   36 in ⁴, ⁵.
        32. But loue...   „   35   37   „   [xxxiii.)
        33. When...   „   36   38   „   (but   misprinted
        34. When Winter...   „   37   38 [*sic*].
        35. Thou canſt...   „   38   39 is 40 in ⁵.
        36. O be not...   „   39   41 in ⁴, ⁵.
        37. Delia...   „   40   42   „
        38. Faire...   „   41   43   „
        39. Reade...   „   42   44   „
        40. My Cynthia...   „   43   45   „
        41. How long...   „   44   46   „
        42. Beautie...   „   45   47   „
        43. I muſt...   „   46   48   „
        44. Drawne...   „   47   O whether, etc., and 44 is 48
                                          in '94, and so ⁴, ⁵, and 50 is 51
                                          in ⁴, ⁵.

        45. Care-charmer...   „   49   51 in ⁴, ⁵.
        46. Set...   „   50   As to the Roman in 51, and
        47. Like as...   „   52   54 in ⁴, ⁵.   [53 in ⁴, ⁵.
        48. None...   „   53   55   „
        49. Vnhappy...   „   54   56   „
        50. Loe here...   „   55   57   „
An Ode...   *ibid.*   *ibid.*
The Complaint of Roſamond...   „   „
A Paſtorall...   „   „

1592—Second Edition.

Title, etc., and Sonnets 1 to 26 same as 1st edition.
                27 Still in the trace...
                28 Oft doe I muſe...
                29—30 as in 1st ed.
                31 To M. P., and 27 of ¹, again marked 31.
                32 (numbered xxx.), My cares...
                33 misprinted xxii. is 28 of ¹.
                34 is 30 of ¹.
                33 (2nd) is 29 of ¹.
                35 is 31 of ¹.
                36 is 32 of ¹.
                37 is 33 of ¹.
                38 is 34 of ¹.

Sonnet 39 is 35 of [1].
40 is 36 of [1].
41 is 37 of [1].
42 is 38 of [1].
43—46 lacking in Bodleian copy.
47 is 43 of [1].
48 is 44 of [1].
49 is 45 of [1].
50 is 46 of [1].
51 is 47 of [1].
52 is 48 of [1].
An Ode...
The Complaint...

Summarily, the first edition contained 50 Sonnets, the second 52, the third 55, the fourth and fifth 57, and following the third (substantially) —ours 60, exclusive of additions in the sequel of this Note from volume of 1591. In the Memorial-Introduction I make remarks on certain of the various readings and alterations and additions and withdrawals.

I would now submit the result of a collation of Thomas Newman's or Thomas Nashe's pre-publication of a considerable proportion of these Sonnets. The selection is headed as though it made a single continuous Poem thus—" The Author of this Poeme, S. D.," and commences with " Goe wayling," etc., for introduction (our Sonnet 2) ; and here in the outset a better reading than the Author's presents itself, viz.—' Goe wayling verfe the infant of my loue ' for ' infants ' ; and in l. 12, ' crueltie ' for ' pitty ' [badly], and ll. 13, 14 run—

> ' Knock at her hard heart : fay, I perifh for her,
> And feare this deed will make the world abhor her.'

Then comes as Sonnet 1 our 1st ; Sonnet 2 our 24th. Sonnet 3 was not reprinted by Daniel, but asserts its authorship. It is as follows :—

> ' The onely birde alone that Nature frames,
> When weary of the tedious life fhee liues,
> By fier dies, yet finds new life in flames :
> Her afhes to her fhape new effence giues.
> For haplefle loe euen with mine owne defires
> I figured on the table of my hart,
> The goodlieft fhape that the worlds eye admires,
> And fo did perifh by my proper arte.

> And ftill I toyle to change the Marble breft
> Of her whofe fweete *Idea* I adore,
> Yet cannot finde her breath vnto my reft ;
> Hard is her heart, and woe is me therefore.
> O bleffed he that ioyes his ftone and arte,
> Vnhappie I to loue a ftonie harte.'

Sonnet 4 is our 3rd, and offers these variations :—
    l. 2, ' . . . and afflicted fongs' for 'lamentable fongs.'
    ll. 4, 5, ' . . . who like to me doe fare
        May moue them, sigh thereat and mone my wrongs.'
    l. 6, ' . . . my foules diftreffe.'
    ll. 7, 8, ' : . . you will note what is awry,
        Whilft blind ones fee no error in my verfe.'
    l. 9, ' . . . hap and errour leades.'
    l. 10, 'the' for 'your.'
    l. 11, ' . . . forrow reads.'

Sonnet 5 is our 11th. In l. 1, for 'winne' it reads 'gaines,' and ll. 9-10 read—
> ' Though frozen will may not be thawed with teares,
> Though my foules Idoll fkorneth all my vowes.'

l. 11, 'to deafned eares.' Sonnet 6 is our 37th, and opens, 'Why doth my Miftres,' and l. 10 reads 'the power of your face'; l. 11, 'To admire '; l. 12 (badly) 'caufe' for 'cafe,' and closes—
> ' I feare your change not flower nor *Hyacinth,*
> Medufa's eye may turne . . .'

Sonnet 7 is our 14th: l. 4 reads 'thefe' for 'thofe'; l. 6, 'ftroke' for 'wound '; l. 8, 'that' for 'this fort '; l. 9, ' I lift' for 'And lift'; l. 10, 'this' for 'the' repeated ; and l. 14, 'Ladie' for 'Delia'—showing delicacy on Nashe's part. Sonnet 8 is our 13th, and reads l. 7, 'goodlieft' for 'faireft'; l. 10, 'fweete *Idea*' for 'fweeteft grace'; and l. 13, 'O bleffed he that ioyes' for 'But happy,' etc. Sonnet 9 is our 27th, and yields these variations—l. 3, 'And clofe the way '; l. 4, 'bitter' for 'better' [very doubtful] ; ll. 5-6—
> ' Whileft garding thus the windowes of my thought
> My freedomes tyrant glorying in hir art ' :

l. 11, 'But (ah) fweete' for 'Small is the victorie.'

Sonnet 10 is our 28th, and blunders in reading 'yeelds . . . who gaines, and 'and figh' (l. 14). Sonnet 11, again, was not accepted by Daniel, but equally again reveals its authorship. It is as follows :—

' The flie Inchanter when to worke his will
And fecret wrong on fome forfpoken wight,
Frames waxe, in forme to reprefent aright
The poore vnwitting wretch he meanes to kill,
And prickes the image fram'd by Magicks fkill,
Whereby to vexe the partie day and night :
Like hath fhe done, whofe fhew bewitcht my fight,
To beauties charmes, her Louers bloud to fpil.
For firft, like waxe fhe fram'd me by her eyes,
Whofe rayes fharp poynted fet vpon my breft,
Martyres my life, and plagues me on this wife,
With lingring paine to perifh in vnreft.
Nought could (faue this) my fweeteft faire fuffice,
    To trie her arte on him that loues her beft.'

Sonnet 12 is our 19th, and has only slight variations, *e.g.*, l. 1, 'treafure' for 'treffes,' and l. 10, 'voyce yeeld to *Hermonius* fpheares.' Sonnet 13 is another that only appears in 1591 volume, but once more is self-authen-ticating. It is as follows :—

' The tablet of my heauie fortunes heere,
Vpon thine Altare (*Paphian* power) I place ;
The greeuous fhipwracke of my trauels deere,
In bulged barke, all perifht in difgrace.
That traitor Loue, was Pilot to my woe,
My Sailes were loofe, fpread with my fighs of griefe,
The twine lights which my haples courfe did fhow,
Hard by th' inconftant fands of falfe reliefe,
Where two bright ftarres which led my view apart,
A Syrens voice allur'd me come fo neare,
To perifh on the marble of her hart,
A danger which my foule did neuer feare :
    Lo thus he fares that trufts a calme too much ;
    And thus fare I whofe credit hath beene fuch.'

Sonnet 14 is our 48th, and presents these various readings :—
    l. 3, '. . . . dies' for 'dries.'
    l. 6, '. . . . the night wandring.'
    l. 7, 'Nor euer hath his impoft paid more . . . .'
    l. 8, '. . . . my foules Queene hath euer beene.'
    ll. 9-11, 'Yet her hard rocke firme fixt for ay removing
                No comfort to my cares fhe euer giueth
                Yet had I . . . . louing.'

l. 12, 'Than to imbrace . . . .'

l. 13, 'I feare . . . . raigning.'

Sonnet 15 is our 15th, and has these readings :—

l. 1, 'If a true . . . .'

l. 3, 'Steruen.'

ll. 9-12, 'If I haue wept the day and fighd the night,
Whilft thrice the Sun approcht his northern bound :
If fuch a faith hath euer wrought aright,
And well deferud, and yet no fauor found.'

ll. 13-14, '. . . . . the whole world it may fee
. . . . . . the moft hurt be.'

Sonnet 16 is our 18th, and only these variations occur : l. 6, 'exacts' for 'exact,' and l. 7, 'So long and pure a faith no fauour.'

Sonnet 17 is the fourth and last of the Sonnets given by Newman and Nashe, but not reprinted by Daniel, albeit as certainly his. It is as follows :—

' Way but the caufe, and giue me leaue to plaine me,
For all my hurt, that my harts Queene hath wrought it ;
Shee whom I loue fo deare, the more to paine me,
Withholds my right, where I haue dearely bought it.
Dearly I bought that was fo highly rated,
Euen with the price of bloud and bodies wafting,
Shee would not yeeld that ought might be abated,
For all fhee faw my Loue was pure and lafting,
And yet now fcornes performance of the paffion,
And with her prefence Iuftice ouer ruleth,
Shee tels me flat her beauty beares no action,
And fo my plea and proces fhe excludeth :
What wrong fhee doth, the world may well perceiue it,
To accept of faith at firft, and then to leaue it.'

Sonnet 18 is our 29th, and gives these various readings :—

ll. 4-5, 'When it had hop'd . . . . . .
My faith of priuiledge could no whit . . . .'

l. 7, 'Whereby fhe had no caufe once to . . . .'

l. 10, 'No comforts liue, w[h]ich falling fpirits erecteth ';

l. 14, 'And by her hand that . . . where I had hope to . . . .'

Sonnet 19 is our 26th, and presents these :—

l. 2, '. . . . thought to thought . . . . leade . . . .'

l. 3, 'Fortunes Orphan, hers and the worlds'

l. 4. 'bad' for 'fad' [very poor]
l. 6. '. . . . . . neuer funne yet.'
l. 7, 'A pleafing griefe impreffed hath . . . .'
ll. 9-10, 'Yet . . . . muft not.'

Sonnet 20 is our 16th, but after the version in Nashes beneath *in loco*. It badly reads in l. 2 'hart' for 'hurt' and 'mooued' for 'inur'd'; in l. 6 of our 16th reads '. . . . mercy (mercie yet my merit)' which is better ; l. 9, 'Yet fince'; l. 10, 'Still forrowes'; and ll. 12-14 run :—

  ' And nothing but her loue and my harts payning :
  Weep howrs, grieue daies, figh months, and ftill mourn yeerly,
  Thus muft I doe becaufe I loue her dearlie.'

Sonnet 21 is also our 21st, and has these variations :—
l. 1, '. . . . bright be doubled . . . .' [bad]
ll. 2, 5, '. . . . cannot fhine through . . . .
    And Difdaines vapors are thus . . . .
    . . . . . . to me quite darkened is,
    Why trouble I the world then with my . . . .
l. 7, ... 'ruthfull' for 'ruthleffe' . . . . [bad].
l. 8, '. . . . my vntuned . . . .'
l. 11, '. . . . ftill hold her moft deare vntill my . . . .

Our Sonnet 22 in Nashe's text opens—
  ' Come Death the Anchor hold of al my thoughts,
  My laft refort whereto my foule appealeth :
  For all too long on earth my fancie dotes,
  Whiles deareft blood my fierie paffions fealeth.'

Sonnet 22 is our 24th, and gives these various readings :—
l. 1, 'fire' for 'fmoake . . . .'
l. 2, 'Thefe are the . . . .'
l. 3, 'And thefe my tyrants cruell minde fulfils.'
ll. 6-8, '. . . . that yet refpects no whit
    My youth, vntimely withered with my teares
    By winter woes . . . .'
l. 11, '. . . . the bliffe . . . .'

Sonnet 23 is our 9th, and offers in l. 1 a much better reading, which we accept in text—' To paint on fluds,' on which see various readings *in loco*. Most of these also excellent :—

  ll. 3-4, 'With prone afpect ftill tending . . . .
    Sad horror, pale greefe, proftrate defpaire.'

ll. 6-8, ' Rife vp to waile, lie down to ſigh, to . . .
With ceaſeles toyle Cares reſtleſſe ſtones . . . .
. . . . and mone . . . . whilſt . . . .'

l. 9, '. . . . to languiſh in ſuch care . . . .'

ll. 10-12, ' Loathing the light, the world, my ſelfe, and all,
With interrupted ſleepes, freſhe grefes repaire
And breathe out horror in perplexed thrall.'

l. 14, ' Loe then . . . .'

Sonnet 24 is our 30th (from 1592 [2]), and gives these variations :—

ll. 2-5, ' My cares drawes on my euerlaſting night
And horrors ſable clowds dims my liues ſunne ;
That my liues ſunne, and thou my worldly light,
Shall riſe no more to me : my daies are donne.'

And these—

ll. 7-8, '. . . . . I'll goe,
And dreſſe a bed of flowers.'

l. 9, ' why that.'

l. 10, '. . . . fault . . . . and . . . .'

l. 13, ' Although the world this deed of hirs may . . . .'

Sonnet 25 is our 32nd, and thus variantly reads—

l. 1, ' my ' for ' this.'

ll. 2-3, '. . . . . . crying
. . . bloud and bloudie trying.'

ll. 12-13, ' My Ocean teares drowne me and quench my . . .
Whiles faith doth bid my cruell Faire adieu.'—[bad].

Sonnet 26 is our 59th, and thus opens, ' To' being a self-correcting misprint for ' Lo,' and ' impreſt ' for ' impreſſe' :—

' To heare the impreſt of a faith not ſaining,
That dutie paies and her diſdaine extorteth :
Theſe beare the meſſage of my wofull paining,
Theſe oliue braunches mercie ſtill exorteth.'

And there are further these :—

l. 5, '. . . . plaints with chaſte deſires . . . .'

l. 9, '. . . . poore ſoule) I liue exild from . . . .'

l. 11, '. . . . liberties . . . .'

ll. 13-14, ' What ſhall I doo but ſigh and waile the while,
My martyrdome exceedes the higheſt ſtile.'

Sonnet **27** is our 38th, and gives these slight verbal various readings :—
   l. 1, 'may' for 'fhall.'
   l. 2, 'And . . . . may . . . .'
   l. 4, '. . . . power not . . . .'
   l. 6, '. . . . the worlds eie doth . . . .'
   l. 7, '. . . . her praife to . . . .'
   l. 8, '. . . . fades the flowers . . . . fed . . . .'
Sonnet **28** (including the Introductory one as 1) is our 36th, and finally presents these variations :—
   l. 1, 'hope for 'hopes.'
   l. 3, 'meane' for 'meanes,' and 'prefumes' for 'prefum'd.'
   l. 4, 'For difdaines thunderbolt made me retire.'
At the close is added, instead of the simple 'S. D.' of the commencement, these words—'Finis, Daniell.'

It may be helpful to add here, collectively, the succession of the 1591 Sonnets, together with the first lines :—
   Goe wayling verfe the infant of my loue,
Sonnet **1**. If fo it hap the Off fpring of my care,
   2. Thefe forrowing fighs, the fmokes of mine annoy ;
   3. The onely birde alone that Nature frames,
   4. Teares, vowes and prayers gaines the hardeft hearts,
   5. Why doth my Miftres credit fo her glaffe,
   6. Thefe amber locks are thofe fame nets (my Deare)
   7. Behold what hap *Pigmalion* had to frame,
   8. Oft and in vaine my rebels thoughts haue ventred,
   9. Raigne in my thoughts, faire hand, fweete eye, rare voice,
   10. The flie Inchanter, when to worke his will,
   11. Reftore thy treafure to the golden ore,
   12. The tablet of my heauie fortunes heere
   13. My *Cinthia* hath the waters of mine eies,
   14. If a true heart and faith vnfained,
   15. Since the firft looke that led me to this error,
   16. Way but the caufe, and giue me leaue to plaine me,
   17. Whilft by her eies purfude, my poore heart flue it
   18. Looke in my griefes, and blame me not to mourne,
   19. Happie in fleepe, waking content to languifh,
   20. If Beautie bright be doubled with a frowne,
   21. Come Death the anchor hold of al my thoughts,
   22. If this be Loue to drawe a wearie breath,
   23. My cares drawes on my euerlafting night,
   24. The Starre of my mifhape impofde my paining

Sonnet 25. To heare the impoft of a faith not faining,

      26. I once may fee when yeares may wrecke my wrong,

      27. Raifing my hope on hills of high defire,

The critical student will perceive that saving four or five bad readings, probably from misreading the MS., the text of these twenty-seven Daniel Sonnets as printed by Newman and Nashe can hold their own against the Author's, and gives no sanction to his condemnation of the 1591 text, albeit his wrath may have been justified by the surreptitious way in which the transcript had been secured. It is well for us that these twenty-seven Sonnets were thus prematurely published. We are (so to say) admitted by them to the Poet's study, and get a vision of him at work and of the processes of his thought and emotion. The four rejected Sonnets are of special biographic interest. But the reader will find more in our 'Memorial-Introduction II.—Critical,' on the various readings, etc., of the "Delian sonnetry."

It only remains to add here the line-arrangements of the three editions:—

1592—FIRST AND SECOND.   1594.

In 1594 edition, the prose-epistle to the Countess of Pembroke is cancelled, and a fresh Sonnet-dedication substituted. I place it after the Prose Epistle and separate from the 'Sonnets to Delia.' On the 'M. P.' and neighbour sonnet of 1592 (2nd ed.)—assigned by various to the Countess of Pembroke in flagrant error—see our 'Memorial-Introduction I.—Biographical.' In the various readings and notes beneath each Sonnet *a* stands for the Quarto of 1623, and, as before noted, [1], [2], [3], [4], [5] for 1592 1st and 2nd, 1594 3rd, 1601 4th, and 1602 5th edition.   A. B. G.

TO THE RIGHT HONOURABLE THE
Ladie *Mary* Counteſſe of Pembroke.

*IGHT Honorable, although I rather
deſired to keep in the private paſſions
of my youth, from the multitude, as
things utterd to my ſelfe, and conſe-
crated to ſilence: yet ſeeing I was
betraide by the indiſcretion of a greedie
Printer, and had ſome of my ſecrets
bewraide to the world, vncorrected: doubting the like of* 10
*the reſt, I am forced to publiſh that which I neuer ment.
But this wrong was not onely doone to mee, but to him
whoſe vnmatchable lines haue indured the like misfortune;
Ignorance ſparing not to commit ſacriledge vpon ſo holy
reliques. Yet* Aſtrophel *flying with the wings of his own
fame, a higher pitch then the groſs-ſighted can diſcerne,
hath regiſtred his owne name in the Annals | of eternitie,
and cannot be diſgraced, howſoeuer diſguiſed. And for
my ſelfe, ſeeing I am thruſt out into the worlde, and that*
my vnboldned Muſe, is forced to appeare ſo rawly in 20
*publique; I deſire onely to bee graced by the countenance
of your protection: whome the foitune of our time hath
made the happie and iudiciall Patroneſſe of the Muſes
(a glory hereditary to your houſe) to preſerue them from
thoſe hidious Beeſtes, Oblivion and Barbariſme. Wherby*

*you doe not onely poſſeſſe the honour of the preſent, but
alſo do bind poſterity to an euer gratefull memorie of your
vertues, wherein you muſt ſurvive your ſelfe. And if
my times heereafter better laboured, ſhall purchaſe grace
in the world, they muſt remaine the monuments of your* 30
*honourable favour, and recorde the zealous duetie of mee,
who am vowed to your honour in all obſeruancy for euer,*

Samuel Danyell.

TO THE RIGHT HONORABLE, THE
Lady Mary, Counteſſe of *Pembrooke*.[1]

ONDER of theſe, glory of other times,
O thou whom Enuy eu'n is forſt t'
admyre :
Great Patroneſs of theſe my humble
Rymes,
Which thou from out thy greatnes
dooſt inſpire :
Sith onely thou haſt deign'd to rayſe them higher,
Vouchſafe now to accept them as thine owne,
Begotten by thy hand, and my deſire,
Wherein my Zeale, and thy great might is ſhowne. 10
And ſeeing this vnto the world is knowne,
O leaue not, ſtill to grace thy worke in mee :
Let not the quickning ſeede be ouer-throwne,
Of that which may be borne to honour thee.
Whereof, the trauaile I may challenge mine,
But yet the glory, (Madam) muſt be thine.   16

[1] 1594 A 1, instead of the Prose Epistle-dedicatory of 1592 [1], [2]—as on
pp. 33—34.

TO DELIA.

SONNET. I.

VNto the boundleffe Ocean of thy beautie,
 Runnes this poore Riuer, charg'd with ftreames
of zeale :
Returning thee the tribute of my dutie,
Which here my loue, my youth, my plaints reueale.
Here I vnclafpe the Booke of my charg'd foule,
 Where I haue caft th'accounts of all my care :
Here haue I fumm'd my fighs, here I inrole
How they were fpent for thee; looke what they are :
Looke on the deere expences of my youth,
 And fee how iuft I reckon with thine eies :
Examine well thy beautie with my truth,
 And croffe my cares ere greater fummes arife.
Reade it (fweet maide) though it be done but fleightly;
Who can fhew all his loue, doth loue but lightly.

accepted from heading ' To Delia.'

 Sonnet **1**. 1. 1, ' boundles ' [1], [2], [3], [4], [5] : , not in [1] ; 1. 2, ' Runs ' [1], [3], [4], [5] : *ibid.*, ' riuer ' [1], [3], [4], [5] ; ' Ryuer ' [2] : *ibid.*, ' zeale : ' [1], [2] ; , [3] ; nothing [4], [5]—the colon accepted : l. 3, ' duetie ' [2] ; ' duty ' [3] : l. 4, ' heere ' [1], [2], and so throughout : *ibid.*, ' playnts ' [1] ; ' reueale.'—period for *nil* accepted from [1], [2], [3], [4], [5] : l. 5, ' booke ' [1], [2], [3], [4], [5] : l. 7, ' fighes ' [1], [2], [3], [4], [5] : *ibid.*, ' enroule [1], [2] ; ' enrole ' [3] ; ' inrole ' [4], [5] : l. 8, ' Howe ' [1], [2] : l. 8, ' thee ; Looke ' [2] ; same in [3], [4], [5], but small ' l '— ; for , accepted : *ibid.*, ' are.' [1], [2], [3] ; : [4], [5] : l. 10, ' thyne eyes ' [1] ; ' thine eyes ' [2], [3] ; ' thine eies ' [4], [5] : l. 11, ' trueth ' [1] : l. 13, no ( ) in [1], [2] : *ibid.*, ' maid ' [3], [4], [5] : *ibid.*, ' doone . . . flightly ' [1], [2], [3] ; ' fleightly ' [4], [5] : l. 14, ' fhewe ' [1], [2].

SONNET. II.

Goe wailing Verſe, the Infants of my loue,
    Mine:ua-like, brought foorth without a mother :
Preſent the Image of the cares I proue,
Witneſſe your Fathers griefe exceedes all other.
Sigh out a Storie of her cruell deedes,
    With interrupted accents of deſpaire :
A Monument that whoſoeuer reedes,
    May iuſtly praiſe, and blame my loueleſſe Faire.
Say her diſdaine hath dryed vp my blood,
    And ſtarued you, in ſuccours ſtill denying :
Preſſe to her eyes, importune me ſome good.
    Waken her ſleeping pitty with your crying,
Knocke at that hard hart, begge till you haue mou'd
        her,
And tell th'vnkinde, how dearely I haue lou'd her.

Sonnet 2. l. 2, 'Mother' [1],[2] : l. 3, 'image' [1],[2] : l. 6, 'diſpayre' [1];
'diſpaire' [2],[3] : l. 12, . for , after 'crying' [1] : l. 12, 'that' accepted for
' her' of [2],[3],[4],[5] : *ibid.*, ' you '[1],[2],[3] accepted for ' ye ' of [4],[5], and ' yee' of *a* :
l. 14, , after 'vnkinde' accepted from [1],[2],[3],[4],[5] (' vnkind ').

SONNET. III.

If ſo it hap, this of-ſpring of my care,
    Theſe fatall Antheames, ſad and mornefull Songs:
Come to their view, who like afflicted are ;
    Let them yet ſigh their owne, and mone my wrongs.
But vntoucht hearts, with vnaffected eie,
    Approach not to behold ſo great diſtreſſe :
Cleere-ſighted you, ſoone note what is awrie,
    Whilſt blinded ones mine errours neuer geſſe.

You blinded foules whom youth and errour leade,
  You out-caft Eaglets, dazeled with your Sunne :
Ah you, and none but you my forrowes reade,
  You beft can iudge the wrongs that fhe hath done.
That fhe hath done, the motiue of my paine,
Who whilft I loue, doth kill me with difdaine.

Sonnet 3. l. 2, 'fad and mornefull ' ¹, ², ³, accepted for 'lamentable'
of ⁴, ⁵ and a : l. 4, 'yet figh their ' ¹, ², accepted for 'Let them figh for
their' of ⁴, ⁵, and 'Ah let them figh theyr' of ³ : l. 6, 'fo great diftreffe'
¹, ², ³, accepted for 'my heauineffe' of ⁴, ⁵, and a : l. 7, qy., after 'Cleere-
fighted'? but as in text in ¹, ², ³, ⁴, ⁵: l. 8, 'ones' ¹, ², ³, accepted for
'foules' of ⁴, ⁵, and a : l. 9, 'errours' ¹, ², ³ : l. 11, 'Ah' ¹, ², ³, accepted
for 'Do' of ⁴, ⁵, and a : l. 12, 'dunne' ¹. ² : l. 13, 'doone' ¹, ².

SONNET. IIII.

Thefe plaintiue Verfe, the Poftes of my defire,
    Which hafte for fuccour to her flow regard :
Beare not report of any flender fire,
  Forging a griefe to winne a fames reward.
Nor are my paffions limnd for outward hew,
  For that no colours can depaint my forrowes :
Delia her felfe, and all the world may view
  Beft in my face, how cares haue tild deepe forrowes.
No Bayes I feeke to decke my mourning brow,
  O cleere-eyde Rector of the holy Hill :
My humble accents beare the Oliue bough,
  Of interceffion but to moue her will.
Thefe lines I vfe, t'vnburthen mine owne hart ;
My loue affects no fame, nor fteemes of Art.

Sonnet 4. l. 2, : accepted from ¹, ², ³ for , of ⁴, ⁵, and a : l. 8, 'how ' ¹, ²,
accepted for 'where ' of ³, ⁴, ⁵ and a, but not 'hath' of ¹, ³ : l. 11, 'craue . . .
bow' ¹, ² : l. 12, 'Of her milde pittie and relenting will' ¹, ² ; 'Of interceffion to a Tyrants will' ³ ; 'Of interceffion but to moue her will ' ⁴, ⁵, as
in a. See errata of ¹ in Note before these Sonnets.

SONNET. V.

VVHilſt youth and error led my wandring
            minde,
And ſet my thoughts in heedleſſe wayes to range :
All vnawares, a Goddeſſe chaſte I finde,
(*Diana*-like) to worke my ſudden change.
For her no ſooner had mine eyes bewraid,
    But with diſdaine to ſee me in that place ;
    With faireſt hand, the ſweet vnkindeſt Maid,
    Caſt water-cold Diſdaine vpon my face.
Which turn'd my ſport into a Harts diſpaire,
    Which ſtill is chac'd, while I haue any breath,
    By mine owne thoughts, ſet on me by my Faire :
    My thoughts (like Houndes) purſue me to my death.
Thoſe that I foſtred of mine owne accord,
Are made by her to murther thus their Lord.

Sonnet 5. l. 4, no ( ) in ¹, ² : l. 5, ' my view ' ¹, ² ; ' mine eye ' ⁴, ⁵ :
l. 7, ' moſt vnkindeſt ' ¹ : l. 8, ' Caſtes ' ¹, ², ³ : l. 12, no ( ) in ¹, ².

SONNET. VI.

FAire is my Loue, and cruell as ſhe's faire ;
        Her brow ſhades frownes, although her eyes
    are ſunny,
    Her ſmiles are lightning, though her pride deſpaire ;
    And her diſdaines are Gall, her fauours Hunny.
A modeſt Maide, deckt with a bluſh of honor,
    Whoſe feete doe tread greene paths of youth and loue,
    The wonder of all eyes that looke vpon her :
    Sacred on earth, deſign'd a Saint aboue.

Chaftitie and Beautie, which were deadly foes,
  Liue reconciled friends within her brow :
  And had fhe pitty to conioyne with thofe,
  Then who had heard the plaints I vtter now ?
For had fhe not beene faire and thus vnkinde,
My Mufe had flept, and none had knowne my minde.

Sonnet 6. l. 1, 'as fh'is' ¹, ², ³ : l. 2, - (hyphen) removed from 'brow fhades' of *a*, not in ¹, ², ³, ⁴, ⁵.

SONNET. VII.

FOr had fhe not beene faire and thus vnkinde,
    Then had no finger pointed at my lightneffe :
  The world had neuer knowne what I doe finde,
  And cloudes obfcure had fhaded ftill her brightneffe.
Then had no Cenfors eye thefe lines furuaid,
  Nor grauer browes haue iudg'd my Mufe fo vaine
  No Sunne my blufh and error had bewraid,
  Nor yet the world haue heard of fuch difdaine.
Then had I walkt with bold erected face,
  No downe-caft looke had fignified my miffe :
  But my degraded hopes, with fuch difgrace
  Did force me grone out griefes, and vtter this.
For being full, fhould I not then haue fpoken,
My fence oppreff'd, had faild, and heart had broken.

Sonnet 7. l. 1, 'For' ¹, ⁴, ⁵, but in ², ³ 'O'—perhaps preferable, albeit the 'For' catches up l. 13 of Sonnet VI.

SONNET. VIII.

THou poore heart facrifiz'd vnto the faireft,
   Haft fent the incenfe of thy fighs to heauen :
  And ftill againft her frownes frefh vowes repaireft,
  And made thy paffions with her beautie euen.
And you mine eyes, the agents of my hart
   Tolde the dumbe meffage of my hidden griefe :
  And oft with carefull turnes, with filent Art,
  Did treate the cruell faire to yeeld reliefe.
And you my Verfe, the Aduocates of Loue,
   Haue followed hard the Proceffe of my cafe :
  And vrg'd that title which doth plainely proue,
  My faith fhould win, if Iuftice might haue place.
Yet though I fee, that nought we doe, can moue,
Tis not difdaine muft make me leaue to loue.

Sonnet 8. l. 8, 'dread' MS. : l. 14, 'leaue'—accepted for 'ceafe' of
[2], [3], [4], [5] and *a.*

SONNET. IX.

IF this be loue, to draw a wearie breath,
   To paint on floods, till the fhore crie to th'aire :
  With downeward lookes, ftill reading on the earth,
  Thefe fad memorials of my loues difpaire :
If this be loue, to warre againft my foule,
   Lie downe to waile, rife vp to figh and grieue,
  The neuer-refting ftone of Care to roule,
  Still to complaine my griefes, whilft none relieue.

If this be loue, to cloathe me with darke thoughts,
  Haunting vntrodden paths to waile apart ;
  My pleaſures horror, Muſicke tragicke notes,
  Teares in mine eyes, and ſorrow at my hart.
If this be loue, to liue a liuing death,
Then doe I loue and draw this wearie breath.

Sonnet 9. l. 1, ⁴, ⁵ drop ' to ' inadvertently : l. 12, ' my ' ¹ : l. 14,
' O then loue I ' ¹, ², ³ : in l. 2, Tieck stupidly proposed ' Pant ' (his
annotated copy of Daniel in B. Museum). ' My name is writ on water '
catches up the ' cry ' better. I accept ' To paint ' of Newman and Nashe
text of 1591 : l. 6, ' me ' and l. 8, ' me ' at close in ¹, ² ; ll. 5, 9, , inserted
after ' loue.'

SONNET. X.

THen doe I loue, and draw this wearie breath,
    For her the cruell Faire, within whoſe brow
I written finde the ſentence of my death,
  In vnkinde Letters ; wrote ſhe cares not how.
Thou powre that rul'ſt the confines of the night,
  Laughter louing Goddeſſe, worldly pleaſures Queene,
  Intenerat that heart that ſets ſo light,
  The trueſt loue that euer yet was ſeene.
And cauſe her leaue to triumph in this wiſe,
  Vpon the proſtrate ſpoyle of that poore hart
  That ſerues a Trophey to her conquering eies,
  And muſt their glory to the world impart.
Once let her know, ſh'hath done enough to proue me,
And let her pitte if ſhe cannot loue me.

Sonnet 10. l. 1, ' O then I loue ' ¹ ; ' O then loue I ' ², ³ ; l. 4,
' wrought ' ¹, ², ³—perhaps preferable : l. 5, ' O thou ' ¹, ², ³ : l. 7, ' Gods ' ;
in l. 11 period.

SONNET. XI.

TEares, vowes, and prayers, winne the hardeſt hart,
    Teares, vowes, and prayers haue I ſpent in vaine;
Teares cannot ſoften flint, nor vowes conuart,
Prayers preuaile not with a quaint diſdaine.
I loſe my teares where I haue loſt my loue,
    I vow my faith, where faith is not regarded ;
    I pray in vaine, a mercileſſe to moue :
So rare a faith ought better be rewarded.
Yet, though I cannot winne her will with teares,
    Though my ſoules Idoll ſcorneth all my vowes ;
    Though all my prayers be to ſo deafe eares,
    No fauour though, the cruell faire allowes,
Yet will I weepe, vow, pray to cruell ſhee :
Flint, froſt, diſdaine, weares, meltes, and yeeldes we
    ſee.

Sonnet 11. In l. 11 the : in ¹, ² obscures the continuous thought, but
perhaps a , after 'though' in l. 12 is better. It is so in Nashe's text of
1591 (*in loco*)—accepted.

SONNET. XII.

MY ſpotleſſe loue houers with pureſt wings,
    About the Temple of the proudeſt frame :
Where blaze thoſe lights faireſt of earthly things,
Which cleere our clouded world with brighteſt flame.
M'ambitious thoughts confined in her face,
    Affect no honor but what ſhe can giue :
My hopes doe reſt in limits of her grace,
I weigh no comfort vnleſſe ſhe relieue.

For fhe that can my heart imparadize,
  Holdes in her faireft hand what deareft is,
  My fortunes wheeles the circle of her eies,
  Whofe rowling grace deigne once a turne of blis.
All my liues fweet confifts in her alone,
So much I loue the moft vnlouing one.

Sonnet 12. l. 1, 'hoouers with white' ¹, ²: ll. 6, 8, 'me' at close in
¹, ²; cf. Sonnet IX., ll. 6, 8 : l. 11, 'wheele' ¹; 'wheele's' ², ³, ⁴, ⁵.

SONNET. XIII.

BEhold what hap *Pigmalion* had to frame
    And carue his proper griefe vpon a ftone ;
  My heauy fortune is much like the fame,
  I worke on flint, and thats the caufe I mone.
For hapleffe loe euen with mine owne defires,
  I figurde on the table of mine hart,
  The faireft forme, that all the world admires,
  And fo did perifh by my proper art.
And ftill I toyle, to change the Marble breft
  Of her, whofe fweeteft grace I do adore,
  Yet cannot finde her breathe vnto my reft,
  Hard is her hart, and woe is me therefore.
But happy he that ioy'd his ftone and art,
Vnhappy I, to loue a ftony hart.

Sonnet 13. l. 6, 'my' ¹, ²: l. 7, 'forme, the worldes eye' ¹, ²—perhaps
preferable, but occurs elsewhere in these Sonnets (see Glossarial-Index *s.v.*).

SONNET. XIIII.

THofe fnary locks, are thofe fame nets (my Deere)
    Wherewith my liberty thou didft furprize ;
  Loue was the flame that fired me fo neere,
  The Dart tranfpearfing, were thofe Chriftall eies.

Strong is the net, and feruent is the flame ;
    Deepe is the wound my fighes can well report :
    Yet do I loue, adore, and prayfe the fame,
    That holds, that burnes, that wounds me in this fort.
And lift not feeke to breake, to quench, to heale,
    The bond, the flame, the wound that feftreth fo,
    By knife, by liquor, or by falue to deale :
    So much I pleafe to perifh in my woe.
Yet leaft long trauailes be aboue my ftrength,
Good DELIA lofe, quench, heale me now at length.

Sonnet 14. l. 1, 'amber'[1], [2]: *ibid.*, no ( ) in [1], [2] : l. 6, 'do'[1]; 'doe'[2], [3] : l. 13, 'Yer'[1]—put in errata.

SONNET. XV.

IF that a loyall hart and faith vnfained,
    If a fweet languifh with a chaft defire,
    If hunger-ftaruen thoughts fo long retained,
    Fed but with fmoke, and cherifht but with fire :
And if a brow with cares chara&ters painted,
    Bewraies my loue, with broken words halfe fpoken
    To her that fits in my thoughts Temple fainted,
    And laies to view my Vultur-gnawne hart open :
If I haue done due homage to her eyes,
    And had my fighes ftill tending on her name ;
    If on her loue my life and honour lyes,
    And fhe (th'vnkindeft maid) ftill fcorns the fame :
Let this fuffice, that all the world may fee
The fault is hers, though mine the hurt muft be.

Sonnet 15. l. 5, 'cara&ters'[1]: l. 8, *a* misprints 'Vultar': l. 13, 'the world yet may fee'[1], [2].

SONNET. XVI.

HAppy in fleepe, waking content to languifh,
    Imbracing clouds by night, in day time
  mourne,
My ioys but fhadowes, touch of truth, my anguifh,
Griefes euer fpringing, comforts neuer borne.
And ftill expecting when fhe will relent,
  Growne hoarce with crying mercy, mercy giue,
  So many vowes, and praiers hauing fpent,
That weary of my life, I loath to liue.
And yet the Hydra of my cares renues
  Still new borne forrowes of her frefh difdaine :
  And ftill my hope the Sommer windes purfues,
Finding no end nor period of my paine.
This is my ftate, my griefes do touch fo neerly,
And thus I liue becaufe I loue her deerly.

Sonnet 16. l. 2, 'morne' [1], [2] :
    ' All things I loath faue her and mine owne anguifh,
    Pleaf'd in my hurt, inur'd to liue forlorne.
      Nought doe I craue, but loue, death, or my Lady,
    Hoarce with crying mercy, mercy yet my merit ;
    So many vowes and prayers euer made I,
    That now at length t' yeelde, meere pittie were it.
      But ftill the *Hydra* of my cares renuing,
    Reuiues new forrowes of her frefh difdayning ;
    Still muft I goe the Summer windes purfuing :
    Finding no ende nor Period of my payning.
      Waile all my life, my griefes do touch fo neerely,
      And thus I liue, becaufe I loue her deerely.'
So in [1], [2], but [2] in last l. reads 'thus' for 'this' of [1] (error) : 'myfelfe' in
l. 8 in [3].

SONNET. XVII.

VVHy ſhould I ſing in verſe, why ſhould I
 frame
Theſe ſad neglećted notes for her deare ſake ?
Why ſhould I offer vp vnto her name,
 The ſweeteſt ſacrifice my youth can make ?
Why ſhould I ſtriue to make her liue for euer,
 That neuer deignes to giue me ioy to liue ?
 Why ſhould m'afflićted Muſe ſo much endeuour,
 Such honour vnto cruelty to giue ?
If her defećts haue purchaſt her this fame,
 What ſhould her vertues do, her ſmiles, her loue ?
 If this her worſt, how ſhould her beſt inflame ?
 What paſſions would her milder fauours moue ?
Fauours (I thinke) would ſence quite ouercome,
And that makes happy Louers euer dombe.

Sonnet 17.   First appeared in [3], and is in [4], [5], and *a*.

SONNET. XVIII.

SInce the firſt looke that led me to this error,
 To this thoughts-maze, to my confuſion tending :
 Still haue I liu'd in griefe, in hope, in terror,
 The circle of my ſorrowes neuer ending.
Yet cannot leaue her loue that holds me hatefull,
 Her eyes exaćt it, though her hart diſdaines me ;
 See what reward he hath that ſerues the vngratefull,
 So true and loyall loue no fauour gaines me.

Still muſt I whet my yong deſires abated,
  Vpon the flint of ſuch a hart rebelling ;
  And all in vaine, her pride is ſo innated,
  She yeelds no place at all for pitties dwelling.
Oft haue I told her that my ſoule did loue her,
(And that with teares) yet all this will not moue her.

Sonnet 18. l. 7, 'th' ¹, ², ³ : l. 4, no ( ) in ¹, ², and so throughout in them—this is XVII. in 1592.

SONNET. XIX.

REſtore thy treſſes to the golden Ore,
  Yeeld *Cithereas* ſonne thoſe Arkes of loue ;
Bequeath the heauens the ſtarres that I adore,
And to th'Orient do thy Pearles remoue,
Yeeld thy hands pride vnto th'Iuory white,
  T' *Arabian* odors giue thy breathing ſweete :
Reſtore thy bluſh vnto *Aurora* bright,
  To *Thetis* giue the honour of thy feete.
Let *Venus* haue thy graces, her reſign'd,
  And thy ſweet voice giue back vnto the Spheares :
But yet reſtore thy fierce and cruell mind,
  To *Hyrcan* Tygres, and to ruthles Beares.
Yeeld to the Marble thy hard hart againe ;
So ſhalt thou ceaſe to plague, and I to paine.

Sonnet 19. See variations in introductory Note to these Delian Sonnets.

SONNET. XX.

VVHat it is to breathe and liue without life :
  How to be pale with anguiſh, red with feare,
T'haue peace abroad, and nought within but ſtrife :
Wiſh to be preſent, and yet ſhun t'appeare :

4

How to be bold far off, and bafhfull neare :
  How to thinke much, and haue no words to fpeake :
  To craue redreffe, yet hold affliction deare :
  To haue affection ftrong, a body weake,
Neuer to finde, and euermore to feeke :
  And feeke that which I dare not hope to finde :
  T'affect this life, and yet this life difleeke :
  Gratefull t'another, to my felfe vnkinde.
This cruell knowledge of thefe contraries,
DELIA my hart hath learnd out of thofe eyes.

Sonnet 20. First appeared in [4], and reprinted in [5].

SONNET. XXI.

IF beauty thus be clowded with a frowne,
  That pitty fhines no comfort to my blis,
And vapours of difdaine fo ouergrowne
That my liues light wholy in-darkned is.
Why fhould I more moleft the world with cries ?
  The ayre with fighes, the earth below with teares ?
  Sith I liue hatefull to thofe ruthleffe eies,
  Vexing with vntun'd moane her dainty eares.
If I haue lou'd her dearer then my breath,
  My breath that calls the heauens to witnes it :
  And ftill muft hold her deare till after death,
  And that all this mooues not her thoughts a whit,
Yet fure fhe cannot but muft thinke a part,
She doth me wrong, to grieue fo true a heart.

Sonnet 21 is XIX. in [1], [2] : l. 4, 'thus wholy darkned' [1], [2], [3] : l. 7,
'Since' [1], [2] : l. 12, 'And if that all this cannot moue' [1] [2], [3] ; ll. 13, 14—
    ' Yet let her fay that fhe hath doone me wrong,
      To vfe me thus and knowe I lou'd fo long ' ([1], [2], [3]).

SONNET. XXII.

COme Time the anchor-hold of my defire,
My laft Refort whereto my hopes appeale,
Caufe once the date of her difdaine t'expire:
Make her the fentence of her wrath repeale.
Rob her faire Brow, breake in on Beauty, fteale
Powre from thofe eyes, which pitty cannot fpare:
Deale with thofe dainty cheekes as fhe doth deale
With this poore heart confumed with difpaire.
This heart made now the profpectiue of care,
By louing her, the cruelft Faire that liues,
The cruelft Fayre that fees I pine for her,
And neuer mercy to thy merit giues.
Let her not ftill triumph ouer the prize
Of mine affections taken by her eies.

Sonnet 22. l. 1, 'death . . . . of all my thoughts' [1], [2], [3]: l. 2, 'foule appealeth' [1], [2]; 'appeales' [3]: l. 3, 'For all too long on earth my fancy dotes' [1], [2], [3]: l. 4, 'Whilft my beft blood my younge defires fealeth' [1], [2]; 'Whilft age vpon my wafted body fteales' [3]: ll. 5—14—

> 'That hart is now the profpectiue of horror,
> That honored hath the cruelft faire that lyueth:
> The cruelft faire, that fees I languifh for her,
> Yet neuer mercy to my merit giueth.
> This is her Lawrell and her triumphes prize,
> To tread me downe with foote of her difgrace:
> Whilft I did builde my fortune in her eyes,
> And laide my liues reft in fo faire a face;
> That reft I loft, my loue, my life and all,
> So high attempts to lowe difgraces fall' ([1], [2]):

in [3] l. 4 is 'That hart being made the profpectiue': 'Tyme' and text of *a*, first in [4] and reprinted in [5].

SONNET. XXIII.

Time, cruell time, come and fubdue that Brow
    Which conquers all but thee, and thee too ftaies
As if fhe were exempt from Syeth or Bow,
From loue or yeares vnfubieĉt to decaies.
Or art thou growne in league with thofe faire eies
    That they may helpe thee to confume our daies ?
    Or doft thou fpare her for her cruelties,
    Being merciles like thee that no man weies ?
And yet thou feeft thy powre fhe difobayes,
    Cares not for thee, but lets thee wafte in vaine,
    And prodigall of howers and yeares betraies
    Beauty and youth t'opinion and difdaine.
Yet fpare her Time, let her exempted be,
She may become more kinde to thee or me.

Sonnet 23. First in ⁴ and reprinted in ⁵ : l. 13, cap. T accepted from
⁴, ⁵.

SONNET. XXIIII.

Thefe forrowing fighes, the fmoake of mine annoy,
    Thefe teares, which heate of facred flame diftils,
Are thofe due tributes that my faith doth pay
Vnto the tyrant, whofe vnkindnes kils.
I facrifife my youth, and blooming yeares
    At her proud feete, and fhe refpeĉts not it ;
    My flower vntimely's withred with my teares :
    And Winter woes, for fpring of youth vnfit.
She thinkes a looke may recompence my care,
    And fo with lookes, prolongs my long-lookt eafe,
    As fhort that bliffe, fo is the comfort rare,
    Yet muft that bliffe my hungry thoughts appeafe.

Thus fhe returnes my hopes fo fruitleffe euer,
Once let her loue indeed, or els eye me neuer.

Sonnet 24. l. 1, 'fmoakes' ¹, ², ³: l. 2, , after 'teares' accepted from ¹, ², ³ : l. 3, 'thefe' ¹, ²; l. 10, 'eafe' ¹, ², ³, accepted for 'cafe' of ⁴, ⁵, and a ; also the hyphen 'long-lookt': l. 14, 'eye me' ¹, ², ³—more quaint and strong—accepted. This is Sonnet xxi. in 1592, and xxii. in ³.

SONNET. XXV.

FAlfe Hope prolongs my euer certaine griefe,
    Traitour to me, and faithfull to my Loue:
A thoufand times it promif'd me reliefe,
Yet neuer any true effect I proue.
Oft when I finde in her no truth at all,
    I banifh her, and blame her trechery,
    Yet foone againe I muft her backe recall,
    As one that dies without her company.
Thus often as I chafe my hope from me,
    Straight-way fhe hafts her vnto DELIAS eies:
    Fed with fome pleafing looke there fhall fhe be,
    And fo fent backe, and thus my fortune lies.
Lookes feed my Hope, Hope fofters me in vaine,
Hopes are vnfure, when certaine is my paine.

Sonnet 25. l. 2, 'Traytrous' ¹; 'Traytours' ².

SONNET. XXVI.

LOoke in my griefes, and blame me not to mourne,
    From care to care that leades a life fo bad ;
Th'Orphan of Fortune, borne to be her fcorne,
Whofe clouded brow doth make my daies fo fad.
Long are their nights whofe cares do neuer fleepe,
    Lothfome their daies, whom no fun euer ioyd,
    Th'impreffion of her eyes do pearce fo deepe,
    That thus I liue both day and night annoyd.

But fince the fweeteft roote yeelds fruite fo fowre,
   Her praife from my complaint I may not part :
   I loue th'effect the caufe being of this powre,
   Ile praife her face, and blame her flinty heart.
Whilft we both make the world admire at vs,
Her for difdaine, and me for louing thus.

Sonnet 26. l. 1, 'morne' [1], [2]—cf. Sonnet XVI., l. 2 : l. 7, 'Her faireft eyes doe penetrate' [1], [2], [3]: l. 9, 'doth yeeld thus much ' [1], [2], [3]; *ibid.*, 'Sith ' [3] : l. 11, 'for that . . . . fuch' [1], [2], [3]: l. 13, 'that we make' [1], [2], [3].

SONNET. XXVII.

OFt and in vaine my rebel thoughts haue ventred,
      To ftop the paffage of my vanquifht hart :
   And fhut thofe waies my friendly foe firft entred,
   Hoping thereby to free my better part.
And whilft I garde thefe windowes of this forte,
   Where my harts theefe to vexe me made her choice:
   And thether all my forces doe tranfporte,
   An other paffage opens at her voice.
Her voyce betraies me to her hand and eye :
   My freedomes tyrants conquering all by arte.
   But ah, what glorie can fhe get thereby,
   With thee fuch powers to plague one filly harte.
Yet my foules foueraigne, fince I muft refigne,
Reigne in my thoughts, my loue and life are thine.

Sonnet 27. From [1] and reprinted in [2], but not in [3], [4], [5], or *a*.

SONNET. XXVIII.

R Aigne in my thoughts faire hand, fweete eye, rare
    voice,
  Poffeffe me whole, my hearts triumvirate :
  Yet heauy heart to make fo hard a choife,
  Of fuch as fpoile thy poore afflicted ftate.
For whilft they ftriue which fhall be Lord of all,
  All my poore life by them is troden downe ;
  They all erect their Trophies on my fall,
  And yeeld me nought that giues them their renowne.
When backe I looke, I figh my freedome paft,
  And waile the ftate wherein I prefent ftand :
  And fee my fortune euer like to laft,
  Finding me rain'd with fuch a heauy hand.
What can I do but yeeld ? and yeeld I doo,
And ferue all three, and yet they fpoile me too.

Sonnet 28. No variations.

SONNET. XXIX.

To M. P.

L Ike as the fpotleffe *Ermelin* diftreft,
  Circumpafi'd round with filth and lothfome mud:
  Pines in her griefe, imprifoned in her neft,
  And cannot iffue forth to feeke her good.
So I inuiron'd with a hatefull want,
  Looke to the heauens ; the heauens yeelde forth no
    grace :
  I fearch the earth, the earth I finde as fkant,
  I view my felfe, my felfe in wofull cafe.

Heauen nor earth will not, my felfe cannot wake
   A way through want to free my foule from care :
   But I muft pine, and in my pining lurke,
   Leaft my fad lookes bewray me how I fare.
My fortune mantled with a clowde f'obfcure ;
Thus fhades my life fo long as wants endure.

Sonnets 29 and 30 appeared only in 1592 ² (E 3 and E 3 verso)—former misnumbered XXXI.. as it follows XXVIII., folio 29 after folio 28. They are accepted and re-inserted. See our Memorial-Introduction on them, and specially on the 'M. P.' of Sonnet 29.

SONNET. XXX.

MY cares draw on mine euerlafting night,
   In horrors fable clowdes fets my liues funne :
   My liues fweet funne, my deareft comforts light,
   Will rife no more to me, whofe day is dunne.
I goe before vnto the Mirtle fhades.
   To attend the prefence of my worlds Deere ;
   And there prepare her flowres that neuer fades,
   And all things fit againft her comming there.
If any afke me why fo foone I came,
   Ile hide her finne and fay it was my lot :
   In life and death Ile tender her good name,
   My life nor death fhal neuer be her blot.
Although this world may feeme her deede to blame,
Th' *Elifian* ghofts fhall neuer know the fame.

SONNET. XXXI.

*Alluding to the Sparrow purſued by a Hawke, that
flew into the boſome of* Zenocrates.

VV Hilſt by thy eies purſu'd, my poore heart
        flew
Into the ſacred Refuge of thy breſt :
Thy rigor in that Sanctuary ſlew
That which thy ſuccring mercy ſhould haue bleſt.
No priuiledge of faith could it protect,
   Faith being with blood, and fiue yeares witnes ſign'd,
   Wherein no ſhew gaue cauſe of leaſt ſufpect,
   For well thou ſaw'ſt my loue and how I pin'd
Yet no mild comfort would thy Brow reueale,
   No lightning lookes which falling hopes erect :
   What bootes to lawes of Succor to appeale ?
   Ladies and Tyrants, neuer lawes refpect.
Then there I die from whence my life ſhould come,
And by that hand whom ſuch deeds ill become.

Sonnet 31.   The heading first in [3] : ll. 1, 3, 'it' at close in [1], [2], [3] ; *ibid.*,
'her' for 'thy' : l. 2, 'boſome of my deereſt' [1], [2], [3] : ll. 3-14—
     ' She there in that ſweete ſanctuary ſlew it,
       Where it preſum'd his ſafetie to be neereſt.
     My priuiledge of faith could not protect it,
       That was with blood and three yeeres witnes ſigned :
       In all which time ſhe neuer could ſufpect it,
       For well ſhe ſawe my loue, and how I pined.
     And yet no comfort would her brow reueale mee,
       No lightning looke, which falling hopes erecteth :
       What bootes to lawes of ſuccour to appeale mee ?
       Ladies and tyrants neuer lawes refpecteth.
     Then there I dye, where hop'd I to haue liuen ;
       And by that hand, which better might haue given' ([1], [2], [3]).

SONNET. XXXII.

THe Starre of my mifhap impof'd this paine
　　To fpend the Aprill of my yeares in griefe:
Finding my fortune euer in the waine
With ftill frefh cares, fupplide with no reliefe.
Yet thee I blame not, though for thee tis done,
　　But thefe weake whings prefuming to afpire,
　　Which now are melted by thine eyes bright fun,
　　That makes me fall from off my hie defire.
And in my fall I crye for helpe with fpeede,
　　No pittying eye lookes backe vpon my feares :
　　No fuccour finde I now when moft I neede,
　　My heates muft drowne in th'Ocean of my teares.
Which ftill muft beare the title of my wrong,
Cauf'd by thofe cruell beames that were fo ftrong.

Sonnet 32 is XXVII. of [1], XXXI. of [2], XXIX. of [3], XXXI. of [4], [5] and *a* : l. 1,
' payning ' [1], [2] : l. 2, ' wayling ' [1], [2] : l. 3, 'That neuer found my fortune
but in wayning ' [1], [2] : l. 4, ' my prefent woes affayling ' [1], [2] : l. 5, ' her
. . . fhe might haue bleft mee ' [1], [2] ; l. 6, ' But my defires wings fo high
afpiring ' [1], [2] : l. 7, ' Now melted with the funne that hath poffeft mee ' [1], [2] :
l. 8, ' Downe now I fall from off my high defiring ' [1], [2] : l. 9, ' doe cry for
mercy fpeedy ' [1], [2] : l. 10, ' mourning ' [1], [2] : l. 11, ' helpe I . . . when now
moft fauour neede I ' [1], [2] : l. 12, ' Th' Ocean of my teares muft drowne
me burning ' [1], [2] : l. 13, ' And this my death chriften her anew ' [1], [2] : l. 14,
' And giue the cruell Faire her tytle dew.'

SONNET. XXXIII.

STill in the trace of one perplexed thought,
　　My ceafles cares continually run on :
Seeking in vaine what I haue euer fought,
One in my loue, and her hard hart ftill one.

I who did neuer ioy in other Sun,
   And haue no ſtars but thoſe, that muſt fulfill
   The worke of rigor, fatally begun
   Vpon this heart, whom cruelty will kill.
Iniurious DELIA yet I loue thee ſtill,
   And will whilſt I ſhall draw this breath of mine,
   Ile tell the world that I deſeru'd but ill,
   And blame my ſelfe t'excuſe that heart of thine.
See then who ſinnes the greater of vs twaine,
I in my loue, or thou in thy diſdaine.

   Sonnet 33. Not in [1], [2]: first in [3] and reprinted in [4], [5] and *a* : [3] is so
different that it must be reproduced here—
        ' Still in the trace of my tormented thought,
          My ceaſeleſſe cares muſt martch on to my death :
          Thy leaſt regard too deerlie haue I bought,
          Who to my comfort neuer deign'ſt a breath.
        Why ſhould'ſt thou ſtop thine eares now to my cryes,
          Whoſe eyes were open, ready to oppreſſe me ?
          Why ſhutt'ſt thou not the cauſe whence al did riſe,
          Or heare me now, and ſeeke how to redreſſe me ?
        Iniurious DELIA, yet Ile loue thee ſtill,
          Whilſt that I breathe in ſorrow of my ſmart :
          Ile tell the world that I deſeru'd but ill,
          And blame my ſelfe for to excuſe thy hart.
        Then iudge who ſinnes the greater of vs twaine,
        I in my loue, or thou in thy diſdaine.'

SONNET. XXXIIII.

OFt do I maruell, whether DELIAS eies,
   Are eyes, or els two radiant ſtarres that ſhine
For how could Nature euer thus deuiſe,
Of earth on earth a ſubſtance ſo diuine.

Starres fure they are, whofe motions rule defires,
  And calme and tempeft follow their afpects :
  Their fweet appearing ftill fuch power infpires,
  That makes the world admire fo ftrange effects,
Yet whether fixt or wandring ftarres are they,
  Whofe influence rule the Orbe of my poore hart ?
  Fixt fure they are, but wandring make me ftray,
  In endles errors, whence I cannot part.
Starres then, not eyes, moue you with a milder view,
Your fweet afpect on him that honours you.

Sonnet 34. Not in [1], [2] : first in [3], and reprinted in [4], [5]. and *a.*

SONNET. XXXV.

A Nd yet I cannot reprehend the flight,
    Or blame th'attempt prefuming fo to fore ;
  The mounting venter for a high delight,
  Did make the honour of the fall the more.
For who gets wealth that puts not from the fhore ?
  Danger hath honor, great defignes their fame,
  Glory doth follow, courage goes before.
And though th'euent oft anfwers not the fame,
Suffice that high attempts haue neuer fhame.
  The meane obferuer (whom bafe fafety keeps)
  Liues without honour, dies without a name,
  And in eternall darkneffe euer fleeps.
And therefore DELIA, tis to me no blot,
To haue attempted, though attaind thee not.

Sonnet 35. Not in [1], [2] : first in [3] (xxx.), and reprinted in [4], [5] and *a.*

SONNET. XXXVI.

R Aifing my hopes on hills of high defire,
   Thinking to fcale the heauen of her hart,
My flender meanes prefum'd too high a part ;
Her thunder of difdaine forft me retire,
And threw me downe to paine in all this fire,
   Where loe I languifh in fo heauy fmart,
   Becaufe th'attempt was farre aboue my art :
   Her pride brook'd not poore foules fhould fo afpire.
Yet I proteft my high defiring will
   Was not to difpoffeffe her of her right :
   Her foueraignty fhould haue remained ftill,
   I onely fought the bliffe to haue her fight.
Her fight contented thus to fee me fpill,
Fram'd my defires fit for her eyes to kill.

Sonnet 36. l. 4, *a* badly inserts 'to' before 'retire': l. 8, 'fhould
come fo nye her ' ¹, ², ³ : l. 9, 'afpyring ' ¹, ², ³.

SONNET. XXXVII.

V V Hy dooft thou DELIA credit fo thy glaffe,
      Gazing thy beauty deign'd thee by the
         fkies :
And doeft not rather looke on him (alas)
   Whofe ftate beft fhewes the force of murdering eies ?
The broken tops of lofty trees declare
   The fury of a mercy-wanting ftorme ;
   And of what force thy wounding graces are,
   Vpon my felfe thou beft mayft finde the forme :

Then leaue thy glaffe, and gaze thy felfe on me,
　　That Mirror fhewes what power is in thy face :
　　To view your forme too much, may danger bee,
　　Narciffus chang'd t'a flower in fuch a cafe.
And you are chang'd, but not t'a Hiacint ;
I feare your eye hath turnd your heart to flint.

Sonnet 37. l. 1, ' O why dooth Delia . . . her ' ¹, ², ³ : l. 2, 'her' for
' thy' and ' thee' ¹, ², ³ : l. 3, 'dooth' ¹, ², ³ : l. 8, 'you . . . may '
¹, ², ³ : ll. 7, 9, 10, 'your.'

SONNET. XXXVIII.

I Once may fee when yeares fhall wreck my wrong,
　　When golden haires fhall change to filuer wier :
　　And thofe bright raies that kindle all this fire,
　　Shall faile in force, their working not fo ftrong :
Then beauty (now the burthen of my fong)
　　VVhofe glorious blaze the world doth fo admire,
　　Muft yeeld vp all to tyrant Times defire ;
　　Then fade thofe flowers that deckt her pride fo long.
VVhen, if fhe grieue to gaze her in her glaffe,
　　Which, then prefents her winter-withered hew,
　　Goe you my verfe, go tell her what fhe was ;
　　For what fhe was, fhe beft fhall find in you.
Your firy heate lets not her glory paffe,
But (Phænix-like) fhall make her liue anew.

Sonnet 38. l. 8, ' which ' ¹, ².

SONNET. XXXIX.

L Ooke DELIA how w'efteeme the halfe blowne
Rofe,
The image of thy blufh and Sommers honor :
Whilft yet her tender bud doth vndifclofe
That full of beauty, time beftowes vpon her.
No fooner fpreads her glory in the ayre,
But ftraight her wide blowne pomp comes to decline :
She then is fcornd that late adornd the Fayre ;
So fade the Rofes of thofe cheeks of thine.
No Aprill can reuiue thy withered flowres,
Whofe fpringing grace adorns thy glory now :
Swift fpeedy Time, feathred with flying houres,
Diffolues the beauty of the faireft brow.
Then do not thou fuch treafure waft in vaine,
But loue now whilft thou maift be lou'd againe.

Sonnet 39. l. 1, 'wee fteeme' [1], [2], [3] : l. 3—
'in . . . greene fhe doth inclofe,
That pure fweete beautie, Time' ([1], [2], [3]) :
l. 6, 'ful-blowne pride is in declyning' [1], [2], [3] : l. 8, 'So clowdes thy
beautie, after fayreft fhining' [1], [2], [3] : l. 10, 'blooming' [1], [2], [3] : *ibid.*, 'thy'
for 'the' misprint of *a*—accepted : l. 13, 'O let not their . . . riches'
[1], [2], [3] : l. 14, 'loue whilft that thou' [1], [2], [3].

SONNET. XL.

B Vt loue whilft that thou maift be lou'd againe,
Now whilft thy May hath fild thy lap with
flowers,
Now whilft thy beauty beares without a ftaine ;
Now vfe the Sommer fmiles, ere Winter lowers.
And whilft thou fpreadft vnto the rifing funne,

The faireſt flowre that euer ſaw the light,
Now ioy thy time before thy ſweet be done.
And (DELIA) thinke thy morning muſt haue night,
And that thy brightnes ſets at length to Weſt,
When thou wilt cloſe vp that which now thou ſhow'ſt,
And thinke the ſame becomes thy fading beſt,
Which then ſhall moſt inuaile and ſhadow moſt.
Men do not wey the ſtalke for that it was,
When once they find her flowre her glory pas.

Sonnet 40. l. 7, 'thy' twice inserted in *a* before ſweet': in [1], [2], spelt
'dunne'—so frequently : l. 12, 'hide it moſt, and couer loweſt' [1], [2], [3].

SONNET. XLI.

VVHen men ſhall find thy flower, thy glory
      paſſe,
And thou with carefull brow ſitting alone :
Receiued haſt this meſſage from thy glaſſe,
That tells the truth, and ſayes that all is gone ;
Freſh ſhalt thou ſee in me the wounds thou madſt,
Though ſpent thy flame, in me the heat remaining,
I that haue lou'd thee thus before thou fadſt,
My faith ſhall waxe, when thou are in thy waining.
The world ſhall finde this myracle in me,
That fire can burne when all the matter's ſpent :
Then what my faith hath bene thy ſelfe ſhall ſee,
And that thou waſt vnkinde, thou mayſt repent.
Thou maiſt repent that thou haſt ſcornd my teares,
When winter ſnowes vpon thy ſable haires.

Sonnet 41. l. 4, 'thee' [1]: l. 11, 'ſhalt' [1], [2], [3]: l. 14, 'golden heares'
[1], [2], [3].

SONNET. XLII.

VV Hen winter fnowes vpon thy fable haires,
  And froft of age hath nipt thy beauties
neere,
When darke fhall feeme thy day that neuer cleares,
 And all lies withred that was held fo deere.
Then take this picture which I here prefent thee,
 Limmed with a Penfill not all vnworthy :
Here fee the gifts that God and nature lent thee,
 Here read thy felfe, and what I fuffred for thee.
This may remaine thy lafting monument,
 Which happily pofterity may cherrifh,
Thefe colours with thy fading are not fpent,
 Thefe may remaine when thou and I fhall perifh.
If they remaine, then thou fhalt liue thereby,
They will remaine, and fo thou canft not die.

Sonnet 42. l. 1, 'golden' [1], [2], [3]: l. 2, 'flowers' [1], [2], [3].

SONNET. XLIII.

T Hou canft not die whilft any zeale abound
  In feeling hearts that can conceiue thefe lines ;
Though thou a *Laura* haft no *Petrarch* found,
 In bafe attire, yet cleerly Beauty fhines.
And I (though borne within a colder clime,)
 Do feele mine inward heat as great (I know it :)
He neuer had more faith, although more rime,
 I loue as well, though he could better fhow it.
But I may adde one feather to thy fame,
 To helpe her flight throughout the faireft Ile,
And if my pen could more enlarge thy name,
 Then fhouldft thou liue in an immortall ftile.

5

For though that *Laura* better limned be,
Suffice, thou fhalt be lou'd as well as fhee.

Sonnet 43. l. 4, , accepted after 'attire' ¹, ², ³.

SONNET. XLIIII.

BE not difpleafd that thefe my papers fhould
    Bewray vnto the world how faire thou art :
Or that my wits haue fhewed the beft they could.
(The chafteft flame that euer warmed hart)
Thinke not (fweet DELIA) this fhall be thy fhame,
    My Mufe fhould found thy praife with mournfull warble :
How many liue, the glory of whofe name
Shall reft in Ife, when thine is grau'd in Marble.
Thou maift in after ages liue efteem'd,
    Vnburied in thefe lines referu'd in purenes ;
Thefe fhall intombe thofe eies, that haue redeem'd
Me from the vulgar, thee from all obfcurenes.
Although my carefull accents neuer moou'd thee,
Yet count it no difgrace that I haue lou'd thee.

Sonnet 44. l. 1, ‘O be not grieu'd’ ¹, ², ³ : ⁴, ⁵ and *a* badly ‘ difplead’ :
l. 7, ‘liues’ ¹, ², ³ : l. 8, ¹ misprinted ‘yee.’

SONNET. XLV.

DELIA, thefe eyes that fo admireth thine,
    Haue feene thofe walls which proud ambition rear'd
To check the world, how they intomb'd haue lien
Within themfelues, and on them ploughs haue ear'd.
Yet neuer found that barbarous hand attaind
    The fpoyle of fame deferu'd by vertuous men :
Whofe glorious actions luckily had gaind
Th'eternall Annals of a happy pen.

And therefore grieue not if thy beauties die,
    Though time do fpoyle thee of the faireft vaile
    That euer yet couered mortality,
    And muft inftarre the Needle, and the Raile.
That Grace which doth more then in woman thee,
Liues in my lines, and muft eternall bee.

Sonnet 45. l. 2, 'the which ambition' [1], [2], [3]: l. 5, 'for all that no' [1], [2], [3]: l. 8, 'Annals' [1]: l. 9, Why then though Delia fade, let that not moue her' [1], [2], [3]: l. 11, 'mortallitie did couer' [1], [2], [3]: l. 12, 'which fhall . . . trayle' [1], [2], [3]: l. 13, 'grace, that vertue, all that feru'd t' in woman' [1], [2], [3]: l. 14, 'Dooth her vnto eternitie affommon' [1], [2], [3].

SONNET. XLVI.

MOft faire and louely Maide, looke from the fhore,
    See thy *Leander* ftriuing in thefe waues:
Poore foule quite fpent, whofe force can do no more,
Now fend forth hope, for now calme pitty faues.
And waft him to thee with thofe louely eies,
    A happy conuoy to a holy Land:
Now fhew thy power, and where thy vertue lies,
    To faue thine owne, ftretch out the faireft hand.
Stretch out the faireft hand, a pledge of peace;
    That hand that darts fo right and neuer miffes:
I fhall forget old wrongs, my griefes fhall ceafe;
    And that which gaue me wounds, Ile giue it kiffes.
Once let the Ocean of my cares finde fhore,
That thou be pleaf'd, and I may figh no more.

Sonnet 46. l. 1, 'Faire and louely' [1], [2], [3]: l. 3, 'fore-fpent' [1]: l. 5, *a* badly mifprints 'waft': l. 11, 'Ile not reuenge . . . wrath' [1], [2], [3]: l. 12, 'For' [1], [2], [3]: [4], [5] print 'gius.'

SONNET. XLVII.

R Ead in my face, a volume of difpaires,
  The wailing Iliads of my tragicke woe :
Drawne with my blood, and painted with my cares,
 Wrought by her hand that I haue honour'd fo.
Who whilft I burne, fhe fings at my foules wrack,
 Looking aloft from turret of her pride :
There my foules tyrant ioyes her, in the fack
 Of her owne feate, whereof I made her guide.
There do thefe fmoakes that from affliction rife,
 Serue as an incenfe to a cruell Dame :
A facrifice thrice-gratefull to her eies,
 Becaufe their power ferue to exact the fame.
Thus ruines fhe (to fatisfie her will,)
The temple, where her name was honour'd ftill.

Sonnet 47. l. 1, , after 'face' accepted [1], [2], [3] : l. 3, 'printed' [1], [2], [3] :
last l., , after 'Temple' accepted [1], [2], [3].

SONNET. XLVIII.

M Y DELIA hath the waters of mine eies,
  The ready handmayds on her grace t'attend :
That neuer fall to ebbe, but euer rife,
 For to their flow fhe neuer grants an end.
Th'Ocean neuer did attend more duly
 Vpon his fouereignes courfe, the nights pale Queene,
Nor payd the impoft of his waues more truly,
 Then mine vnto her cruelty hath beene.

Yet nought the rocke of that hard heart can moue,
  Where beat thefe teares with zeale, and fury driues :
  And yet I'd rather languifh for her loue,
  Then I would ioy the faireft fhe that liues.
And if I finde fuch pleafure to complaine,
What fhould I do then, if I fhould obtaine ?

Sonnet 48. 1. 1, 'Cynthia' [1], [2]: l. 2, 'attending' [1], [2], [3]: *a* badly 'but neuer dries' from [4], [5]; [3] giues the true reading 'but euer rife'—accepted : l. 4, 'ending' [1], [2], [3]: l. 8, 'to her in truth haue euer beene' [1], [2], [3]: *ibid.*, 'Deitie become' [3]: l. 10, 'thefe' accepted [1], [2], [3]: *a* badly 'their' from [4], [5]: *ibid.*, 'driueth' [1], [2], [3]: l. 11, 'for' [1], [2], [3]: 'I'd' for 'I': l. 12, 'liueth' [1], [2], [3]: ll. 13, 14—

> ' I doubt to finde fuch pleafure in my gayning,
>   As now I tafte in compas of complayning' ([1], [2], [3]).

SONNET. XLIX.

How long fhall I in mine afflicion mourne ?
  A burden to my felfe, diftreft in minde :
When fhall my interdicted hopes returne,
From out difpaire, wherein they liue confinde ?
When fhal her troubled brow charg'd with difdaine
  Reueale the treafure which her fmiles impart ?
When fhall my faith the happines attaine,
  To breake the Ife that hath congeald her heart ?
Vnto her felfe, her felfe my loue doth fommon,
  (If loue in her hath any power to moue,)
And let her tell me as fhe is a woman,
  Whether my faith hath not deferu'd her loue ?
I know her heart cannot but iudge with me,
Although her eyes my aduerfaries be.

Sonnet 49. l. 1, 'morne' [1], [2]—cf. Sonnet XVI., l. 2 : l. 5, 'troubled' in errata [1], as dropped : ll. 13, 14—

> ' I knowe fhe cannot but muft needes confeffe it,
>   Yet deignes not with one fimple figne t'expreffe it ' ([1], [2], [3]).

SONNET. L.

BEautie (sweet Loue) is like the morning dew,
    Whose short refresh vpon the tender greene :
Cheeres for a time, but till the Sunne doth shew,
And straight tis gone as it had neuer beene.
Soone doth it fade that makes the fairest florish,
    Short is the glory of the blushing Rose :
The hew which thou so carefully dost norish,
    Yet which at length thou must be forc'd to lose.
When thou surcharg'd with burthen of thy yeeres,
    Shalt bend thy wrinckles homeward to the earth,
And that in Beauties leafe expir'd, appeares
    The date of Age, the Kalends of our death.
But ah ! no more, this must not be foretold,
For women grieue to thinke they must be old.

Sonnet 50. ll. 11, 12—
        ' When tyme hath made a passport for thy feares,
          Dated in age . . .' ([1], [2], [3]) :
l. 13, ' hath beene often tolde ' [1], [2], [3] : l. 14, ' And.'

SONNET. LI.

I Must not grieue my Loue, whose eies would reede
    Lines of delight, whereon her youth might smile :
Flowers haue a time before they come to seede,
And she is yong, and now must sport the while.
Ah sport (sweet Maide) in seafon of these yeares,
    And learne to gather flowers before they wither :
And where the sweetest blossomes first appeares,
    Let loue and youth conduct thy pleafures thither.

Lighten foorth fmiles to cleere the clouded aire,
  And calme the tempeft which my fighs doo raife :
  Pitty and fmiles doe beft become the faire,
  Pitty and fmiles muft onely yeeld thee praife.
Make me to fay, when all my griefes are gone,
Happy the heart that figh'd for fuch a one.

Sonnet 51. l. 3, ' a ' dropped by *a* inadvertently : l. 5, ' Ah,' [1], [2], [3] accepted for ' And ' of *a* and [4], [5] : l. 12, ' fhall yeeld thee lafting ' [1], [2], [3] : l. 13, ' I hope ' [1], [2], [3].

SONNET. LII.

At the Authors going into Italie.

ANd whither (poore forfaken) wilt thou goe,
  To goe from forrow, and thine owne diftreffe ?
When euery place prefents like face of woe,
  And no remoue can make thy forrowes leffe ?
Yet goe (forfaken) leaue thefe Woods, thefe plaines,
  Leaue her and all, and all for her that leaues
  Thee and thy Loue forlorne, and both difdaines :
  And of both, wrongfull deemes, and ill conceiues.
Seeke out fome place, and fee if any place
  Can giue the leaft releafe vnto thy griefe :
  Conuay thee from the thought of thy difgrace,
  Steale from thy felfe, and be thy cares owne thiefe.
But yet, what comforts fhall I hereby gainè ?
Bearing the wound, I needes muft feele the paine.

Sonnet 52. Not in [1], [2] : heading accepted from [3] : l. 1, ' O Whether ' [3].

SONNET. LIII.

¶ *This Sonnet was made at the Author's beeing in Italie.*

DRawne with th'atractiue vertue of her eyes,
    My toucht heart turnes it to that happy coft:
My ioyfull North, where all my fortune lies,
The leuell of my hopes defired moft,
There where my *Delia* fairer then the Sunne,
    Deckt with her youth whereon the world doth fmile,
Ioyes in that honor which her eyes haue wonne,
Th'eternall wonder of our happy Ile.
Florifh faire *Albion*, glory of the North,
    Neptunes beft darling, held betweene his armes:
Diuided from the world, as better worth,
    Kept for himfelfe, defended from all harmes.
Still let difarmed peace decke her and thee:
And Mufe-foe *Mars*, abroad farre foftred bee.

Sonnet 53. Heading from ³ accepted: l. 5, *a* badly misprints 'were':
l. 6, 'fmyleth' ¹, ², ³: l. 7, 'beautie wonne' ¹, ², ³: l. 8, 'Thˢ eternall
volume which her fame compyleth' ¹, ²: l. 10, 'Neptunes darling' ¹, ²:
ibid., misprinted 'arme' in *a*.

SONNET. LIIII.

CAre-charmer Sleepe, fonne of the fable night,
    Brother to death, in filent darknes borne:
Relieue my languifh, and reftore the light,
With darke forgetting of my care returne.
And let the day be time enough to mourne
    The fhipwracke of my ill aduentred youth:
Let waking eyes fuffice to waile their fcorne,
Without the torment of the nights vntruth.

Ceafe dreames, th'Images of day defires,
  To modell forth the paffions of the morrow :
  Neuer let rifing Sunne approue you liers,
  To adde more griefe to aggrauate my forrow.
Still let me fleepe, imbracing clouds in vaine,
And neuer wake to feele the dayes difdaine.

Sonnet 54. l. 5, 'morne' ¹, ², as before : l. 9, 'th' ymagery of our day' ¹, ², ³.

SONNET. LV.

LEt others fing of Knights and Palladines ;
  In aged accents, and vntimely words :
  Paint fhadowes in imaginary lines,
  VVhich well the reach of their high wits records ;
But I muft fing of thee, and thofe faire eies,
  Autentique fhall my verfe in time to come,
  VVhen yet th'vnborne fhall fay, Lo where fhe lies,
  VVhofe beauty made him fpeake that elfe was
    dombe.
Thefe are the Arkes, the Trophies I erect,
  That fortifie thy name againft old age :
  And thefe thy facred vertues muft protect,
  Againft the darke and times confuming rage.
Though th'error of my youth in them appeare,
Suffice, they fhew I liu'd and lou'd thee deare.

Sonnet 55. l. 13, 'they fhall difcouer' ¹, ², ³ : l. 14, 'was thy louer' ¹, ², ³.

SONNET. LVI.

A S to the Roman that would free his Land,
      His error was his honour and renowne :
And more the fame of his miftaking hand,
    Then if he had the tyrant ouer-throwne.
So DELIA, hath mine error made me knowne,
    And my deceiu'd attempt, deferu'd more fame ;
    Then if I had the victory mine owne :
    And thy hard heart had yeelded vp the fame.
And fo likewife, renowmed is thy blame,
    Thy cruelty, thy glory ; O ftrange cafe
    That errors fhould be grac'd that merit fhame,
    And finne of frownes bring honour to the face.
Yet happy DELIA that thou waft vnkind,
Though happier far if thou wouldft change thy mind.

   Sonnet 56.   First in [3]: l. 14, 'yet'[3].

SONNET. LVII.

L Ike as the Lute delights or els diflikes,
      As is his art that playes vpon the fame :
So founds my Mufe according as fhe ftrikes
On my heart-ftrings high tun'd vnto her fame.
Her touch doth caufe the warble of the found,
    VVhich here I yeeld in lamentable wife :
    A wayling defcant on the fweeteft ground,
    VVhofe due reports giue honor to her eyes.

Elfe harfh my ftile, vntunable my Mufe,
  Hoarce founds the voyce that prayfeth not her
    name ;
  If any pleafing relifh here I vfe,
  Then iudge the world her beauty giues the fame.
For no ground els could make the Muficke fuch,
Nor other hand could giue fo true a touch.

Sonnet 57. l. 1, 'that ioyes' [1], [2], [3] : ll. 13, 14—
  'O happie ground that makes . . . .
  And bleffed hand that giues fo fweete' ([1], [2], [3]).

SONNET. LVIII.

NOne other fame mine vnambitious Mufe,
  Affected euer, but t'eternize thee :
All other honors doe my hopes refufe,
Which meaner priz'd and momentary bee.
For God forbid I fhould my Papers blot,
  With mercenary lines, with feruile Pen :
  Praifing vertues in them that haue them not,
  Bafely attending on the hopes of men.
No, no, my Verfe refpects not *Thames* nor *Theaters*,
  Nor feekes it to be knowne vnto the Great,
  But *Auon* rich in fame, though poore in waters,
  Shall haue my Song, where *Delia* hath her feat:
Auon fhall be my *Thames*, and fhe my Song,
No other prouder Brookes fhall heare my wrong.

Sonnet 58. l. 11, 'rich' [1], [2], [3], accepted for 'poore' of [3], [4], [5], and *a* ;
also 'though' for 'and ' : l. 14, 'Ile found her name the Ryuer all along
[1], [2], [3].

SONNET. LIX.

VNhappy Pen, and ill-accepted lines
        That intimate in vaine my chafte defire :
My chafte defire, which from darke forrow fhines,
Inkindled by her eyes celeftiall fire.
Celeftiall fire, and vnrefpecting powres
    Which pitty not the wounds made by their might,
    Shew'd in thefe lines, the worke of carefull houres,
    The facrifice here offred to her fight.
But fince fhe weighs them not, this refts for me,
    Ile mone my felfe, and hide the wrong I haue :
    And fo content me that her frownes fhould be
    To m'infant ftile the Cradle, and the Graue.
What though my Mufe no honor get thereby,
Each Bird fings to her felfe, and fo will I.

Sonnet 59. l. 1, 'papers' [1], [2], [3] : l. 2, 'defiers' [1], [2], [3]: l. 3, 'defiers, the euer burning tapers' [1], [2], [3] : l. 4, 'fiers' [1], [2], [3] : l. 5, 'fiers' [1], [2], [3] : l. 6, 'That deigne not view the glory of your' [1], [2], [3] : l. 7, 'In humble lines' [1], [2], [3] : l. 8, 'I offer' [1], [2], [3] : l. 9, 'fith' [1], [2], [3] : *ibid.*, 'fcornes her owne' [1], [2], [3] : l. 13, 'felfe' [1], [2], [3].

SONNET. LX.

LO here the impoft of a faith entire
        Which loue doth pay, and her difdaine extorts:
    Behold the meffage of a chaft defire
    Which tells the world how much my griefe imports.
Thefe tributary paffions, beauties due,
    I fend those eyes the cabinets of loue :
    That Cruelty her felfe might grieue to view
    Th'affliction her vnkind difdaine doth moue.

And how I liue caſt downe from off all myrth,
 Penſiue alone, onely but with Diſpaire :
 My ioyes abortiue, periſh in their byrth.
 My griefes long liu'd, and care ſucceeding care.
This is my ſtate, and DELIAS heart is ſuch,
I ſay no more, I feare I ſayd too much.

Sonnet 60. l. 1, 'vnfaining' [1], [2], [3] : l. 2, 'That loue hath paide . . . .
extortes' [1], [2], [3] : l. 3, 'my iuſt complayning' [1], [2], [3] : l. 4, 'That ſhewes
. . . imported' [1], [2], [3] : l. 5, 'plaintes fraught with deſire' [1], [2], [3] : l. 7,
'The Paradice whereto my hopes aſpire' [1], [2], [3] : ll. 8, 9—
        'From out this hell, which mine afflictions proue.
        Wherein I thus doe liue caſt downe from myrth ' ([1], [2], [3]) :
l. 10, 'none but deſpayre about mee' [1], [2], [3] : l. 11, 'periſht at' [1], [2], [3]—
'periſht' accepted for 'periſh' from [4], [5] and *a* : l. 12, 'carres . . . will
not dye without mee' [1], [2], [3] : 'Finis' [1], [2], [3] : l. 14, qu.—'I've '?

The Ode and other related Poems appended will be found under 'IX.
Occasional Poems.'

III.

THE COMPLAINT OF ROSAMOND.

1592.

NOTE.

As shown by the title-pages of 1592 (1st and 2nd edition), the 'Complaint of Rofamond' accompanied the 'Sonnets to Delia'; and so in [3], [4], [5], and *a*. Our text (as throughout) is the 4to of 1623; but underneath the various readings, additions, etc., of the earlier texts are recorded.

In 1594 edition (Malone 354) on last leaf (verso) the following notes are written :—

EPITAPHIUM.

Hic jacet in tombo Rofa mundi non Rofa munda.
Non redolet fed olet, quæ redolere folet.

Heer lyes intoumbd w^th^in this compaſt ſtone,
ffayre *Rofamond*, not nowe the world's fayre rofe;
Who whilome fweeteſt fmelt, follow'd by none,
Doth nowe wth deadly ſtaunch infeſt ye nofe.

F. L.

AND

This marble ſtone doth heere enclofe
The worlds fayre not now fweete rofe,
In whome too late the worlds repofe
Doth nowe wth ſtinch offende the nofe.

F.d.

See Memorial-Introduction on Mr. J. Payne Collier's reprints of the early texts of the ' Complaint.'

A. B. G

THE
COMPLAINT OF
Rofamond.

OVt from the horror of infernall deepes,
  My poore afflicted ghoft comes here to plain it,
Attended with my fhame that neuer fleepes,
The´fpot wherewith my kind, and youth did ftaine it.
My body found a graue where to containe it :
  A fheete could hide my face, but not my fin,
  For Fame findes neuer Tombe t'inclofe it in.

And which is worfe, my foule is now denied,
Her tranfport to the fweet Elifian reft,
The ioyfull bliffe for Ghofts repurified,   10
The euer-fpringing Gardens of the bleft :
Caron denies me waftage with the reft.
  And faies my foule can neuer paffe the Riuer,
  Till Louers fighs on earth fhall it deliuer.

So fhall I neuer paffe ; for how fhould I
Procure this facrifice amongft the liuing ?
Time hath long fince worne out the memorie
Both of my life, and liues vniuft depriuing :
Sorrow for me is dead for aye reuiuing.
  Rofamond hath little left her but her name,   20
  And that difgrac'd, for time hath wrong'd the fame.

l. 4, , accepted from ¹, ² : also : after ' it ' for . : l. 9, ' Elifean ' ¹ : l. 18,
: for , ¹, ², ³.

No Mufe fuggefts the pitty of my cafe,
Each Pen doth ouerpaffe my iuft complaint,
Whilft others are prefer'd, though farre more bafe ;
Shores wife is grac'd, and paffes for a Saint ;
Her Legend iuftifies her foule attaint.
    F er well-told tale did fuch compaffion finde,
    That fhe is pafs'd, and I am left behinde.

Which feene with griefe, my miferable Ghoft,
(Whilome inuefted in fo faire a vaile,   30
Which whilft it liu'd, was honoured of the moft,
And being dead, giues matter to bewaile,)
Comes to follicite thee, (whilft others faile)
    To take this tafke, and in thy wofull fong
    To forme my cafe, and regifter my wrong.

Although I know thy iuft lamenting Mufe,
Toill'd in th'afflicion of thine owne diftreffe,
In others cares hath little time to vfe,
And therefore maift efteeme of mine the leffe :
Yet as thy hopes attend happy redreffe,   40
    The ioyes depending on a womans grace,
    So moue thy minde a wofull womans cafe.

Delia may hap to deigne to reade our Story,
And offer vp her fighs among the reft,
Whofe merit wculd fuffice for both our glory,
Whereby thou might'ft be grac'd and I be bleft ;
That indulgence would profit me the beft.
    Such powre fhe hath by whom thy youth is led,
    To ioy the liuing, and to bleffe the dead.

1. 27, hyphen accepted ¹, ², ³: l. 33, 'fince' ¹, ², ³: l. 37, 'affliction'
accepted ¹, ², ³, for 'affection': l. 43, 'deynge' ¹, ².

So I (through beauty) made the wofull'ſt wight,   50
By beauty might haue comfort after death :
That dying faireſt, by the faireſt might
Finde life aboue on earth, and reſt beneath.
She that can bleſſe vs with one happy breath,
   Giue comfort to thy Muſe to doe her beſt,
   That thereby thou mayſt ioy, and I might reſt.

Thus ſaid : forthwith mou'd with a tender care,
And pitty (which my ſelfe could neuer find,)
What ſhe deſir'd, my Muſe deign'd to declare,
And therefore, will'd her boldly tell her mind.   60
And I (more willing) tooke this charge aſſign'd,
   Becauſe her griefes were worthy to be knowne,
   And telling hers, might hap forget mine owne.

Then write (quoth ſhe) the ruine of my youth,
Report the downe-fall of my ſlippry ſtate :
Of all my life reueale the ſimple truth,
To teach to others what I learnt too late.
Exemplifie my frailtie, tell how Fate
   Keepes in eternall darke our fortunes hidden,
   And ere they come to know them tis forbidden. 70

For whilſt the Sun-ſhine of my fortune laſted,
I ioy'd the happieſt warmth, the ſweeteſt heate
That euer yet imperious beauty taſted,
I had what glory euer fleſh could get :
But this faire morning had a ſhamefull ſet.
   Diſgrace dark'd honour, ſinne did cloude my brow,
   As note the ſequell, and Ile tell thee how.

l. 65, : ¹, ², ³ for , .

The bloud I ſtain'd, was good and of the beſt,
My birth had honour, and my beauty fame :
Nature and Fortune ioyn'd to make me bleſt.   80
Had I had grace t'haue knowne to vſe the ſame.
My education ſhew'd from whence I came,
　　And all concurr'd to make me happy furſt,
　　That ſo great hope might make me more accurſt.

Happy liu'd I whilſt parents eye did guide
The indiſcretion of my feeble wayes,
And Countrey-home kept me from being eide,
Where beſt vnknowne I ſpent my ſweeteſt daies :
Till that my friends mine honour ſought to raiſe
　　To higher place, which greater credit yeelds,   90
　　Deeming ſuch beauty was vnfit for fields.

From Countrey then to Court I was prefer'd
From calme to ſtormes, from ſhore into the deepes :
There where I periſh'd, where my youth firſt err'd,
There where I loſt the floure which honour keepes,
There where the worſer thriues, the better weepes ;
　　Ah me (poore wench) on this vnhappy ſhelfe,
　　I grounded me, and caſt away my ſelfe.

There whereas fraile and tender beauty ſtands,
With all aſſaulting powres inuironed ;   100
Hauing but prayers and weake feeble hands
To hold their honours Fort vnuanquiſhed ;
There where to ſtand, and be vnconquered,
　　Is to b'aboue the nature of our kinde,
　　That cannot long for pitty be vnkinde.

l. 98, , ¹, ², ³, accepted : ll. 99—105 first inserted in ⁴ are reprinted in ⁵,
though left out in 1599 edition, but again in 1605.

For thither com'd, when yeeres had arm'd my youth,
With rareft proofe of beauty euer feene :
When my reuiuing eie had learnt the truth,
That it had powre to make the winter greene,
And floure affections whereas none had beene ;   110
   Soone could I teach my brow to tyrannize,
   And make the world doe homage to mine eyes.

For age I faw (though yeeres with cold conceit,
Congeal'd their thoughts againft a warme defire,)
Yet figh their want, and looke at fuch a baite ;
I faw how youth was waxe before the fire ;
I faw by ftealth, I fram'd my looke a lyre.
   Yet well perceiu'd, how Fortune made me then
   The enuie of my fexe, and wonder vnto men.

Looke how a Comet at the firft appearing,   120
Drawes all mens eyes with wonder to behold it ;
Or as the faddeft tale at fudden hearing,
Makes filent liftning vnto him that told it,
So did my fpeech when Rubies did vnfold it ;
   So did the blazing of my blufh appeare,
   T'amaze the world, that holdes fuch fights fo deere.

Ah beauty Syren, faire enchaunting good,
Sweet filent Rhetorique of perfwading eyes :
Dombe Eloquence, whofe powre doth moue the bloud,
More then the words or wifedome of the wife ;   130
Still harmony, whofe Diapafon lyes
   Within a brow, the key which paffions moue,
   To rauifh fence, and play a world in loue.

What might I then not doe whofe powre was fuch ?
What cannot women doe that know their powre ?
What women knowes it not (I feare too much)
How bliffe or bale lyes in their laugh or lowre ?
Whilft they inioy their happy blooming flowre,
   Whilft Nature decks them in their beft attires
   Of youth and beauty, which the world admires. 140

Such one was I, my beauty was mine owne,
No borrowed blufh which bank-rot beauties feeke :
That new-found fhame, a finne to vs vnknowne,
Th'adulterate beauty of a falfed cheeke :
Vilde ftaine to honour, and to women eeke,
   Seeing that time our fading muft detect,
   Thus with defect to couer our defect.

Impietie of times, Chaftities abator,
Falfhood, wherein thy felfe thy felfe denieft :
Treafon to counterfeit the feale of Nature,   150
The ftampe of heauen, impreffed by the higheft.
Difgrace vnto the world, to whom thou lieft,
   Idoll vnto thy felfe, fhame to the wife,
   And all that honour thee Idolatrife.

Farre was that finne from vs whofe age was pure,
VVhen fimple beauty was accounted beft,
The time when women had no other lure
But modeftie, pure cheekes, a vertuous breft :
This was the pompe wherewith my youth was bleft.
   Thefe were the weapons which mine honour wonne,
   In all the conflicts which mine eyes begunne.   161

l. 139, 'her' (*bis*) 'proper fayre' [1], [2], [3] : l. 140, 'Which cheeres the
worlde, ioyes each fight, fweetens th'ayre' [1], [2], [3] (in [2] misprinted 'arye') :
l. 152, , [1], [2], [3], for . : l. 158, : [1], [2], [3] for . : l. 160, spelt 'wunne' [1], [2] : 'wun' [3].

VVhich were not fmall; I wrought on no meane obie&,
A Crowne was at my feete, Scepters obey'd me :
VVhom Fortune made my King, Loue made my Subie&,
VVho did command the Land, moft humbly pray'd me:
Henry the fecond, that fo highly weigh'd me,
   Found well (by proofe) the priuiledge of beauty,
   That it had powre to counter-maund all duty.

For after all his victories in *France*,
And all the triumphs of his honour wonne :   170
Vnmatcht by fword, was vanquifht by a glancé,
And hotter warres within his breaft begunne.
VVarres, whom whole legions of defires drew on :
   Againft all which, my chaftitie contends,
   VVith force of honour, which my fhame defends.

No Armour might be found that could defend,
Tranfpearcing raies of criftall poynted eyes :
No ftratagem, no reafon could amend,
No not his age ; (yet old men fhould be wife)
But fhewes deceiue, outward appearance lies.   180
   Let none for feeming fo, thinke Saints of others,
   For all are men, and all haue fuckt their mothers.

VVho would haue thought a Monarch would haue euer
Obey'd his hand-maide of fo meane eftate ;
Vulture ambition feeding on his liuer,
Age hauing worne his pleafures out of date.
But hap comes neuer, or it comes too late,
   For fuch a dainty which his youth found not,
   Vnto his feeble age did chaunce allot.

l. 163, : ¹, ², ³ for ,: and so l. 165 : l. 170, 'Tryumphing in the honour
of his deedes ' ¹, ², ³ : l. 172, ' bofome breedes ' ¹, ², ³ : l. 173, 'defires feedes'
¹, ², ³ : l. 174, ' oppofes' ¹, ², ³ : l, 175, 'The fielde of honour vertue neuer
lofes ' ¹, ², ³ : l. 184, 'a ftate ' ¹, ².

Ah Fortune, neuer abfolutely good,   190
For that fome croffe ftill counter-checks our lucke ;
As here behold th'incompatible blood,
Of age and youth was that whereon we ftucke :
VVhofe lothing, we from Natures breafts doe fucke,
 As oppofite to what our bloud requires ;
 For equall age, doth equall like defires.

But mighty men, in higheft honour fitting,
Nought but applaufe and pleafure can behold :
Sooth'd in their liking, careleffe what is fitting,
May not be fuffred once to thinke the'are old :   200
Not trufting what they fee, but what is told.
 Miferable fortune to forget fo farre
 The ftate of flefh, and what our frailties are.

Yet muft I needs excufe fo great defe&ct ;
For drinking of the *Lethe* of mine eies,
H'is forc'd forget himfelfe, and all refpe&ct
Of maiefty, whereon his ftate relies :
And now of loues and pleafures muft deuife.
 For thus reuiu'd againe, he ferues and fu'th,
 And feekes all meanes to vndermine my youth. 210

Which neuer by affault he could recouer,
So well incamp'd in ftrength of chafte defires :
My cleane-arm'd thoughts repell'd an vnchafte louer.
The Crowne that could command what it requires,
I leffer priz'd then Chaftities attires.
 Th'vnftained vaile, which innocents adornes,
 Th'vngathred Rofe, defended with the thornes.

l. 195, ; ¹, ², ³ for , .

And fafe mine honor ftood, till that in truth,
One of my Sexe, of place and nature bad,
Was fet in ambufh to intrap my youth. 220
One in the habit of like frailtie clad,
One who the liu'ry of like weakeneffe had.
 A feeming Matron, yet a finfull Monfter,
 As by her words the Chafter fort may confter.

She fet vpon me with the fmootheft fpeech
That Court and age could cunningly deuife :
Th'one authentique, made her fit to teach,
The other learn'd her how to fubtilife.
Both were enough to circumuent the wife.
 A document that well might teach the fage, 230
 That there's no truft in youth, nor hope in age.

Daughter (faid fhe) behold thy happy chance,
That haft the lot caft downe into thy lap,
Whereby thou may'ft thy honor great aduance,
Whilft thou (vnhappy) wilt not fee thy hap :
Such fond refpect thy youth doth fo inwrap,
 T'oppofe thy felfe againft thine owne good fortune,
 That poynts thee out, and feemes thee to importune.

Dooft thou not fee, how that thy King (thy *Ioue*)
Lightens forth glory on thy darke eftate : 240
And fhowers downe gold and treafure from aboue,
Whilft thou dooft fhut thy lap againft thy Fate ?
Fie Fondling fie, thou wilt repent too late
 The error of thy youth ; that canft not fee
 What is the Fortune that doth follow thee.

    l. 230, ' may ' ¹, ², ³: l. 232, ' faith ' ¹, ².

Thou muſt not thinke thy flower can alwayes flouriſh,
And that thy beauty will be ſtill admired ;
But that thoſe raies which all theſe flames doe nouriſh,
Cancell'd with Time, will haue their date expired,
And men will ſcorne what now is ſo deſired.   250
    Our frailties doome is written in the flowers,
    Which flouriſh now, and fade ere many howers.

Reade in my face the ruines of my youth,
The wracke of yeeres vpon my aged brow ;
I haue beene faire (I muſt confeſſe the truth)
And ſtood vpon as nice reſpeEts as thou ;
I loſt my time, and I repent it now.
    But were I to beginne my youth againe,
    I would redeeme the time I ſpent in vaine.

But thou haſt yeeres and priuiledge to vſe them,   260
Thy priuiledge doth beare Beauties great ſeale ;
Beſides, the Law of Nature doth excuſe them,
To whom thy youth may haue a iuſt appeale.
Eſteeme not Fame more then thou doſt thy weale.
    Fame (whereof the world ſeemes to make ſuch choice)
    Is but an Eccho, and an idle voice.

Then why ſhould this reſpeEt of honor bound vs,
In th'imaginarie liſts of Reputation ?
Titles which cold ſeueritie hath found vs,
Breath of the vulgar, foe to recreation :   270
Melancholies opinion, Cuſtomes relation ;
    Pleaſures plague, beauties ſcourge, hell to the faire,
    To leaue the ſweet for Caſtles in the aire.

l. 256, 'thow ' ¹, ², ³.

Pleafure is felt, opinion but conceau'd,
Honor, a thing without vs, not our owne :
Whereof we fee how many are bereau'd,
Which fhould haue reap'd the glory they had fowne :
And many haue it, yet vnworthy, knowne.
   So breathes his blaft this many-headed beaft,
   Whereof the wifeft haue efteemed leaft.   280

The fubtill City-women, better learned,
Efteeme them chafte enough that beft feeme fo :
Who though they fport, it fhall not be difcerned,
Their face bewraies not what their bodies do ;
Tis warie walking that doth faflyeft go,
   With fhew of Vertue, as the cunning knowes :
   Babes are beguild with fweets, and men with fhowes.

Then vfe thy tallent, youth fhall be thy warrant,
And let not honor from thy fports detra&ct :
Thou muft not fondly thinke thy felfe tranfparant, 290
That thofe who fee thy face can iudge thy fa&ct ;
Let her haue fhame that cannot clofely a&ct.
   And feeme the chafte, which is the chiefeft arte,
   For what we feeme each fees, none knowes our hart.

The mightie who can with fuch finnes difpence,
In fteed of fhame doe honors great beftow,
A worthie author doth redeeme th'offence,
And makes the fcarlet finne as white as fnow.
The Maieftie that doth defcend fo low,
   Is not defilde, but pure remaines therein :   300
   And being facred, fan&ctifies the fin.

l. 279, 'blafts' [1], [2] : l. 291, 'the' [1], [3] : l. 294, 'fees' [1], [3], accepted for 'fee' : ll. 295—301 from [1], [2], [3] : l. 298, misprinted 'sarelet.'

What, dooſt thou ſtand on this, that he is old ?
Thy beautie hath the more to worke vpon ;
Thy pleaſures want ſhall be ſupplide with gold,
Cold age dotes moſt when heate of youth is gone :
Enticing words preuaile with ſuch a one.
    Alluring ſhewes moſt deepe impreſſion ſtrikes,
    For age is prone to credit what it likes.

Here interrupt, ſhe leaues me in a doubt,
When loe beganne the cumbat in my blood :   310
Seeing my youth inuiron'd round about,
The ground vncertaine where my reaſons ſtood ;
Small my defence to make my party good,
    Againſt ſuch powers which were ſo ſurely laid,
    To ouerthrow a poore vnſkilfull Maide.

Treaſon was in my bones, my ſelfe conſpiring,
To ſell my ſelfe to luſt, my ſoule to ſin :
Pure-bluſhing ſhame was euen in retiring,
Leauing the ſacred hold it glori'd in.
Honor lay proſtrate for my fleſh to win,   320
    When cleaner thoughts my weakeneſſe gan vpbray
    Againſt my ſelfe, and ſhame did force me ſay ;

Ah *Roſamond*, what doth thy fleſh prepare ?
Deſtruction to thy dayes, death to thy fame :
Wilt thou betray that honor held with care,
T'entombe with blacke reproch a ſpotted name ?
Leauing thy bluſh the colours of thy ſhame ?
    Opening thy feete to ſinne, thy ſoule to luſt,
    Graceleſſe to lay thy glory in the duſt ?

l. 321, 'can' ¹, ². See Glossarial-Index, *s.v.*

Nay firſt let th'earth gape wide to ſwallow thee, 330
And ſhut thee vp in boſome with her dead,
Ere Serpent tempt thee taſte forbidden Tree,
Or feele the warmth of an vnlawfull bed ;
Suffring thy ſelfe by luſt to be miſled ;
   So to diſgrace thy ſelfe and grieue thine heires,
   That *Cliffords* race ſhould ſcorne thee one of theirs.

Neuer wiſh longer to enioy the Aire,
Then that thou breath'ſt the breath of Chaſtitie :
Longer then thou preſeru'ſt thy ſoule as faire
As is thy face, free from impuritie. 340
Thy face, that makes th'admir'd in euery eie,
   Where Natures care ſuch rarities inroule ;
   Which vſ'd amiſſe, may ſerue to damne thy ſoule.

But what ? he is my King, and may conſtraine me,
Whether I yeeld or not, I liue defamed.
The World will thinke Authoritie did gaine me,
I ſhall be iudg'd his Loue, and ſo be ſhamed :
We ſee the faire condemn'd, that neuer gamed.
   And if I yeeld, tis honorable ſhame,
   If not, I liue diſgrac'd, yet thought the ſame. 350

What way is left thee then (vnhappy Maide)
Whereby thy ſpotleſſe foote may wander out
This dreadfull danger, which thou ſeeſt is laide,
Wherein thy ſhame doth compaſſe thee about ?
Thy ſimple yeeres cannot reſolue this doubt.
   Thy Youth can neuer guide thy foote ſo euen,
   But (in deſpite) ſome ſcandall will be giuen.

Thus ftood I ballanc'd equally precize,
Till my fraile flefh did weigh me downe to fin ;
Till world and pleafure made me partialize,   360
And glittering pompe my vanitie did win,
When to excufe my fault my lufts begin.
    And impious thoughts alledg'd this wanton claufe,
    That though I finn'd, my finne had honeft caufe.

So well the golden balles caft downe before me,
Could entertaine my courfe, hinder my way :
Whereat my wretchleffe youth ftooping to ftore me,
Loft me the Goale, the Glory and the Day.
Pleafure had fet my well fchool'd thoughts to play,
    And bade me vfe the vertue of mine eies,   370
    For fweetly it fits the faire to wantonife.

Thus wrought to finne, foone was I train'd from Court,
T'a follitarie Grange, there to attend
The time the King fhould thither make refort,
Where he Loues long-defired worke fhould end.
Thither he daily meffages doth fend,
    With coftly Iewels (Orators of Loue,)
    Which (ah, too well men know) doe women moue.

The day before the night of my defeature,
He greetes me with a Cafket richly wrought ;   380
So rare, that Arte did feeme to ftriue with Nature,
T'expreffe the cunning Worke-mans curious thought ;
The myfterie whereof I prying fought,
    And found engrauen on the lid aboue,
    Amymone, how fhe with *Neptune* ftroue.

l. 367, 'rechleffe' [1], [2], [3].

Amymone, old *Danaus* faireſt Daughter,
As ſhe was fetching water all alone
At *Lerna* : whereas *Neptune* came and caught her :
From whom ſhe ſtriu'd and ſtruggled to be gone,
Beating the aire with cries and piteous mone ;   390
   But all in vaine, with him ſhe's forc'd to go ;
   Tis ſhame that men ſhould vſe poore maidens ſo.

There might I ſee deſcribed how ſhe lay,
At thoſe proude feete, not ſatisfied with prayer:
Wayling her heauy hap, curſing the day,
In aĉt ſo pitious to expreſſe deſpaire.
And by how much more grieu'd, ſo much more faire.
   Her teares vpon her cheekes (poore carefull Gerle,)
   Did ſeeme againſt the Sunne Chriſtall and Pearle :

Whoſe pure cleere ſtreames (which lo ſo faire appeares)
Wrought hotter flames (O miracle of Loue   401
That kindles fire in water, heate in teares,
And makes negleĉted beauty mightier proue,
Teaching afflĉted eyes affeĉts to moue ;)
   To ſhew that nothing ill becomes the faire,
   But cruelty, which yeelds vnto no prayer.

This hauing view'd, and therewith ſomething moued,
Figured I finde within the other ſquares,
Transformed *Io, Ioues* deerely loued,
In her afflĉtion how ſhe ſtrangely fares.   410
Strangely diſtreſſ'd (O beauty, borne to cares)
   Turn'd to a Heiffer, kept with iealous eyes,
   Alwayes in danger of her hatefull ſpies.

l. 390, ' Beating ' ¹, ², ³, accepted for ' Bathing ' of *a* : l. 391, ' ſh'is ' ¹, ², ³:
l. 404,) inserted instead of after l. 401 at ' Loue ' : l. 406, ' that ' ¹, ², ³ :
l. 408, ' found ' ¹, ².

Thefe prefidents prefented to my view,
Wherein the prefage of my fall was fhowne,
Might haue fore-warn'd me well what would enfue,
And others harmes haue made me fhun mine owne.
But Fate is not preuented, though foreknowne.
    For that muft hap, decreed by heauenly powers,
    Who worke our fall, yet make the fault ftill ours. 420

Witneffe the world, wherein is nothing rifer,
Then miferies vnken'd before they come :
Who can the Characters of chaunce decipher,
Written in cloudes of our concealed dome ?
Which though perhaps haue beene reueal'd to fome,
    Yet that fo doubtfull (as fucceffe did proue them)
    That men muft know they haue the Heau'ns aboue
      them.

I faw the finne wherein my foote was entring,
I faw how that difhonour did attend it,
I faw the fhame whereon my flefh was ventring,   430
Yet had I not the power for to defend it.
So weake is fence, when error hath condemn'd it.
    We fee what's good, and thereto we confent,
    But yet we choofe the worft, and foone repent.

And now I come to tell the worft of ilneffe,
Now drawes the date of mine affliction neere.
Now when the darke had wrapt vp all in ftilneffe,
And dreadfull blacke had difpoffeft the cleere,
Com'd was the Night (mother of fleepe and feare)
    Who with her fable-mantle friendly couers   440
    The fweet-ftolne fport of ioyfull meeting Louers.

ll. 433-4, ' vs ' ¹, ² : added ' confent,' ' repent.'

When lo, I ioy'd my Louer, not my Loue,
And felt the hand of luft moft vndefired :
Enforc'd th'vnprooued bitter fweet to proue,
Which yeeldes no naturall pleafure when tis hired.
Loue's not conftrain'd, nor yet of due required.
 Iudge they who are vnfortunately wed,
 What tis to come vnto a loathed bed.

But foone his age receiu'd his fhort contenting,
And fleepe feal'd vp his languifhing defires :   450
When he turnes to his reft, I to repenting,
Into my felfe my waking thought retires :
My nakedneffe had prou'd my fences liers.
 Now opned were mine eyes to looke therein ;
 For firft we tafte the fruit, then fee our fin.

Now did I finde my felfe vnparadif'd,
From thofe pure fields of my fo cleane beginning :
Now I perceiu'd how ill I was aduif'd,
My flefh gan loathe the new-felt touch of finning ;
Shame leaues vs by degrees, not at firft winning. 460
 For Nature checks a new offence with loathing,
 But vfe of finne doth make it feeme as nothing.

And vfe of finne did worke in me a boldneffe,
And loue in him, incorporates fuch zeale,
That iealoufie increaf'd with ages coldneffe,
Fearing to loofe the ioy of all his weale ;
Or doubting time his ftealth might elfe reueale,
 H'is driuen to deuife fome fubtill way,
 How he might fafelyeft keepe fo rich a pray.

l. 454, ; added for , : and so ll. 466, 474, 482.

A ftately Pallace he forthwith did build,   470
Whofe intricate innumerable wayes
With fuch confufed errours, fo beguilde
Th'vnguided Entrers, with vncertaine ftrayes,
And doubtfull turnings, kept them in delayes ;
    With booteleffe labor leading them about,
    Able to finde no way, nor in, nor out.

Within the clofed bofome of which frame,
That feru'd a Centre to that goodly Round,
Were lodgings, with a Garden to the fame,
With fweeteft flowers that eu'r adorn'd the ground, 480
And all the pleafures that delight hath found,
    T'entertaine the fenfe of wanton eies ;
    Fuell of Loue, from whence lufts flames arife.

Here I inclof'd from all the world afunder,
The Minotaure of fhame kept for difgrace,
The Monfter of Fortune, and the worlds wonder,
Liu'd cloiftred in fo defolate a cafe :
None but the King might come into the place,
    With certaine Maides that did attend my neede,
    And he himfelfe came guided by a threed.   490

O Iealoufie, daughter of Enuie and Loue,
Moft wayward iffue of a gentle Sire ;
Foftred with feares, thy fathers ioyes t'improue,
Mirth-marring Monfter, borne a fubtill lier ;
Hatefull vnto thy felfe, flying thine owne defire :
    Feeding vpon fufpeft that doth renue thee,
    Happy were Louers if they neuer knew thee.

Thou haſt a thouſand Gates thou entereſt by,
Condemning trembling paſſions to our hart ;
Hundred ey'd *Argus*, euer waking Spie,   500
Pale Hagge, infernall Furie, pleaſures ſmart,
Enuious Obſeruer, prying in euery part ;
   Suſpicious, fearefull, gazing ſtill about thee,
   O would to God that loue could be without thee.

Thou didſt depriue (through falſe ſuggeſting feare)
Him of content, and me of libertie :
The onely good that women hold ſo deere,
And turnſt my freedome to captiuitie,
Firſt made a priſoner, ere an enemie.
   Enioyn'd the ranſome of my bodies ſhame,   510
   Which though I paid, could not redeeme the ſame.

What greater torment euer could haue beene,
Then to inforce the faire to liue retir'd ?
For what is beauty if it bee not ſeene ?
Or what is't to be ſeene if not admir'd ?
And though admir'd, vnleſſe in loue deſir'd ?
   Neuer were cheekes of Roſes, locks of Amber,
   Ordain'd to liue impriſon'd in a Chamber.

Nature created beauty for the view,
(Like as the Fire for heate, the Sunne for light :)   520
The faire doe hold this priuiledge as due
By ancient Charter, to liue moſt in ſight,
And ſhe that is debar'd it, hath not right.
   In vaine our friends from this, doe vs dehort,
   For Beauty will be where is moſt reſort.

l. 515, 'vnleſſe' ¹, ², ³ : l. 524, 'in this vſe dehorting' ¹, ², ³ : l. 525
'reſorting' ¹, ², ³.

Witneffe the faireft ftreetes that Thames doth vifit,
The wondrous concourfe of the glittring Faire :
For what rare woman deckt with beauty is it,
That thither couets not to make repaire ?
The follitary Countrey may not ftay her.   530
  Here is the centre of all beauties beft,
  Excepting *Delia*, left t'adorne the Weft.

Here doth the curious with iudiciall eies,
Contemplate Beauty glorioufly attired :
And herein all our chiefeft glory lies,
To liue where we are praif'd and moft defired.
O how we ioy to fee our felues admired,
  Whilft niggardly our fauours we difcouer :
  We loue to be belou'd, yet fcorne the Louer.

Yet would to God my foote had neuer mou'd   540
From Countrey-fafety, from the fields of reft :
To know the danger to be highly lou'd,
And liue in pompe to braue among the beft :
Happy for me, better had I beene bleft,
  If I vnluckily had neuer ftraide,
  But liu'd at home a happy Countrey Maide.

Whofe vnaffe&ted innocencie thinkes
No guilefull fraude, as doth the Courtly liuer :
Shee's deckt with truth ; the Riuer where fhe drinkes
Doth ferue her for her glaffe, her Counfell-giuer ;   550
She loues fincerely, and is loued euer.
  Her dayes are peace, and fo fhe ends her breath,
  (True life that knowes not what's to die till death.)

l. 531, mis-spelt 'beatties,' and l. 532, 'Delea' in *a* : l. 549, ; for
, inserted.

So fhould I neuer haue beene regiftred,
In the blacke booke of the vnfortunate :
Nor had my name inrol'd with maides mifled,
Which bought their pleafures at fo hie a rate.
Nor had I taught, (through my vnhapy fate)
    This Leffon (which my felfe learn't with expence)
    How moft it hurts, that moft delights the fence. 560

Shame followes finne, difgrace is duely giuen,
Impietie will out, neuer fo clofely done :
No walles can hide vs from the eye of Heauen,
For fhame muft end what wickedneffe begun ;
Forth breakes reproch when we leaft thinke thereon,
    And this is euer proper vnto Courts,
    That nothing can be done, but Fame reports.

Fame doth explore what lies moft fecret hidden,
Entring the Clofet of the Pallace dweller :
Abroade reuealing what is moft forbidden.   570
Of truth and falfhood both an equall teller,
Tis not a guard can ferue for to expell her.
    The Sword of Iuftice cannot cut her Wings,
    Nor ftop her mouth from vtt'ring fecret things.

And this our ftealth fhe could not long conceale,
From her whom fuch a forfeit moft concerned :
The wronged Queene, who could fo clofely deale,
That fhe the whole of all our practife learned,
And watcht a time when leaft it was difcerned,
    In abfence of the King to wreake her wrong,   580
    With fuch reuenge as fhe defired long.

The Labyrinth ſhe entred by that Threed,
That ſeru'd a conduƈt to my abſent Lord,
Left there by chance, reſeru'd for ſuch a deed,
Where ſhe ſurpriz'd me whom ſhe ſo abhor'd.
Enrag'd with madneſſe, ſcarce ſhe ſpeakes a word,
　　But flies with eager furie to my face,
　　Offring me moſt vnwomanly diſgrace.

Looke how a Tygreſſe that hath loſt her Whelpe,
Runnes fiercely ranging through the Woods aſtray: 590
And ſeeing her ſelfe depriu'd of hope or helpe,
Furiouſly aſſaults what's in her way,
To ſatisfie her wrath, (not for a pray)
　　So fell ſhe on me in outragious wiſe,
　　As could Diſdaine and Iealouſie deuiſe.

And after all her vile reproches vſde,
She forc'd me take the Poyſon ſhe had brought,
To end the life that had her ſo abuſde,
And free her feares, and eaſe her iealous thought.
No cruelty her wrath could leaue vnwrought,　　600
　　No ſpitefull aƈt that to Reuenge is common ;
　　(No beaſt being fiercer then a iealous woman.)

Here take (ſaith ſhe) thou impudent vncleane,
Baſe graceleſſe Strumpet, take this next your heart ;
Your Love-ſicke heart, that ouer-charg'd hath beene
With Pleaſures ſurfeit, muſt be purg'd with Art.
This potion hath a power that will conuart
　　To naught, thoſe humors that oppreſſe you ſo.
　　And (Gerle) Ile ſee you take it ere I go.

l. 608, 'nought' ².

What, ftand you now amaz'd, retire you backe ?   610
Tremble you (Minion ?) come, difpatch with fpeed ;
There is no helpe, your Champion now you lacke,
And all thefe teares you fhed will nothing fteed ;
Thofe dainty fingers needes muft doe the deed.
   Take it, or I will drench you elfe by force,
   And trifle not, left that I vfe you worfe.

Hauing this bloody doome from hellifh breath,
My wofull eyes on euery fide I caft :
Rigor about me, in my hand my death,
Prefenting me the horror of my laft :   620
All hope of pitty and of comfort paft.
   No meanes, no power ; no forces to contend,
   My trembling hands muft giue my felfe my end.

Thofe hands that beauties minifters had bin,
They muft giue death, that me adorn'd of late,
That mouth that newly gaue confent to fin,
Muft now receiue deftruction in thereat,
That body which my luft did violate,
   Muft facrifice it felfe t'appeafe the wrong.
   (So fhort is pleafure, glory lafts not long.)   630

And fhe no fooner faw I had it taken,
But forth fhe rufhes (proud with victorie)
And leaues m'alone, of all the world forfaken,
Except of Death, which fhe had left with me.
(Death and my felfe alone together be.)
   To whom fhe did her full reuenge refer.
   Oh poore weake conqueft both for him and her.

ll. 617—770 first appeared in ³, and reprinted in ⁴ and ⁵ : also in 1599
and 1605.

Then ſtraight my Conſcience ſummons vp my ſinne,
T'appeare before me in a hideous face ;
Now doth the terror of my ſoule beginne,   640
When eu'ry corner of that hatefull place
Dictates mine error, and reueales diſgrace ;
    Whilſt I remaine oppreſt in euery part,
    Death in my body, Horror at my hart.

Downe on my bed my loathſome ſelfe I caſt,
The bed that likewiſe giues in euidence
Againſt my ſoule, and tels I was vnchaſt ;
Tels I was wanton, tels I followed ſence,
And therefore caſt, by guilt of mine offence ;
    Muſt here the right of Heauen needes ſatisfie,   650
    And where I wanton lay, muſt wretched die.

Here I beganne to waile my hard miſhap,
My ſudden, ſtrange vnlookt for miſery,
Accuſing them that did my youth intrap,
To giue me ſuch a fall of infamy.
And poore diſtreſſed *Roſamond* (ſaid I)
    Is this thy glory got, to die forlorne
    In Deſarts where no eare can heare thee mourne ?

Nor any eye of pitty to behold
The wofull end of my ſad tragedie ;   660
But that thy wrongs vnſeene, thy tale vntold,
Muſt here in ſecret ſilence buried lie.
And with thee, thine excuſe together die.
    Thy ſinne reueal'd, but thy repentance hid,
    Thy ſhame aliue, but dead what thy death did.

Yet breathe out to thefe Walles the breath of mone,
Tell th'Aaire thy plaints, fince men thou canft not tell.
And though thou perifh defolate alone,
Tell yet thy felfe, what thy felfe knowes too well :
Vtter thy griefe wherewith thy foule doth fwell.   670
   And let thy heart pitty thy hearts remorfe,
   And be thy felfe the mourner and the corfe.

Condole thee here, clad all in blacke difpaire,
With filence onely, and a dying bed ;
Thou that of late, fo flourifhing, fo faire,
Did'ft glorious liue, admir'd and honored :
And now from friends, from fuccour hither led,
   Art made a fpoyle to luft, to wrath, to death,
   And in difgrace, forc'd here to yeeld thy breath.

Did Nature (for this good) ingeniate,   680
To fhew in thee the glory of her beft ;
Framing thine eye the ftarre of thy ill fate,
Making thy face the foe to fpoyle the reft ?
O Beautie thou an enemie profeft
   To Chaftitie and vs that loue thee moft,
   Without thee, how w'are loath'd, and with thee loft ?

You, you that proude with libertie and beautie,
(And well may you be proude that you be fo)
Glitter in Court, lou'd and obferu'd of dutie ;
Would God I might to you but ere I goe   690
Speake what I feele, to warne you by my woe,
   To keepe your feete in cleanly paths of fhame,
   That no inticing may diuert the fame.

l. 680 ('ô for thys ') ³ : l. 687, ' O you ' ³.

See'ng how againſt your tender weakeneſſe ſtill,
The ſtrength of wit, and gold, and all is bent ;
And all th'aſſaults that euer might or ſkill,
Can giue againſt a chaſte and cleane intent :
Ah let not greatneſſe worke you to conſent.
    The ſpot is foule, though by a Monarch made,
    Kings cannot priuiledge what God forbade.   700

Locke vp therefore the treaſure of your loue,
Vnder the ſureſt keyes of feare and ſhame :
And let no powers haue power chaſte thoughts to moue
To make a lawleſſe entry on your fame.
Open to thoſe the comfort of your flame,
    Whoſe equall loue ſhall march with equall pace,
    In thoſe pure wayes that leade to no diſgrace.

For ſee how many diſcontented beds,
Our owne aſpiring, or our Parents pride
Haue cauſ'd, whilſt that ambition vainely weds   710
Wealth and not loue, honor and nought beſide :
Whilſt married but to titles, we abide
    As wedded Widowes, wanting what we haue,
    When ſhadowes cannot giue vs what we craue.

Or whilſt we ſpend the freſheſt of our time,
The ſweet of youth in plotting in the ayre ;
Alas, how oft we fall, hoping to clime ;
Or whither as vnprofitably faire,
Whilſt thoſe decayes which are without repaire,
    Make vs negleƈted, ſcorned and reprou'd.   720
    (And O what are we, if we be not lou'd ?)

Faften therefore vpon occafions fit,
Left this, or that, or like difgrace as mine,
Doe ouer-take your youth or ruine it,
And cloude with infamie your beauties fhine :
Seeing how many feeke to vndermine
    The treafurie that's vnpoffeft of any :
    And hard tis kept that is defired of many.

And flie (O flie) thefe Bed-brokers vncleane,
(The Monfters of our Sexe) that make a pray   730
Of their owne kinde, by an vnkindely meane ;
And euen (like Vipers) eating out a way
Through th'wombe of their owne fhame, accurfed they
    Liue by the death of Fame, the gaine of fin,
    The filth of luft, vncleanneffe wallowes in.

As if t'were not inough that we (poore we)
Haue weakeneffe, beautie, gold and men our foes,
But we muft haue fome of our felues to be
Traitors vnto our felues, to ioyne with thofe ?
Such as our feeble forces doe difclofe,   740
    And ftill betray our caufe, our fhame, our youth,
    To luft, to folly, and to mens vntruth ?

Hatefull confounders both of bloud and lawes,
Vilde Orators of fhame, that pleade delight :
Vngracious agents in a wicked caufe,
Factors for darkeneffe, meffengers of night,
Serpents of guile, Deuils, that doe inuite
    The wanton tafte of that forbidden tree,
    Whofe fruit once pluckt, will fhew how foule we bee.

l. 736, ' O is it ' ².

You in the habite of a graue afpect,   750
(In credit by the truft of yeeres) can fhoe
The cunning wayes of luft, and can direct
The faire and wilie wantons how to goe,
Hauing (your lothefome felues) your youth fpent fo.
 And in vncleanneffe euer haue beene fed,
 By the reuenue of a wanton bed.

By you haue beene the innocent betraide,
The blufhing fearefull, boldned vnto fin,
The wife made fubtill, fubtill made the maide,
The hufband fcorn'd, difhonored the kin :   760
Parents difgrac'd, children infamous bin.
 Confuf'd our race, and falfified our blood,
 Whilft fathers fonnes poffeffe wrong fathers good.

This, and much more, I would haue vttered then,
A teftament to be recorded ftill,
Sign'd with my bloud, fubfcrib'd with Confcience Pen,
To warne the faire and beautifull from ill.
Though I could wifh (by th'example of my will)
 I had not left this note vnto the faire,
 But dide inteftate to haue had no heire.   770

But now, the poyfon fpread through all my vaines,
Gan difpoffeffe my liuing fences quite :
And nought-refpecting death (the laft of paines)
Plac'd his pale colours (th'enfigne of his might)
Vpon his new-got fpoyle before his right ;
 Thence chac'd my foule, fetting my day ere noone,
 When I leaft thought my ioyes could end fo foone.

l. 768, 'And ô I wifh': l. 771, 'The poyfon foone difperc'd' [1], [2]:
l. 772, 'Had' [1], [2], [3]: l. 773, 'When naught' [1], [2]; 'and naught' [3]; hyphen
inserted.

And as conuaide t'vntimely funerals,
My fcarce cold corfe not fuffred longer ftay,
Behold, the King (by chance) returning, fals   780
T'incounter with the fame vpon the way,
As he repair'd to fee his deareft ioy.
      Not thinking fuch a meeting could haue beene,
      To fee his Loue, and feeing bin vnfeene.

Iudge thofe whom chance depriues of fweeteft treafure,
What tis to lofe a thing. we hold fo deere :
The beft delight, wherein our foule takes pleafure,
The fweet of life, that penetrates fo neere.
What paffions feeles that heart, inforc'd to beare
      The deepe impreffion of fo ftrange a fight,   790
      That ouerwhelmes vs, or confounds vs quite ?

Amaz'd he ftands, nor voice nor body fteares,
Words had no paffage, teares no iffue found,
For forrow fhut vp words, wrath kept in teares ;
Confuf'd affects each other doe confound.
Oppreft with griefe, his paffions had no bound :
      Striuing to tell his woes, words would not come ;
      For light cares fpeake, when mightie griefes are dombe.

At length, extremitie breakes out a way,
Through which, th'imprifoned voice with teares attended,
Wailes out a found that forrowes doe bewray :   801
With armes a-croffe, and eyes to heauen bended,
Vaporing out fighs that to the fkies afcended.
      Sighs (the poore eafe calamitie affords)
      Which ferue for fpeech when forrow wanteth words.

l. 791, ' Tongue, pen, nor art, can neuer fhew a right ' [1], [2], [3] : l. 799,
'away' [1], [2] (bad).

O Heauens (quoth he) why doe mine eyes behold
The hatefull raies of this vnhappy Sunne?
Why haue I light to fee my finnes controld,
With bloud of mine owne fhame thus vildely done?
How can my fight endure to looke thereon?   810
   Why doth not blacke eternall darkeneffe hide,
   That from mine eyes, my heart cannot abide?

What faw my life wherein my foule might ioy;
What had my dayes whom troubles ftill afflicted,
But onely this, to counterpoize annoy?
This ioy, this hope, which Death hath interdicted;
This fweet, whofe loffe hath all diftreffe inflicted;
   This, that did feafon all my fowre of life,
   Vext ftill at home with broiles, abroade in ftrife.

Vext ftill at home with broiles, abroade in ftrife,   820
Diffenfion in my bloud, iarres in my bed:
Diftruft at boord, fufpecting ftill my life,
Spending the night in horror, daies in dread;
(Such life hath Tyrants, and this life I led.)
   Thefe miferies goe mafk'd in glittering fhowes,
   Which wife men fee, the vulgar little knowes.

Thus as thefe paffions doe him ouerwhelme,
He drawes him neere my body to behold it.
And as the Vine married vnto the Elme
With ftrict imbraces, fo doth he infold it: 830
And as he in his carefull armes doth hold it,
   Viewing the face that euen death commends,
   On fenceleffe lippes, millions of kiffes fpends.

l. 807, 'Sonne' [1], [2], [3]: l. 817, 'afflicted' [1], [2].

Pittifull mouth (faith he) that liuing gaueſt
The ſweeteſt comfort that my ſoule could wiſh :
O be it lawfull now, that dead thou haueſt,
This ſorrowing farewell of a dying kiſſe ;
And you faire eyes, containers of my bliſſe,
   ·Motiues of Loue, borne to be matched neuer,
   Entomb'd in your ſweet circles, ſleepe for euer. 840

Ah, how me thinkes I ſee Death dallying ſeekes,
To entertaine it ſelfe in Loues ſweet place ;
Decayed Roſes of diſcoloured cheekes,
Doe yet retaine deere notes of former grace :
And vgly Death ſits faire within her face ;
   Sweet remnants reſting of Vermillian red,
   That Death it ſelfe doubts whether ſhe be dead.

Wonder of beautie, oh receiue theſe plaints,
Theſe obſequies, the laſt that I ſhall make thee :
For loe, my ſoule that now already faints,   850
(That lou'd thee liuing, dead will not forſake thee)
Haſtens her ſpeedy courſe to ouer-take thee.
   Ile meete my death, and free my ſelfe thereby,
   For (ah) what can he doe that cannot die ?

Yet ere I die, thus much my ſoule doth vow,
Reuenge ſhall ſweeten death with eaſe of minde :
And I will cauſe Poſterity ſhall know,
How faire thou wert about all women kinde ;
And after-Ages Monuments ſhall finde,
   Shewing thy beautïes title, not thy name,   860
   Roſe of the world, that ſweetned ſo the fame.

l. 834, ' quoth ' ¹, ², ³ : l. 845, ' ougly ' ¹, ² : l. 849, ' The ' ¹, ².

This faid, though more defirous yet to fay,
(For forrow is vnwilling to giue ouer)
He doth repreffe what griefe would elfe bewray,
Left he too much his paffions fhould difcouer ;
And yet refpect fcarce bridles fuch a Louer,
    So farre tranfported that he knowes not whither,
    For Loue and Maieftie dwell ill togither.

Then were my Funerals not long deferred,
But done with all the rites pompe could deuife,   870
At *Godftow*, where my body was interred,
And richly tomb'd in honorable wife :
Where yet as now fcarce any note defcries
    Vnto thefe times, the memory of me,
    Marble and Braffe fo little lafting be.

For thofe walles which the credulous deuout,
And apt-beleeuing ignorant did found ;
With willing zeale, that neuer call'd in doubt,
That time their workes fhould euer fo confound,
Lie like confufed heapes as vnder-ground.   880
    And what their ignorance efteem'd fo holy,
    The wifer ages doe account as folly.

And were it not thy fauourable lines
Re-edified the wracke of my decayes,
And that thy accents willingly affignes
Some farther date, and giue me longer daies,
Few in this age had knowne my beauties praife.
    But thus renew'd, my fame redeemes fome time,
    Till other ages fhall neglect thy Rime.

l. 865. 'might' ¹, ² : l. 867, 'whether' ¹, ².

Then when Confufion in her courfe fhall bring   890
Sad defolation on the times to come :
When mirthleffe *Thames* fhall haue no Swanne to fing,
All Muficke filent, and the Mufes dombe.
And yet euen then it muft be knowne to fome,
 That once they flourifht, though not cherifht fo,
 And *Thames* had Swannes as well as euer *Po*.

But here an end, I may no longer ftay,
I muft returne t'attend at *Stygian* flood :
Yet ere I goe, this one word more I pray,
Tell *Delia*, now her figh may doe me good,   900
And will her note the frailtie of our blood.
 And if I paffe vnto thofe happy bankes,
 Then fhe muft haue her praife, thy Pen her thankes.

So vanifht fhe, and left me to returne
To profecute the tenor of my woes,
Eternall matter for my Mufe to mourne :
But (yet) the world hath heard too much of thofe,
My youth fuch errors muft no more difclofe.
 Ile hide the reft, and grieue for what hath beene ;
 Who made me knowne, muft make me liue vnfeene.
           910

ll. 902, 904, 'thee' added : l. 914, 'vanifht' accepted from ¹, ², for ³ and
a 'vanquifht.'

FINIS.

8

IV.

A LETTER FROM OCTAUIA TO MARCUS ANTONIUS.

1599.

NOTE

This 'Letter from Octauia' was first published in the 'Poeticall Essayes' of 1599, and was reprinted in the folios of 1601 and 1602, and also in 1605, 1607, 1611 onward to *a*. Exceptionally, a collation of the successive editions reveals practically no variations.   A. B. G.

To the right Honourable and moſt
vertuous Lady, the Lady MARGARET
Counteſſe of Cumberland.[1]

Lthough the meaner ſort (whoſe
thoughts are plac'd
As in another Region, farre below
The ſphere of greatneſſe) cannot
rightly taſte
What touch it hath, nor right her
paſſions know :
Yet haue I here aduentur'd to beſtow
Words vpon griefe, as my griefes comprehend ;
And made this great afflicted Lady ſhow,   10
Out of my feelings, what ſhe might haue pend.
And here the fame, I bring forth, to attend
Vpon thy reuerent name, to liue with thee
Moſt vertuous Lady, that vouchſaf'ſt to lend
Eare to my notes, and comfort vnto mee,
That one day may thine owne faire vertues ſpread,
B'ing Secretary now but to the dead.   17

[1] See Memorial-Introduction for notice of this 'Fair Lady.'

The Argument.

Pon the *second agreement (the first*
being broken through iealousie of a
disproportion of eminencie) betweene
the Triumuiri Octauius Cæsar, Marcus
Antonius, & Lepidus: Octauia *the*
sister of Octauius Cæsar, *was maried*
to Antonius, *as a lincke to combine*
that which nere yet, the greatest strength
of Nature, or any power of nearest respect could long 10
hold together, who made but the instrument of others
ends, and deliuered vp as an Ostage, to serue the oppor-
tunity of aduantages, met not with that integrity she
brought : but as highly preferred to affliction, encountred
with all the grieuances that beate vpon the misery of
greatnesse, exposed to stand betwixt the diuerse tending
humours of vnquiet parties. For Antonie *hauing yet*
vpon him the fetters of Ægypt, layd on by the power of
a most incomparable beauty, could admit no new Lawes
into the state of his affection, or dispose of himselfe, being 20
not himselfe, but as hauing his heart turned Eastward,
whither the poynt of his desires were directed, toucht
with the strongest allurements that ambition, and a
licentious soueraignty could draw a man vnto : could
not truly descend to the priuate loue of a ciuill nurtred

l. 8, 'neuer' 1601.

*Matron, whoſe entertainment bounded with modeſty, and
the nature of her education, knew not to clothe her
affeƈtions in any other colours, then the plaine habit of
truth : wherein ſhe euer ſuted all her aƈtions, and vſed
all her beſt ornaments of Honeſtie, to winne the good* 30
*liking of him that held her, but as a Curtaine, drawne
betweene him and* Oƈtauius, *to ſhadow his other purpoſes
withall : which the ſharpe ſight of an equally iealous
ambition could ſoone pierce into, and as eaſily looke
thorow, and ouer bloud and nature, as he to abuſe it :
and therefore, to preuent his aſpiring, he armes his forces,
either to reduce* Antonie *to the ranke of his eſtate, or
elſe to diſranke him out of ſtate and all. When* Oƈtauia
by the imployment of Antonie *(as being not yet ready to
put his fortune to her tryall) throwes her ſelfe, great* 40
*with childe, and as big with ſorrow, into the trauell of a
moſt labourſome reconciliation : taking her iourney from
the fartheſt part of* Greece, *to finde* Oƈtauius, *with whom
her care and teares were ſo good agents, that they effeƈted
their Commiſſion beyond all expeƈtation : and for that
time quite diſarmed their wrath, which yet long could
not hold ſo. For* Antonius *falling into the relapſe of his
former diſeaſe, watching his opportunity, got ouer againe
into* Ægvpt, *where he ſo forgot himſelfe, that hee quite
put off his owne nature, and wholly became a prey* 50
*to his pleaſures, as if he had wound himſelfe
out of the reſpeƈt of Countrey, bloud and
alliance ; which gaue to* Oƈtauia *the
cauſe of much affliƈtion, and
to mee, the Argument of
this Letter.* 56

A Letter ſent from *Oƈtauia* to
her huſband *Marcus Antonius*
into Ægypt.

I

O thee (yet deere) though moſt dis-
loyall Lord,
Whom impious loue keeps in a
barbarous land,
Thy wronged wife *Oƈtauia* ſendeth
word
Of th'vnkind wounds receiued by thy
hand :
Great *Antony*, O let thine eyes afford
But to permit thy heart to vnderſtand
The hurt thou doſt, and doe but reade her teares,
That ſtill is thine though thou wilt not be hers.

2

Although perhaps, theſe my complaints may come
Whilſt thou in th'armes of that inceſtuous Queene,
The ſtaine of Ægypt, and the ſhame of Rome
Shalt dallying ſit, and bluſh to haue them ſeene :
Whilſt proud diſdainfull ſhe, geſſing from whome
The meſſage came, and what the cauſe hath beene,
Will ſcorning ſay, Faith this comes from your Deere,
Now Sir you muſt be ſhent for ſtaying heere.

3

From her indeede it comes, delitious Dame,
(Thou royall Concubine and Queene of luft)
Whofe armes yet pure, whofe breafts are voyde of blame,
And whofe moft lawfull flame proues thine vniuft :
Tis fhe that fends the meffage of thy fhame,
And his vntruth that hath betraid her truft :
Pardon, deare Lord, from her thefe forrowes are,
Whofe bed brings neither infamie nor warre.

4

And therefore heare her words, that too too much
Hath heard the wrongs committed by thy fhame,
Although at firft my truft in thee was fuch,
As it held out againft the ftrongeft fame :
My heart would neuer let in once a touch
Of leaft beleefe, till all confirm'd the fame :
That I was almoft laft that would belieue,
Becaufe I knew me firft that moft muft grieue.

5

How oft haue poore abufed I tooke part
With Falfhood, onely for to make thee true ?
How oft haue I argued againft my heart,
Not fuffering it to know that which it knew ?
And for I would not haue thee what thou art,
I made my felfe, vnto my felfe vntrue :
So much my loue labour'd againft my finne,
To fhut out feare which yet kept feare within.

6

For I could neuer thinke th'afpiring mind
Of worthy and victorious *Anthonie*,
Could be by fuch a Syren fo declind,
As to be traind a prey to Luxury :
I could not thinke my Lord would be s'vnkind,
As to defpife his Children, *Rome* and me :
But O how foone are they deceiu'd that truft,
And more their fhame that will be fo vniuft.

7

But now that certaine fame hath open laid
Thy new relapfe, and ftrange reuolt from me,
Truth hath quite beaten all my hopes away,
And made the paffage of my forrowes free ;
For now poore heart, there's nothing in the way
Remaines to ftand betwixt Defpaire and thee :
All is throwne downe, there comes no fuccours new,
It is moft true, my Lord is moft vntrue.

8

And now I may with fhame inough pull in
The colours I aduanced in his grace,
For that fubduing powre, that him did win,
Hath loft me too, the honour of my face :
Yet why fhould I, bearing no part of finne,
Beare fuch a mighty part of his difgrace ?
Yes, though it be not mine, it is of mine :
And his renowne being clipf'd, mine cannot fhine.

9

Which makes me, as I doe, hide from the eye
Of the mifiudging vulgar that will deeme,
That fure there was in me fome reafon why
Which made thee thus, my bed to difefteeme :
So that alas, poore vndeferuing I,
A caufe of thy vncleane deferts fhall feeme,
Though luft takes neuer ioy in what is due,
But ftill leaues knowne delights to feeke out new.

10

And yet my brother *Cæfar* laboured,
To haue me leaue thy houfe, and liue more free :
But God forbid *Octauia* fhould be led,
To leaue to liue in thine, though left by thee.
The pledges here of thy forfaken bed,
Are ftill the obiects that remember me
What *Antony* was once, although falfe now,
And is my Lord, though he neglect his vow.

11

Thefe walles that here doe keepe me out of fight,
Shall keepe me all vnfpotted vnto thee,
And teftifie that I will doe thee right ;
Ile neuer ftaine thy houfe, though thou fhame me :
The now fad Chamber of my once delight,
Shall be the Temple of my pietie,
Sacred vnto the faith I reuerence,
Where I will pay my teares for thy offence.

12

Although my youth, thy abfence, and this wrong
Might draw my bloud to forfeit vnto fhame;
Nor neede I fruftrate my delights fo long,
That haue fuch meanes to carry fo the fame,
Since that the face of greatneffe is fo ftrong,
As it diffolues fufpect, and beares out blame;
Hauing all fecret helpes that long thereto,
That feldome wants there aught, but will to do.

13

Which yet to doe, ere luft this heart fhall frame,
Earth fwallow me aliue, Hell rap me hence :
Shall I, becaufe difpif'd, contemne my fhame,
And adde difgrace to others impudence ?
What can my powre, but giue more powre to fame ?
Greatneffe muft make it great incontinence :
Chambers are falfe, the bed and all will tell,
No doore keepes in their fhame that doe not well.

14

Hath greatneffe aught peculiar elfe alone,
But to ftand faire and bright aboue the bafe ?
What doth diuide the Cottage from the Throne,
If vice fhall lay both leuell with difgrace?
For if vncleanneffe make them but all one,
What priuiledge hath Honour by his place ?
What though our finnes goe braue and better clad
They are as thofe in ragges, as bafe, as bad.

15

I know not how, but wrongfully I know
Hath vndifcerning cuftome plac'd our kind
Vnder defert, and fet vs farre below
The reputation to our fexe affign'd :
Charging our wrong reputed weakneffe, how
We are vnconftant, fickle, falfe, vnkinde :
And though our life with thoufand proofes fhewes no,
Yet fince ftrength faies it, weakeneffe muft be fo.

16

Vnequall partage to b'allow'd no fhare
Of power to doe of lifes beft benefit :
But ftand, as if we interdicted were
Of vertue, action, liberty and might :
Muft you haue all, and not vouchfafe to fpare
Our weakneffe any int'reft of delight ?
Is there no portion left for vs at all,
But fufferance, forrow, ignorance and thrall ?

17

Thrice happy you, in whom it is no fault,
To know, to fpeake, to doe, and to be wife :
Whofe words haue credit, and whofe deedes, though
    naught,
Muft yet be made to feeme farre otherwife :
You can be onely heard, whilft we are taught
To hold our peace, and not to exercife
The powers of our beft parts, becaufe your parts
Haue with our freedome robb'd vs of our harts.

18

We, in this prifon of our felues confin'd,
Muft here fhut vp with our owne paffions liue,
Turn'd in vpon vs, and denied to find
The vent of outward meanes that might relieue :
That they alone muft take vp all our mind,
And no room left vs, but to thinke and grieue :
Yet oft our narrowed thoughts looke more direct
Then your loofe wifdomes born with wild neglect.

19

For, fhould we to (as God forbid we fhould)
Carry no better hand on our defires
Then your ftrength doth, what int'reft could
Our wronged patience pay you for your hires ?
What mixture of ftrange generations would
Succeede the fortunes of vncertaine Sires ?
What foule confufion in your bloud and race
To your immortall fhame and our difgrace ?

20

What ? are there barres for vs, no bounds for you ?
Muft Leuitie ftand fure, though Firmeneffe fall ?
And are you priuiledg'd to be vntrue,
And we no grant to be difpenf'd withall ?
Muft we inuiolable keepe your due,
Both to your loue, and to your falfhood thrall ?
Whilft you haue ftretch't your luft vpon your will,
As if your ftrength were licenc'd to doe ill.

21

O if you be more ſtrong, then be more iuſt,
Cleere this ſuſpition, make not the world to doubt,
Whether in ſtrong or weake be better truſt,
If frailty or elſe valour be more ſtout :
And if we haue ſhut in our hearts from luſt,
Let not your bad example let them out,
Thinke that there is like feeling in our bloud :
If you will haue vs good, be you then good.

22

Is it, that loue doth take no true delight
In what it hath, but ſtill in what it would,
Which drawes you on to doe vs this vnright,
Whilſt feare in vs, of looſing what we hold,
Keepes vs in ſtill to you, that ſet vs light,
So that, what you vnties, doth vs infolde ?
Then Loue, tis thou that doſt confound vs ſo,
To make our truth the occaſion of our wo.

23

Diſtreſſed woman kind, that either muſt
For louing looſe your loues, or get neglect :
Whilſt wantons are more car'd for then the iuſt,
And falſhood cheriſht, Faith without reſpect :
Better ſhe fares in whom is leſſe truſt,
And more is lou'd that is in more ſuſpect.
Which (pardon me) ſhewes no great ſtrength of mind
To be moſt theirs, that vſe you moſt vnkind

24

Yet well it fits, for that finne euer muft
Be tortur'd with the racke of his owne frame ;
For he that holdes no faith, fhall find no truft,
But fowing wrong, is fure to reape the fame :
How can he looke to haue his meafure iuft,
That fils deceit, and reckons not of fhame,
And being not pleaf'd with what he hath in lot,
Shall euer pine for that which he hath not ?

25

Yet if thou couldft not loue, thou mightft haue fem'd
Though to haue feem'd, had likewife beene vniuft :
Yet fo much are leane fhewes of vs efteem'd,
That oft they feede, though not fuffice our truft :
Becaufe our nature grieueth to be deem'd
To be fo wrong'd, although we be, and muft,
And it's fome eafe yet to be kindly vf'd
In outward fhew, though fecretly abuf'd.

26

But woe to her that both in fhew defpif'd
And in effect difgrac'd, and left forlorne,
For whom no comforts are to be deuif'd,
Nor no new hopes can euermore be borne :
O *Antony*, could it not haue fuffiz'd
That I was thine, but muft be made her fcorne
That enuies all her bloud, and doth deuide
Thee from thy felfe, onely to ferue her pride ?

9

27

What fault haue I committed that fhould make
So great diflike of me and of my loue ?
Or doth thy fault but an occafion take
For to diflike what moft doth it reproue ?
Becaufe the confcience gladly would miftake
Her owne mifdeeds which fhe would faine remoue ;
And they that are vnwilling to amend,
Will take offence, becaufe they will offend.

28

Or hauing runne beyond all pardon quite,
They flie and ioyne with finne as wholly his,
Making it now their fide, their part, their right,
And to turne backe, would fhew t'haue done amiffe :
For now they thinke, not to be oppofite
To what obraides their fault, were wickedneffe :
So much doth folly thruft them into blame,
That euen to leaue off fhame, they count it fhame.

29

Which doe not thou, deere Lord, for I doe not
Purfue thy fault, but fue for thy returne
Backe to thy felfe, whom thou haft both forgot
With me, poore me, that doth not fpight, but mourne :
And if thou couldft as well amend thy blot
As I forgiue, thefe plaints had beene forborne :
And thou fhouldft be the fame vnto my hart
Which once thou were, not that which now thou art.

30

Though deepe doth fit the hard recouering fmart
Of that laft wound (which God grant be the laft)
And more doth touch that tender feeling part
Of my fad foule, then all th'vnkindneffe paft :
And *Antony*, I appeale to thine owne hart,
(If th'heart which once was thine thou yet ftill haft)
To iudge if euer woman that did liue
Had iufter caufe, then wretched I, to grieue.

31

For comming vnto *Athens*, as I did,
Weary and weake with toyle, and all diftreft,
After I had with forrow compaffed
A hard confent, to grant me that requeft :
And how my trauell was confidered,
And all my care and coft, thy felfe knowes beft :
That wouldft not moue one foote from luft for me,
That had left all was deere to come to thee.

32

For firft what great adoe had I to win
M'offended brother *Cæfars* backward will ?
And praid, and wept, and cride to ftay the finne
Of ciuill rancor rifing twixt you ftill :
For in what cafe fhall wretched I be in,
Set twixt both, to fhare with both your ill ?
My bloud faid I with either of you goes,
Who euer win, I fhall be fure to lofe.

33

For what fhame fhould fuch mighty perfons get,
For two weake womens caufe to difagree ?
Nay, what fhall I that fhall be deem'd to fet
Th'inkindled fire, feeming inflam'd for me ?
O if I be the motiue of this heate,
Let thefe vnguilty hands the quenchers be,
And let me trudge to mediate an accord,
The agent twixt my brother and my Lord.

34

With prayers, vowes and teares, with vrging hard
I wrung from him a flender grant at laft,
And with the rich prouifions I prepar'd
For thy (intended Parthian warre) made hafte,
Weighing not how my poore weake body far'd,
But all the tedious difficulties paft :
And came to *Athens* ; whence I *Niger* fent,
To fhew thee of my comming and intent.

35

Whereof, when he had made relation,
I was commanded to approach no neare ;
Then fent I backe, to know what fhould be done
With th'horfe, and men, and money I had there :
Whereat perhaps when fome remorfe begun
To touch thy foule, to thinke yet what we were,
Th'inchantreffe ftrait ftept twixt thy heart and thee,
And intercepts all thoughts that came of mee.

36

She armes her teares, the ingins of deceit
And all her batterie, to oppofe my loue,
And bring thy comming grace to a retreit,
The powre of all her fubtilty to proue :
Now pale and faint fhe languifhes, and ftrait
Seemes in a found, vnable more to moue :
Whilft her inftructed fellowes ply thine eares
With forged paffions, mixt with fained teares.

37

Hard-hearted Lord, fay they, how canft thou fee
This mighty Queene, a creature fo diuine
Lie thus diftreft, and languifhing for thee,
And onely wretched, but for being thine ?
Whilft bafe *Octauia* muft intitled be
Thy wife, and fhe efteem'd thy Concubine :
Aduance thy heart, raife it vnto his right,
And let a Scepter bafer paffions quit.

38

Thus they affaile thy natures weakeft fide,
And worke vpon th'aduantage of thy minde,
Knowing where iudgement ftood leaft fortified,
And how t'incounter folly in her kinde :
But yet the while, O what doft thou abide,
Who in thy felfe fuch wraftling thoughts doft finde ?
In what confufed cafe is thy foule in,
Rackt betwixt pitty, forrow, fhame and fin ?

39

I cannot tell, but fure I dare beleeue
My trauels needs muft fome compaffion moue :
For no fuch locke to bloud could Nature giue
To fhut out Pitty, though it fhut out Loue :
Confcience muft leaue a little way to grieue
To let in horror comming to reproue
The guilt of thine offence that cauf'd the fame,
For deepeft wounds the hand of our owne fhame.

40

Neuer haue vniuft pleafures beene compleete,
In ioyes intire, but ftill feare kept the dore,
And held backe fomething from that full of fweete,
To interfowre vnfure delights the more :
For neuer did all circumftances meete
With thofe defires which were conceiu'd before :
Some thing muft ftill be left to checke our finne,
And giue a touch of what fhould not haue bin.

41

Wretched Mankinde, wherfore hath nature made
The lawfull vndelightfull, th'vniuft fhame ?
As if our pleafure onely were forbade,
But to giue fire to luft, t'adde greater flame ;
Or elfe, but as ordained more to lade
Our heart with paffions to confound the fame ;
Which though it be, yet adde not worfe to ill,
Do, as the beft men do, bound thine owne will.

42

Redeeme thy felfe, and now at length make peace
With thy diuided heart oppreft with toile :
Breake vp this warre, this breft-diffention ceafe,
Thy paffions to thy paffions reconcile :
I do not onely feeke my good t'increafe,
But thine owne eafe, and liberty : the while
Thee in the circuit of thy felfe confine,
And be thine owne, and then thou wilt be mine.

43

I know my pittied loue, doth aggrauate
Enuy and Wrath for thefe wrongs offered :
And that my fuffrings adde with my eftate,
Coales in thy bofome, hatred on thy head :
Yet is not that, my fault, but, my hard fate,
Who rather wifh to haue beene vnpitied
Of all but thee, then that my loue fhould be
Hurtfull to him that is fo deere to me.

44

Cannot the bufie world let me alone,
To beare alone the burthen of my griefe,
But they muft intermeddle with my mone,
And feeke t'offend me with vnfought reliefe ?
Whilft my afflictions labour to moue none
But onely thee, muft Pitty play the thiefe,
To fteale fo many hearts to hurt my hart,
And moue a part againft my deereft part ?

45

Yet all this fhall not preiudice my Lord,
If yet he will but make returne at laft ;
His fight fhall raze out of the fad' record
Of my inrowled griefe all that is paft :
And I will not fo much as once afford
Place for a thought to thinke I was difgrac'd :
And pitty fhall bring backe againe with me
Th'offended harts that haue forfaken thee.

46

And therefore come deere Lord, left longer ftay
Do arme againft thee all the powres of fpight,
And thou be made at laft the wofull pray
Of full inkindled wrath, and ruin'd quite :
But what prefaging thought of bloud doth ftay
My trembling hand, and doth my foule affright ?
What horror do I fee, prepar'd t'attend
Th'euent of this ? what end vnleffe thou end ?

47

With what ftrange formes and fhadowes ominous
Did my laft fleepe, my grieu'd foule intertaine ?
I dreamt, yee O dreames are but friuolous,
A sea horse.   And yet Ile tell it, and God grant it vaine.
Me thought a mighty *Hippopotamus*
From *Nilus* floating, thrufts into the maine,
Vpon whofe backe, a wanton Mermaide fate,
As if fhe rul'd his courfe, and fteer'd his fate.

48

With whom t'incounter, forth another makes,
Alike in kind, of ftrength and powre as good :
At whofe ingrappling, *Neptunes* mantle takes
A purple colour, dyde with ftreames of bloud ;
Whereat this looker on amaz'd, forfakes
Her Champion there, who yet the better ftood :
But fe'ing her gone, ftrait after her he hies,
As if his heart and ftrength lay in her eyes.

49

On followes Wrath vpon Difgrace and Feare,
Whereof th'euent forfooke me with the night
But my wak'd cares, gaue me : thefe fhadowes were
Drawne but from darkeneffe to inftruct the light.
Thefe fecret figures, natures meffage beare
Of comming woes, were they defciphered right ;
But if as cloudes of fleepe thou fhalt them take,
Yet credite Wrath and Spight that are awake.

50

Preuent, great fpirit, the tempefts that begin,
If Luft and thy Ambition haue left way
But to looke out, and haue not fhut all in,
To ftop thy iudgement from a true furuay
Of thy eftate, and let my hart within
Confider in what danger thou doft lay
Thy life and mine, to leaue the good thou haft,
To follow hopes with fhadowes ouercaft.

5 1

Come, come away from wrong, from craft, from toile,
Poſſeſſe thine owne with right, with trueth, with peace :
Breake from theſe ſnares, thy iudgment vnbeguile,
Free thine owne torment, and my griefe releaſe.
But whither am I carried all this while
Beyond my ſcope, and know not when to ceaſe ?
Words ſtill with my increaſing ſorrowes grow :
I know t'haue ſaid too much, but not enow.
Wherefore no more, but onely I commend
To thee the hart that's thine, and ſo I end.

Finis.

V.

A PANEGYRIKE CONGRATVLATORIE

TO

THE KING

(*JAMES I.*).

1603.

NOTE.

In the gift-folio of 1601 in the Bodleian and other copies, this 'Panegyrike' is found, so that it was probably privately printed and presented before the King arrived in England; albeit the 1601 volume is evidently made up of earlier and later printed pieces. A holograph MS. of this 'Panegyrike' is in the British Museum (Royal MSS. A 18. 72). So far as appears it was first published in 1603 :—" A Panegyrike congratulatorie to the King's Maieftie; alfo certaine epiftles"—folio [British Museum, 837 K 9 (1)]. In the same year it was re-issued with a new general title-page, and 'Defence of Ryme' added : 'Printed by V. S. for E. Blount' [*Ibid.* 644, K 8 (2) folio]. Another (8vo) edition bears the same date (*Ibid.* 1076, f. 2). It was also contemporarily reprinted at Edinburgh (4to, 1603). The special title-page in the 1601 volume is given opposite this. It is within the wood-cut border of the others. Unlike his 'Delia' and 'Funerall Poeme' for Devonshire, the Author seems to have left the 'Panegyrike' unaltered, save in the slight variations and margin-note recorded in their places, and in st. 30. See our Memorial-Introduction on this 'Panegyrike.'

A. B. G.

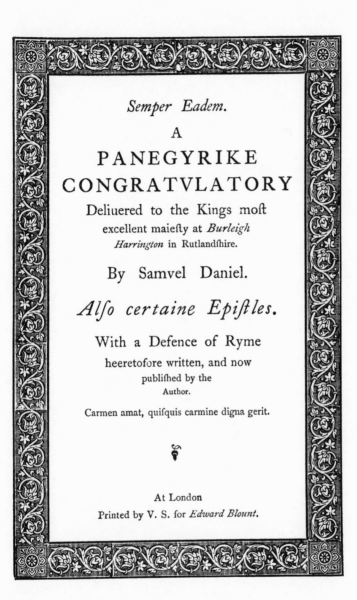

Semper Eadem.

A

PANEGYRIKE
CONGRATVLATORY

Deliuered to the Kings moſt
excellent maieſty at *Burleigh*
Harrington in Rutlandſhire.

By Samvel Daniel.

Alſo certaine Epiſtles.

With a Defence of Ryme

heeretofore written, and now
publiſhed by the
Author.

Carmen amat, quiſquis carmine digna gerit.

At London
Printed by V. S. for *Edward Blount.*

A PANEGYRIKE
CONGRATVLATORIE
to the Kings moſt excellent
Maieſtie.

1

Oe here the glory of a greater day
  Then *England* euer heretofore could
   ſee
  In all her daies ! When ſhe did moſt
   diſplay
  The enſignes of her pow'r, or whenas
   ſhe
  Did ſpread her ſelfe the moſt, and
   moſt did ſway
Her ſtate abroade, yet could ſhe neuer be
Thus bleſt at home, nor euer come to grow
To be intire in her full Orbe till now.

2

And now ſhe is, and now in peace therefore
Shake hands with Vnion, O thou mighty State,
Now thou art all *Great-Britaine* and no more,
No Scot, no Engliſh now, nor no debate ;
No borders but the Ocean and the ſhore :
No wall of *Adrian* ſerues to ſeparate
Our mutuall loue, nor our obedience,
Being Subiects all to one imperiall Prince.

St. 2, l. 3, ' great Brittaine ' 1601.

3

What heretofore could neuer yet be wrought
By all the fwords of pow'r, by bloud, by fire,
By ruine and diftruction ; here is brought
To paffe with peace, with loue, with ioy, defire :
Our former bleffed vnion hath begot
A greater vnion that is more intire,
And makes vs more our felues, fets vs at one
With Nature that ordain'd vs to be one.

4

Glory of men, this haft thou brought to vs,
And yet haft brought vs more then this by farre ;
Religion comes with thee, peace, righteoufneffe,
Iudgement and iuftice, which more glorious are
Then all thy Kingdomes ; and art more by this
Then Lord and Sou'raigne, more then Emperor
Ouer the hearts of men that let thee in
To more then all the pow'rs on earth can win.

5

God makes thee King of our eftates, but we
Doe make thee King of our affection,
King of our loue : a paffion borne more free,
And moft vnfubiect to dominion :
And know, that *England* which in that degree
Can loue with fuch a true deuotion,
Thofe that are leffe then Kings ; to thee muft bring
More loue, who art fo much more then a King.

St. 3 in *a*, l. 3, ' to paffe ' ends l. 3 (error).

6

And King of this great Nation, populous,
Stout, valiant, pow'rfull both by Sea and Land,
Attemptiue, able, worthy, generous,
Which ioyfully embraces thy command ;
A people tractable, obfequious,
Apt to be fafhion'd by thy glorious hand
To any forme of honor, t'any way
Of high attempts, thy vertues fhall affay.

7

A people fo inur'd to peace, fo wrought
To a fucceffiue courfe of quietneffe,
As th'haue forgot (and O, b'it ftill forgot)
The nature of their ancient ftubbornneffe :
Time altred hath the forme, the meanes, and brought
The State to that proportion'd euenneffe,
As 'tis not like againe 'twill euer come
(Being vf'd abroad) to draw the fword at home.

8

This people, this great State, thefe hearts adore
Thy Scepter now, and now turne all to thee,
Touch't with as pow'rfull zeale, and if not more,
(And yet O more, how could there euer be
Then vnto her, whom yet we doe deplore
Amidft our ioy !) And giue vs leaue if we
Reioyce and mourne, that cannot without wrong
So foone forget her we enioy'd fo long.

9

Which likewife makes for thee, that yet we holde
True after death, and bring not this refpeɛt
To a new Prince for hating of the olde ;
Or from defire of change, or from negleɛt ;
Whereby, O mighty Soueraigne, thou art tolde
What thou and thine are likely to expeɛt
From fuch a faith, that doth not hafte to runne
Before their time to an arifing Sunne.

10

And let my humble *Mufe*, whom fhe did grace,
Beg this one grace for her that now lies dead,
That no vile tongue may fpot her with difgrace,
Nor that her fame become disfigured :
O let her reft in peace, that rul'd in peace ;
Let not her honour be difquieted
Now after death : but let the Graue inclofe
All but her good, and that it cannot clofe.

11

It addes much to thy glory and our grace,
That this continued current of our loue
Runnes thus to thee, all with fo fwift a pace ;
And that from peace to peace we doe remoue
Not as in motion put from out our place,
But in one courfe, and doe not feeme to moue,
But in more ioy then euer heretofore ;
And well we may, fince thou wilt make vs more.

12

Our loue we fee concurres with Gods great loue,
Who onely made thy way, thy paffage plaine,
Leuell'd the world for thee, did all remoue,
That might the fhew but of a let retaine :
Vnbarr'd the *North*, humbled the *South*, did moue
The hearts of all the right to entertaine ;
Held other ftates embroil'd, whofe enuie might
Haue foftred factions to impugne thy right :

13

And all for thee, that we the more might praife
The glory of his powre, and reuerence thine,
Whom he hath raif'd to glorifie our dayes,
And make this Empire of the *North* to fhine
Againft all th'impious workings, all th'affayes
Of vile difnatur'd Vipers, whofe defigne
Was to embroile the State, t'obfcure the light,
And that cleere brightneffe of thy facred right.

14

To whofe reproch, fince th'iffue and fucceffe
Doth a fufficient marke of fhame returne,
Let no Pen elfe blazon their ouglineffe ;
Be it enough, that God and men doe fcorne
Their proiects, cenfures, vaine pretendences :
Let not our children, that are yet vnborne,
Find there were any offred to conteft,
Or make a doubt to haue our Kingdome bleft.

15

Burie that queſtion in th'eternall graue
Of darkneſſe, neuer to be ſeene againe :
Suffice we haue thee whom we ought to haue,
And t'whom all good men knew did appertaine
Th'inheritance thy ſacred birth-right gaue,
That needed n'other ſuffrages t'ordaine
What onely was thy due, nor no decree
To be made know'n, ſince none was known but thee.

16

Witneſſe the ioy, the vniuerſall cheere,
The ſpeede, the eaſe, the will, the forwardneſſe
Of all this great and ſpacious State, how deere
It held thy title and thy worthineſſe :
Haſte could not poſt ſo ſpeedy any where,
But Fame ſeem'd there before in readineſſe,
To tell our hopes, and to proclaime thy name ;
O greater then our hopes, more then thy fame !

17

What a returne of comfort doſt thou bring
Now at this freſh returning of our bloud,
Thus meeting with the opening of the Spring,
To make our ſpirits likewiſe to imbud !
What a new ſeaſon of incouraging
Biginnes t'inlength the dayes diſpoſ'd to good !
What apprehenſion of recouerie
Of greater ſtrength, of more abilitie !

18

The pulfe of *England* neuer more did beat
So ftrong as now : nor euer were our harts
Let out to hopes fo fpacious and fo great
As now they are : nor euer in all parts
Did we thus feele fo comfortable heat,
As now the glory of thy worth imparts :
The whole compleƈtion of the Common-wealth,
So weake before, hop'd neuer for more health.

19

Could'ft thou but fee from *Douer* to the Mount,
From *Totnes*, to the *Orcades*, what ioy,
What cheere, what triumphs, and what deere account
Is held of thy renowne this bleffed day :
A day which we and ours muft euer count
Our folemne feftiuall, as well we may.
And though men thus court Kings ftill which are new,
Yet doe they more, where they find more is due.

20

They feare the humours of a future Prince,
Who either loft a good or felt a bad,
But thou haft cheer'd vs of this feare long fince,
We know thee more, then by report we had :
We haue an euerlafting euidence
Vnder thy hand, that now we need not dread
Thou wilt be otherwife in thy defignes
Then there thou art in thofe iudiciall lines.

St. 18, l. 5, *a* misprints ' freely.'

21

It is the greateft glory vpon earth
To be a King, but yet much more to giue
The inftitution with the happy birth
Vnto a King, and teach him how to liue :
VVe haue, by thee, far more then thine owne worth,
That doth encourage, ftrengthen and relieue
Our hopes in the fucceffion of thy blood,
That like to thee, they likewife will be good.

22

VVe haue an earneft, that doth euen tie
Thy Scepter to thy word, and binds thy Crowne
(That els no band can binde) to ratifie
VVhat thy religious hand hath there fet downe,
VVherein thy all commanding Soueraigntie
Stands fubiect to thy Pen and thy renowne ;
There we behold thee King of thine owne hart,
And fee what we muft be, and what thou art.

23

There great *Exemplare*, *Prototipe*, of Kings,
VVe finde the good fhall dwell within thy Court ;
Plaine zeale and truth, free from bafe flatterings,
Shall there be entertain'd, and haue refort ;
Honeft difcretion, that no cunning brings,
But counfels that lie right, and that import,
Is there receiu'd, with thofe whofe care attends
Thee and the State more then their priuate ends.

24

There grace and fauour fhall not be difpof'd,
But by proportion, euen and vpright ;
There are no mightie Mountaines interpof'd
Betweene thy beames and vs, t'imbarre thy light ;
There Maiefty liues not as if inclof'd
Or made a prey t'a priuate benefit :
The hand of Pow'r deales there her owne reward,
And thereby reapes the whole of mens regard.

25

There is no way to get vp to refpeɛt,
But onely by the way of worthineffe ;
All paffages that may feeme indireɛt
Are ftopt vp now, and there is no acceffe
By groffe corruption, bribes cannot effeɛt
For th'vndeferuing any offices ;
Th'afcent is cleane, and he that doth afcend
Muft haue his meanes as cleane as is his end.

26

The deeds of worth and laudable defarts
Shall not now paffe thorow the ftraight report
Of an imbafing tongue, that but imparts
What with his ends and humours fhall comport :
The Prince himfelfe now heares, fees, knowes what parts
Honor and Vertue aɛts, and in what fort :
And thereto giues his grace accordingly,
And cheeres vp other to the like thereby.

27

Nor fhall we now haue vfe of flatterie,
For he knowes falfhood farre more fubtill is
Then truth, bafeneffe then libertie,
Feare then loue, t'inuent thefe flourifhes :
And Adulation now is fpent fo nie
As that it hath no colours to expreffe
That which it would, that now we muft be faine
T'vnlearne that Arte, and labour to be plaine.

28

For where there is no eare to be abuf'd
None will be found that dare t'informe a wrong :
The infolent deprauer ftands confuf'd :
The impious Atheift feemes to want a tongue,
Transform'd into the fafhion that is vf'd.
All ftriue t'appeare like thofe they liue among,
And all will feeme compof'd by that fame fquare
By which they fee the beft and greateft are.

29

Such pow'r hath thy example and refpect,
As that without a fword, without debate,
Without a noife (or feeling in effect)
Thou wilt difpofe, change, forme, accommodate
Thy Kingdome, people, rule, and all effect
Without the leaft conuulfion of the State;
That this great paffage and mutation will
Not feeme a change, but onely of our ill.

30

We fhall continue and remaine all one,
In Law, in Iuftice, and in Magiftrate ;
Thou wilt not alter the foundation
Thy Anceftors haue laid of this Eftate,
Nor grieue thy Land with innouation,
Nor take from vs more then thou wilt collate ;
Knowing that courfe is beft to be obferu'd,
Whereby a State hath longeft beene preferu'd.

31

A King of *England* now moft graciouflie,
Remits the iniuries that haue beene done
T'a King of Scots, and makes his clemencie
To checke them more then his correction ;
Th'annointed bloud that ftain'd moft fhamefully
This ill feduced State, he lookes thereon
With th'eye of griefe, not wrath, t'auenge the fame,
Since th'Authors are extinct that cauf'd that fhame.

32

Thus mightie riuers quietly doe glide,
And doe not by their rage their powers profeffe,
But by their mightie workings, when in pride
Small *Torrents* roare more lowd, and worke much leffe :
Peace, greatneffe beft becomes: calme power doth guide
With a farre more imperious ftatelineffe,
Then all the fwords of violence can doe,
And eafier gaines thofe ends fhe tends vnto.

St. 30. We fhall continue one, and be the fame
In Law, in Iuftice, Magiftrate and forme,
Thou wilt not touch the fundamentall frame
Of their Eftate thy Anceftors did forme
But with a reuerence of their glorious fame
Seek onely the corruptions to reforme (1601 folio).

33

Then *England*, thou haſt reaſon thus to cheare,
Reaſon to ioy and triumph in this wiſe,
When thou ſhalt gaine ſo much, and haue no feare
To loſe ought els but thy deformities ;
When thus thou ſhalt haue health and be ſet cleare
From all thy great infectious maladies,
By ſuch a hand that beſt knowes how to cure,
And where moſt lie thoſe griefes thou doſt endure.

34

When thou ſhalt ſee there is another grace
Then to be rich ; another dignitie
Nam vbi cupi- Then money ; other meanes for place
do diuitiarum Then gold ; wealth ſhall not now make
inuaſit, neque
diſciplina, honeſtie ;
neque artes
bonæ neque When thou ſhalt ſee the eſtimation baſe
ingenium
vllum ſatis Of that which moſt afflicts our miſerie :
pollet. Without the which, elſe could'ſt thou neuer ſee
Our wayes laid right, nor men themſelues to bee.

35

By which improuement we ſhall gaine much more
Then by *Peru*, or all diſcoueries :
For this way to imbaſe, is to inſtore
The treaſure of the Land, and make it riſe.
This is the onely key t'vnlocke the dore,
To let out plenty, that it may ſuffice :
For more then all this Ile, for more increaſe
Of ſubiects then by thee, there can increaſe.

36

This fhall make roome and place enough for all,
Which otherwife would not fuffice a few,
And by proportion Geometricall
Shall fo difpofe to all what fhall be due,
As that without corruption, wrangling, brawle,
Intrufion, wrefting, and by meanes vndue,
Defert fhall haue her charge, and but one charge,
As hauing but one body to difcharge.

37

Whereby the all in-cheering Maieftie
Shall come to fhine at full in all her parts,
And fpread her beames of comfort equally,
As being all alike to like defarts :
For thus to checke, imbafe and vilifie
Th'efteeme of wealth, will fafhion fo our hearts
To worthy ends, as that we fhall by much
More labour to be good then to be rich.

38

This will make peace with *Law*, reftore the *Bar*,
T'her ancient filence, where contention now
Makes fo confuf'd a noife ; this will debar
The foftring of debate, and ouerthrow
That ougly Monfter, that foule rauener,
Extortion, which fo hideoufly did grow,
By making prey vpon our mifery,
And wafting it againe as wickedly.

39

The ftrange examples of impou'rifhments,
Of facriledge, exaaction and of wafte,
Shall not be made, nor held as prefidents
For times to come, but end with th'ages paft :
Whenas the State fhall yeeld more fuppliments
(Being well imploy'd) then Kings can well exhauft ;
This golden Meadow lying ready ftill
Then to be mow'd, when their occafions will.

40

Fauour, like pitie, in the hearts of men
Haue the firft touches euer violent :
But foone againe it comes to languifh, when
The motiue of that humour fhall be fpent :
But being ftill fed with that which firft hath been
The caufe thereof, it holdes ftill permanent,
And is kept in by courfe, by forme, by kinde,
And time begets more ties that ftill more binde.

41

The broken frame of this difioynted State,
Being by the bliffe of thy great Grandfather
Henry the feuenth, reftor'd to an eftate
More found then euer, and more ftedfafter,
Owes all it hath to him, and in that rate
Stands bond to thee that art his fucceffer :
For without him it had not beene begunne,
And without thee we had beene now vndone.

42

He, of a priuate man, became a King,
Hauing indur'd the weight of tyrannie,
Mourn'd with the world, complain'd, and knew the thing
That good men wifh for in their miferie
Vnder ill Kings, faw what it was to bring
Order and forme to the recouerie
Of an vnruly State ; conceiu'd what cure
Would kill the caufe of this diftemp'rature.

43

Thou, borne a King, haft in thy State endur'd
The fowre affronts of priuate difcontent
With fubiects broiles ; and euer beene enur'd
To this great myfterie of gouernment :
Whereby thy Princely wifdome hath allur'd
A State to peace, left to thee turbulent,
And brought vs an addition to the frame
Of this great worke, fquar'd fitly to the fame.

44

And both you (by the all-working Prouidence,
That fafhions out of dangers, toyles, debates,
Thofe whom it hath ordained to commence
The firft, and great eftablifhments of States)
Came when your aide, your powers experience
(Which out of iudgement beft accommodates
Thefe ioynts of rule) was more then moft defir'd,
And when the times of neede the moft requir'd.

St. 43, l. 1, *a* misprints ' Then.'

45

And as he laid the modell of this frame,
By which was built fo ftrong a worke of State,
As all the powers of changes in the fame,
All that exceffe of a difordinate
And luftfull Prince, nor all that after came,
Nor child, nor ftranger, nor yet womens fate,
Could once difioynt the couplements, whereby
It held together in iuft Symetry.

46

So thou likewife art come as fore-ordaind,
To reinforce the fame more really,
Which oftentimes hath but beene entertain'd
By the onely ftile and name of Maiefty ;
And by no other counfells oft attain'd
Thofe ends of her inioy'd tranquility,
Then by this forme, and by the incumbrances
Of neighbour States that gaue it a fucceffe.

47

That hadft thou had no title (as thou haft
The onely right, and none hath els a right)
We yet muft now haue bin inforc'd t'haue caft
Our felues into thy armes, to fet all right,
And to auert confufion, bloudfhed, wafte,
That otherwife vpon vs needes muft light :
None but a King, and no King els befide
Could now haue fau'd this State from being deftroid'.

48

Thus hath the hundred yeeres brought backe againe
The facred bloud lent to adorne the *North*,
And here return'd it with a greater gaine,
And greater glory then we fent it forth.
Thus doth th'all-working Prouidence retaine,
And keepe for great effects the feede of worth,
And fo doth point the ftops of time thereby,
In periods of vncertaine certainty.

49

Margaret of *Richmond* (glorious Grandmother
Vnto that other precious *Margaret*,
From whence th'Almighty worker did transfer
This branch of peace, as from a roote well fet)
Thou Mother, Author, Plotter, Counfeller
Of vnion, that didft both conceiue, beget
And bring forth happineffe to this great State,
To make it thus intirely fortunate.

50

O couldft thou now but view this faire fucceffe,
This great effect of thy religious worke,
And fee therein how God hath pleaf'd to bleffe
Thy charitable counfels and to worke
Still greater good out of the bleffedneffe
Of this conioyned *Lancafter* and *Yorke* :
Which all conioyn'd within, and thofe fhut out
Whom nature and their birth had fet without.

St. 48, margin-note from 1601 folio—" It is iuft a hundred yeares fince the
Lady Margaret was married to James the fourth King of Scots."

51

How much haſt thou bound all poſterities
In this great worke to reuerence thy name !
And with thee, that religious, faithfull, wife
And learned *Mourton*, who contriu'd the fame,
And firſt aduiſ'd, and did fo well aduife
As that the good fucceſſe that thereof came
Shew'd well, that holy hands, cleane thoughts, cleere harts
Are onely fit to act fuch glorious parts.

52

But *Muſe*, thefe deare remembrances muſt be
In their conuenient places regiſtred,
When thou ſhalt bring ſterne diſcord to agree,
And bloudy warre into a quiet bed :
Which worke muſt now be finiſhed by thee,
That long hath laine vndone, as deſtined
Vnto the glory of thefe dayes : for which
Thy vowes and Verfe haue laboured fo much.

53

Thou euer haſt oppofed all thy might
Againſt contention, furie, pride and wrong,
Perfwading ſtill to hold the courfe of right ;
And peace hath beene the burden of thy fong :
And now thy felfe ſhalt haue the benefit
Of quietneſſe, which thou haſt wanted long ;
And now ſhalt haue calme peace, and vnion
With thine owne warres, and now thou muſt go on.

54

Onely the ioy of this fo deare a thing
Made me looke backe vnto the caufe, whence came
This fo great good, this bleffing of a King,
When our eftate fo much requir'd the fame :
When we had need of pow'r for the well ordering
Of our affaires, need of a fpirit to frame
The world to good, to grace and worthineffe,
Out of this humour of luxurioufneffe.

55

And brings vs backe vnto our felues againe,
Vnto our ancient natiue modeftie ;
From out thefe forren finnes we entertaine,
Thefe lothefome furfets, ougly gluttonie ;
From this vnmanly and this idle vaine
Of wanton and fuperfluous brauery :
The wracke of Gentry, fpoyle of Nobleneffe ;
And fquare vs by thy temp'rate foberneffe.

56

When Abftinence is fafhion'd by the Time,
It is no rare thing to be abftinent,
But then it is, when th'age full fraught with crime
Lies proftrate vnto all mifgouernment.
And who is not licencious in the prime
And heate of youth, nor then incontinent
When out of might he may, he neuer will ;
No power can tempt him to that tafte of ill.

57

Then what are we t'expe&t from fuch a hand
That doth this fterne of faire example guide ?
Who will not now fhame to haue no command
Ouer his lufts ?   Who would be feene t'abide
Vnfaithfull to his vowes, to infringe the band
Of a moft facred knot which God hath tide ?
Who would now feeme to be difhonoured
With th'vncleane touch of an vnlawfull bed ?

58

What a great checke will this chafte Court be now
To wanton Court debaufht with luxury ;
Where we no other Miftreffes fhall know
But her to whom we owe our loyalty ?
Chafte Mother of our Princes, whence do grow
Thofe righteous iffues, which fhall glorifie
And comfort many Nations with their worth,
To her perpetuall grace that brought them forth.

59

We fhall not feare to haue our wiues diftain'd,
Nor yet our daughters violated here
By an imperiall luft, that being vnrain'd,
Will hardly be refifted any where.
He will not be betrai'd with eafe, nor train'd
With idle reft, in foft delights to weare
His time of life : but knowes whereto he tends,
How worthy minds are made for worthy ends.

60

And that this mighty worke of vnion now
Begun with glory, muft with grace run on,
And be fo clof'd, as all the ioynts may grow
Together firme in due proportion :
A worke of power and Iudgement, that muft fhow
All parts of wifedome and difcretion
That man can fhew, that no cloud may impaire
This day of hope, whofe morning fhewes fo faire.

61

He hath a mighty burden to fuftaine,
Whofe fortune doth fucceed a gracious Prince,
Or where mens expectations entertaine
Hopes of more good, and more beneficence :
But yet he vndergoes a greater paine,
A more laborious worke, who muft commence
The great foundation of a gouernment,
And lay the frame of Order and Content.

62

Efpecially where mens defires do runne
A greedy courfe of eminency, gaine,
And priuate hopes, weighing not what is done
For the Republicke, fo themfelues may gaine
Their ends, and where few care who be vndone,
So they be made, whil'ft all do entertaine
The prefent motions that this paffage brings
With th'infancy of change, vnder new kings.

63

So that the weight of all feemes to relie
Wholly vpon thine owne difcretion ;
Thy iudgement now muft only rectifie
This frame of pow'r thy glory ftands vpon
From thee muft come ; that thy pofterity
May ioy this peace, and hold this vnion :
For whil'ft all worke for their owne benefit,
Thy only worke muft keepe vs all vpright.

64

For, did not now thy full maturity
Of yeeres and wifdome, that difcerne what fhowes,
What arte and colours may deceiue the eye,
Secure our truft that that cleere iudgement knowes
Vpon what grounds depend thy Maiefty,
And whence the glory of thy greatneffe growes ;
We might diftruft left that a fide might part
Thee from thy felfe, and fo furprize thy heart.

65

Since th'art but one, and that againft thy breft
Are laid all th'ingins both of fkill and wit,
And all th'affaults of cunning are addreft
With ftratagems of Art to enter it,
To make a prey of grace, and to inueft
Their pow'rs within thy loue, that they might fit
And ftir that way which their affection tends,
Refpecting but themfelues and their owne ends.

66

And fee'ng how difficult a thing it is
To rule, and what ftrength is requir'd to ftand
Againft all th'interplac'd refpondences
Of combinations, fet to keepe the hand
And eye of power from out the Prouinces
That Auarice may draw to her command;
Which, to keepe hers, fhe others vowes to fpare,
That they againe to her might vfe like care.

67

But God, that raif'd thee vp to act this part,
Hath giuen thee all thofe powers of worthines,
Fit for fo great a worke, and fram'd thy heart
Difcernable of all apparences ;
Taught thee to know the world, and this great Art
Of ord'ring man, *Knowledge of Knowledges ;*
That from thee men might reckon how this State
Became reftor'd, and was made fortunate.

68

That thou the firft, with vs, in name, might'ft be
The firft in courfe, to fafhion vs a new,
VVherein the times hath offred that to thee,
VVhich feldome t'other Princes could accrue :
Thou haft th'aduantage only to be free
T'imploy thy fauours where they fhall be due,
And to difpofe thy grace in generall,
And like to *Ioue*, to be alike to all.

St. 68, in margin of 1601 folio, ' *Eft Iupiter omnibus idem.*'

69

Thy fortune hath indebted thee to none,
But t'all thy people vniuerfally,
And not to them, but for their loue alone,
Which they account is placed worthily :
Nor wilt thou now fruftrate their hopes, wheron
They reft, nor they faile in their loyalty ;
Since no Prince comes deceiued in his truft,
But he that firft deceiues, and proues vniuft.

70

Then fince we are in this fo faire a way
Of Reftauration, Greatneffe and Command,
Curfed be he that caufes the leaft ftay
In this faire worke, or interrupts thy hand ;
And curfed he that offers to betray
Thy graces or thy goodneffe to withftand ;
Let him be held abhorr'd, and all his race
Inherit but the portion of difgrace.

71

And he that fhall by wicked Offices
Be th'author of the leaft difturbancy,
Or feeke t'auert thy godly purpofes,
Be euer held the fcorne of infamy :
And let men but confider their fucceffe
Who Princes loues abuf'd prefumptuoufly :
They fhall perceiue their ends do ftill relate,
That fure God loues them not whom men do hate.

72

And it is iuſt, that they who make a prey
Of Princes fauours, in the end againe
Be made a prey to Princes, and repay
The ſpoiles of miſery with greater gaine ;
Whoſe ſacrifices euer do allay
The wrath of men, conceiu'd in their diſdaine :
For that their hatred proſecuteth ſtill,
More than ill Princes, thoſe that make them ill.

73

But both thy iudgement and eſtate doth free
Thee from theſe powers of feare and flattery
The conquerours of Kings, by whom we ſee
Are wrought the acts of all impiety :
Thou art ſo ſet, as th'haſt no cauſe to be
Iealous, or dreadfull of diſloyalty ;
The pedeſtall whereon thy greatneſſe ſtands,
Is built of all our hearts, and all our hands.

St. 73, l. 7, misprinted 'the.'

VI.

A Fvnerall Poeme Vpon the Death of the late noble Earle of Deuonſhire.

1606.

NOTE.

The Earl of Devonshire died on 3rd April, 1606, and this 'Fvnerall Poeme,' which appeared originally as a thin quarto, having a title-page printed in white letters on a black ground, may be dated in the same year, though without date anywhere. The title-page thus runs :—

A Fvnerall Poeme

Vpon the Death of

the late noble Earle

of Deuonſhire. (11 *leaves.*)

An exemplar is in the British Museum. It is found in all the collective editions after 1606. A collation of the quarto of 1623 with this original edition—never before done—abundantly rewards us. At the bottom of the pages lines and whole passages left out by the Author on revision are recorded, and some re-introduced into the text. Passages in the quarto of 1623 not in the original edition are also noted. The 1607 edition supplies in margin an important name. See Memorial-Introduction on this nobleman, and for an original and unpublished letter from Daniel to him. A. B. G.

A
FVNERALL
POEME.
Vpon the Death of the late noble
Earle of Deuonſhire.

OW that the hand of death hath layd
    thee there,
Where neither greatneſſe, pompe, nor
    grace, we ſee,
Nor any differences of earth ; and
    where
No vaile is drawne betwixt thy ſelfe
    and thee :

Now *Deuonſhire* that thou art but a name,   10
And all the reſt of thee beſides is gone,
When men conceiue thee not, but by the fame
Of what thy vertue, and thy worth haue done :

ll. 7-13 in the original edition are as follows :—
        Where all muſt be, and leuel'd thee with th' Earth—
        Where men are all of them alike, and where
        There are no ſeu'rall roomes for ſtate or birth :
        Now thou haſt nothing left thee but a name
        (O noble *Deuonſhire*) and all is gone
        With thee, except the memorie, and fame
        Of what thy vertue . . . hath . . .

Now fhal my verfe which thou in life didft grace,
(And which was no difgrace for thee to do)
Not leaue thee in the graue, that ougly place
That few regard, or haue refpeft vnto,
Where all attendance, and obferuance ends,
Where all the Sunfhine of our fauour fets,
Where what was ill, no countenance defends,   20
And what was good, th'vnthankfull world forgets.
Here fhalt thou haue the feruice of my pen
(The tongue of my beft thoughts) and in this cafe
I cannot be fuppofde to flatter, when
I fpeake behinde thy backe, not to thy face :
Men neuer footh the dead but where they do
Find liuing tyes, to hold them therevnto.
And I ftand cleere from any other chaine
Then of my loue which freeborne, draws free breath.
The benefit thou gau'ft me to fuftaine   30
My humble life, I loofe it by thy death.
Nor was it fuch, as it could lay on me
Any exaftion of refpeft fo ftrong,
As t'inforce m'obferuance, beyond thee,
Or make my confcience differ from my tongue.
Let thofe be vaffals to fuch feruices
Who have their hopes, or whofe defires are hye,
For me I haue my ends, and know it is
    For I haue learnt it is the property
    For free men to fpeake truth, for flaues to lye.   40

l. 16, 'darkefome'; ll. 26-7 not in original edition; l. 28, 'And am vntide'; ll. 36-8 accepted from original edition; l. 40—Here in the original edition a very striking but scarcely wrought-out passage is found, as follows :—

And if miftaken by the Parralax
And diftance of my ftanding too farre off

And therefore I fincerely will report
Firft how thy parts were faire conuaid within,
How that braue minde was built and in what fort
All thy contexture of thy heart hath beene,
Which was fo nobly fram'd, fo well compof'd
As vertue neuer had a fairer feate,
Nor could be better lodg'd nor more repof'd,
Then in that goodly frame ; where all things fweete,
And all things quiet, held a peacefull reft ;
Where paffion did no fuddaine tumults raife   50
That might difturbe her, nor was euer breft
Contain'd fo much, and made fo little noyfe;

I heretofore might erre, and men might tax
My being to free of prayfes, without proofe.
But here it is not fo, and yet the choyce
Of thofe I made did yeald the greateft fhow
Of honour and of worth, and had the voyce
Of prefent times their virtues to allow.
And if they naue not made them good, it is
No fault of mine, nor ought it to be layd
To difrepute thefe my obferuances :
True prayfes doe adorne, the falfe obrayd,
  And oftentimes to greatneffe we are glad
To attribute thofe parts we wifh they had.
But *Deuonfhire* I here ftand cleere with thee,
I haue a manumiffion to be free,
I owe thee nothing, and I may be bold
To fpeake the certaine truth of what I know :
There is no power remaines in thee, to hold
The tongues of men, that will be talking now :
And now being dead may anatomife,
And open here all that thou wert within,
Shew how thy minde was built, and in what wife
All the contexture . . . [See l. 39.]

       l. 48, mifprinted ' thing.'

That by thy filent modeftie is found
The emptieft veffells make the greateft found.
For thou fo well difcernd'ft thy felfe, had'ft read
Man and his breath fo well, as made thee force
The leffe to fpeake, as being ordain'd to fpread
Thy felfe in action, rather than difcourfe ;
Though thou hadft made a generall Suruey
Of all the beft of mens beft knowledges,   60
And knew as much as euer learning knew,
Yet did it make thee truft thy felfe the leffe,
And leffe prefume ; and yet when being mou'd
In priuate talke to fpeake, thou didft bewray
How fully fraught thou wert within, and prou'd
That thou didft know what euer wit could fay ;
Which fhew'd thou hadft not bookes as many haue
For oftentation, but for vfe, and that
Thy bounteous memory was fuch, as gaue
A large reuenue of the good, it gat.   70
Witneffe fo many volumes whereto thou
Haft fet thy notes vnder thy learned hand,
And markt them with that print as will fhew how
The point of thy conceiuing thoughts did ftand ;
That none would thinke if all thy life had beene,
Turn'd into leifure, thou couldft haue attain'd
So much of time, to haue peruf'd and feene,
So many volumes that fo much contain'd.
Which furniture may not be deem'd leaft rare
Amongft thofe ornaments that fweetly dight   80
Thy folitary *Wanfteed*, where thy care
Had gathered all what heart or eyes delight.

l. 56, 'fmoake' ; 'the' for 'thee' ; l. 59,'furuiew' ; ll. 81-2, in margin,
' *The Library at Wanfteed.*'

And whereas many others haue, we fee
All things within their houfes worth the fight,
Except themfelues, that furniture of thee
And of thy prefence, gaue the beft delight.
With fuch a feafon, fuch a temprature
Wert thou compof'd, as made fweetnes one,
And held the tenor of thy life ftill fure,
In confort with thy felfe in perfect tone ;   90
And neuer man had heart more truely feru'd
Vnder the regiment of his owne care
And was more at command, and more obferu'd
The colours of that modefty he bare
Then that of thine, in whom men neuer found
That any fhew, or fpeech obfcene, could tell
Of any veine thou hadft that was vnfound,
Or motion of thy powers, that turn'd not well.
And this was thy prouifion laid within,
Thus wert thou to thy felfe, and now remaines.   100
VVhat to the world thou outwardly haft beene,
VVhat the dimenfion of that fide containes,
Which likewife was fo goodly and fo large
As fhewes that thou wert borne t'adorne the dayes
Wherein thou liu'ft, and alfo to difcharge
Thofe parts which Englands and thy fame fhould raife ;
Although in peace, thou feem'dft to be all peace
Yet being in warre, thou wert all warre, and there
As in thy fpheere thy fpirits did neuer ceafe
To moue with indefatigable care   110
And nothing feem'd more to arride thy heart
Nor more inlarge thee into iollity,

ll. 87-98 not in original edition.

Then when thou faweft thy felfe in armour girt,
Or any act of armes like to be nye.
The *Belgique* warre firft tride thy martiall fpirit,
And what thou wert and what thou wouldft be found
And markt thee there according to thy merit
With honors ftampe, a deepe and noble wound.
And that fame place that rent from mortall men
Immortall *Sidney*, glory of the field   120
And glory of the Mufes, and their pen
(VVho equall bare the *Caduce* and the *Shield*)
Had likewife bin thy laft, had not the fate
Of *England* then referu'd thy worthy blood,
Vnto the preferuation of a State
That much concern'd her honour and her good ;
And thence return'd thee to inioy the blis
Of grace and fauour in *Elizaes* fight
(That miracle of women) who by this
Made thee be held according to thy right;   130
Which faire and happy blefling thou mightft well
Haue farre more raif'd had not thine enemy
Retired priuacy, made thee to fell
Thy greatnes for thy quiet, and deny
To meet faire Fortune, when fhe came to thee.
For neuer man did his preferment fly,
And had it in that emminent degree,
As thou, as if it fought thy modefty.
For that which many, whom ambition toyles
And tortures with their hopes, hardly attaine   140

l. 128, 'eyes'; l. 130—

'. . . held, and made thee to arife
Vnto a note more hye, which thou . . .';

l. 413, 'quiet' accepted for *a*'s mifprint 'quite;' l. 138, mifprinted 'fought.'

With all their thrufts, & fhouldring-plots, and wiles
VVas eafily made thine, without thy paine.
And without any priuate malicing
Or publique greeuance, euery good man ioy'd
That vertue could come cleere to any thing,
And faire deferts to be fo fairely pay'd.
Thofe benefits that were beftow'd on thee
VVere not like fortunes fauours, they could fee.
Eliza's cleere-eied iudgement is renown'd
For making choice of thy ability: 150
But it will euerlaftingly redound
Vnto the glory, and benignity
Of *Britaines* mighty Monarch, that thou wert
By him aduanced for thy great defert ;
It being the fairer worke of maiefty
With fauour to reward, than to employ.
And as thou faidft that naught thy heart did grieue,
In death fo much, as that time would not yeeld
Thee meanes to fhew thy zeale, that thou mightft liue
T'haue done but one dayes feruice in the field,   160
And that faire bed of honour died vpon,
And with thy bloud haue feald thy gratefulneffe
To fuch a royall Maifter.   Who had done
So much for thee t'aduance thy feruices ;
Which were indeed of that defeart, as they
Might afke their grace themfelues : yet do we fee
That to fucceffe, defert hath not a way
But vnder Princes that moft gracious be,

l. **149**, hyphen accepted from original edition ; l. **151**, misprinted 're-
bound'; ll. **157-65** accepted and re-inserted from the original edition ;
l. **165** in 1623 reads, 'Although thy feruices, were fuch as they'; l. **166**,
'although' for 'yet do.'

For without thy great valour we had loft
The deareft purchafe euer *England* made: 170
And made with fuch profufe exceeding coft
Of bloud and charge, to keepe and to inuade :
As commutation paid a deerer price
For fuch a peece of earth, and yet well paid
And well aduentur'd for, with great aduice,
And happily to our dominions laid ;
Without which out-let, *England* thou hadft bin
From all the reft of th'earth fhut out, and pent
Vnto thy felfe, and forft to keepe within,
Inuiron'd round with others gouernment;   180
Where now by this, thy large imperiall Crowne
Stands boundleffe in the Weft, and hath a way
For noble times, left to make all thine owne
That lyes beyond it, and force all t'obay.
And this important peece, like t'haue beene rent
From off thy ftate, did then fo tickle ftand,
As that no ioynture of the gouernment
But fhooke, no ligament, no band
Of order and obedience, but were then
Loofe and in tottering, when the charge   190
Thereof was laid on *Montioy*, and that other men
Checkt by example fought to put it off.
And he out of his natiue modefty
(As being no vndertaker) labours too
To haue auoided that which his ability
And Englands *Genius* would haue him do

l. 169, 'For when our kingdom ftood in ftate t' haue loft '; l. 170, 'that
it' for 'euer'; l. 171, ' And what it bought with that'; l. 173, ' As neuer
nation '; mifprinted ' communation '; l. 177, 'hadft ' for 'haft '—accepted ;
l. 180, 'Inuiron'd with incroching'; l. 183, 'leaft' for 'left'; l. 192,
'checkt' accepted for 'chokt' of *a*; l. 196, 'to' in error before 'do' in *a*.

Alleadging how it was a charge vnfit
For him to vndergo, feeing fuch a one
As had more power and meanes t'accomplifh it
Then he could haue, had there fo little done.   200
VVhofe ill fucceffe (confidering his great worth,
Was fuch as could that mifchiefe be withftood,
It had beene wrought) did in it felfe bring forth
Difcouragement that he fhould do leffe good.

   The ftate replide, it was not lookt he fhould
Reftore it wholy to it felfe againe,
But only now if poffible he could
In any fafhion but the fame retaine
So that it did not fall a funder quite,
Being thus difhiuered in a defperate plight.   210

   With courage on he goes, doth exiquute
With counfell, and returnes with victory ;
But in what noble fafhion he did fute
This action, with what wit and induftry,
Is not to be difgracde in this fmall carde :
It afkes a fpacious Mappe of more regarde.

l. 197, ' And did aleadge it ' ; ll. 201-4 in original edition read—

     ' Whofe ill fucceffe (for that he knew his worth
     So great, as if there could haue beene redreffe,
     He had effected it) in him brought forth
     Difcouragement, that he fhould there do leffe.'

l. 206, ' being fo dis-rent ' ; ll. 207-8—

     ' And only now, if poffibly he could
     But hold it vp, it was fufficient '—

' fufficient ' rhyme-word to ' disrent ' in l. 206 ; l. 211, ' execute ' ; l. 212, ' With ' accepted for ' Which ' ; ll. 215-90 not in original edition, which has only the following :—

     ' There is no roome to place it in this ftreight.
     Time, and my prefent griefes, do difappoint

Here is no roome to tell with what ftrange fpeed
And fecrecy he vfed to preuent
The enemies defignes, nor with what heed
He marcht before report, where what he ment   220
Fame neuer knew her felfe till it was done,
His drifts and Rumor feldome being all one ;
Nor will this place conueniency afford
To fhew how he, when difmall winter ftormes
Keepes peace, and makes Mars fheath his fword,
Toyles him abroad, and noble act performes ;
Nor how by maftring difficulties fo
In times vnufuall, and by paffage hard
He brauely came to difappoint his foe,
And many times furprif'd him vnprepared.   230
   Yet let me touch one point of that great Act,
That famous fiege, the Mafter-worke of all,
Where no diftreffe nor difficulties lackt
T'afflict his weary tyred Campe with all.
That when inclof'd by powerfull enemies
One either fide, with feeble troupes he lay
Intrencht in myre, in colde, in miferies ;
Kept waking with Alarumes night and day.
There were, who did aduife him, to withdraw
His army to fome place of fafe defence,   240
From the apparent perill which they faw
Was to confound them, or to force them thence.

My willingnes.   Befides being of that weight
Tis finne to place it in a narrower point,
And better now fay nothing then to fay
But little ; there remaines for this behind,
A *Trophey* to b'erected that will ftay
To all pofterityes, and keepe in minde
That glorious worke, which did a kingdome faue,
Kept the Crowne whole & made the Peace we haue.'

For now the Spaniard had poſſeſt three ports
The moſt important of this Ile ſay they,
And ſooner freſh ſupplyments, Spaine tranſports
To them then England can to vs conuay ;
The Reble is in heart, and now is ioyn'd
With ſome of them already, and doth ſtand
Here ouer vs, with chiefeſt ſtrength combin'd
Of all the deſperate forces of the land ;   250
And how vpon theſe diſaduantages
Your doubtfull troupes will fight your *Honour guess.*
Th'vndaunted *Montioy* hereto anſwers this.

My worthy friends, the charge of this great ſtate
And kingdome to my faith committed is,
And I muſt all I can ingeniate
To anſwere for the ſame, and render it
Vpon as faire a reckning as I may ;
But if from hence I ſhall once ſtirre my feete,
The kingdome is vndone, and loſt this day.   260
    All will fly thither where they find is hart,
    And feare ſhal haue none ſtand to take his part ;
    And how ſhal we anſwere our Country then
At our returne, nay anſwere our owne fame ?
Which howſoeuer we haue done like men
Will be imbranded with the marke of blame.
And ſince we here are come vnto the point
For which we toild ſo much and ſtaid ſo long,
Let vs not now our trauailes diſappoint
Of th'honour which doth thereunto belong.   270
We cannot ſpend our blood more worthily
Then in ſo faire a cauſe, and if we fall

l. 252, spelt ' ges.'

We fall with glory, and our worth thereby
Shalbe renowned, and held deare of all.
And for my part I count the field to be
The honourableſt bed to die vpon ;
And here your eies this day either ſee
My body laid, or els this aɛtion done.
    The Lord the chiefe and ſoueraigne Generall
      Of Hoſts, makes weake to ſtand, the ſtrong to
        fall.   280
With which braue reſolution he ſo warm'd
Their ſhaking courage, as they all in one
Set to that noble worke ; which they perform'd
As gallantly as euer men haue done.
Of which tis better nothing now to ſay,
Then ſay too little : For there reſts behind
A Trophey to b'ereɛted, that will ſtay
To all poſterities, and keepe in minde
That glorious aɛt which did a kingdome ſaue,
Kept the Crowne whole and made the peace we
    haue.   290
    And now I will omit to ſhew therefore,
His management of publike buſineſſes :
Which oft are vnder fortunes conduɛt more
Then ours, and tell his priuate carriages ;
VVhich on his owne diſcretion did relie,
VVherewith his ſpirit was furniſht happely.
    Milde, affable, and eaſie of acceſſe
He was, but with a due reſeruednes :
So that the paſſage to his fauours lay
Not common to all commers, nor yet was   300

    l. 291, 'here' for 'now'; l. 292, 'buſ'neſſes '; ll. 285-90—see foot-
note on pp. 179-80.

So naïrow, but it gaue a gentle way
To fuch as fitly might or ought to paffe :
Nor fold he fmoke, nor tooke he vp to day
Commodities of mens attendances,
And of their hopes, to pay them with delay,
And intertaine them with faire promifes.
But as a man that lou'd no great commerce
With bufineffe, and with noife, he euer flies
That Maze of many waies, which might difperfe
Him, into other mens vncertainties.   310
And with a quiet calme fincerity,
H'effeɛts his vndertakings really.
His tongue and heart did not turne-backes, but went
One way, and kept one courfe with what he ment.
He vf'd no mafke at all, but euer ware
His honeft inclination open fac'd,
The friendfhips that he vou'd, moft conftant were,
And with great iudgment, and difcretion plac'd.
    And *Deuonfhire* thy faith hath her reward,
Thy nobleft friends do not forfake thee now,   320
After thy death, but beare a kind regard,
Vnto thine honour in the Graue, and fhow,
That worthineffe, which merits to remaine
Among th'examples of integrity ;
Whereby themfelues no doubt fhall alfo gaine,
A like regard vnto their memory.
    Now muttering enuy, what canft thou produce
To darken the bright lufter of fuch parts ?
Caft thy pure ftone, exempt from all abufe.
Say what defeɛts could weigh downe thefe deferts ? 330

l. 308, ' bufineffe.'

Summon detraction, to obiect the worſt
That may be told, and vtter all it can.
It cannot find a blemiſh to b'inforſt,
Againſt him, other, then he was a man,
And built of fleſh and blood, and did liue here
Within the region of infirmity ;
VVhere all perfections neuer did appeare,
To meet in any one ſo really,
But that his frailty euer did bewray
Vnto the world, that he was ſet in clay.   340
But yet his vertues, and his worthineſſe
Being ſeene ſo farre aboue his weakneſſe,
Muſt euer ſhine, whilſt th'other vnder ground,
With his fraile part, ſhall neuer more be found
And *gratitude*, and *charity* I know,
Will keepe no note, nor memory will haue,
Of any fault committed, but will now
Be pleaſd, to bring all within his Graue.
Seeing only ſuch ſtand euer baſe and low
That ſtrike the dead, or mutter vnder-hand :   350
And as dogges bark at thoſe they do not know,
So they at ſuch they do not vnderſtand.
The worthier ſort, who know we do not liue
With perfect men, will neuer be ſo vnkinde ;
They will the right to the diſceaſed giue,
Knowing themſelues muſt likewiſe leaue behind,

---

l. 334, , for . accepted ; ll. 341-4 re-inserted and accepted from original
edition ; ll. 347-8 accepted for *a*'s—

> ' Of ought, but of his worthy vertues now
> Which ſtill will liue ; the reſt lies in his graue ' ;

l. 349, 'lie' for 'ſtand' ; l. 354, 'be ſo vnkinde' accepted for 'ſ'vnkind' ;

Thofe that will cenfure them.   And they know how,
The Lyon being dead euen Hares infult.
And will not vrge a paffed error now,
Whenas he hath no party to confult,   360
Nor tongue, nor aduocate, to fhew his minde :
They rather will lament the loffe they finde,
By fuch a noble member of that worth,
And know how rare the world fuch men brings forth.
For neuer none had heart more truly feru'd,
Vnder the regiment of his own care,
And was none at command, and none obferu'd
The coullours of that honefty he bare,
Then that of his : who neuer more was knowne ;
To vfe immodeft act, or fpeech obfcene,   370
Or any leuity that might haue fhowne,
The touch but of a thought that was vncleane.
So that what euer he hath done amiffe,
Was vnderneath a fhape that was not knowne ;
As *Iupiter* did no vnworthineffe,
But was in other formes, not in his owne.
   But let it now fufficient be, that I,
The laft Scene of his act of life bewray ;
Which giues th'applaufe to all, doth glorifie
The worke.   For t'is the euening crownes the day. 380
This action of our death efpecially
Shewes all a man.   Here only is he found.
With what munition he did fortifie
His heart, how good his furniture hath bin.
And this did he performe in gallant wife :
In this did he confirme his worthineffe.

l. 359, 'a paffed error' accepted for 'an imperfection'; ll. 365-76 re-
inserted and accepted from original edition.

For on the morrow after the furprife
That ficknes made on him with fierce acceffe,
He told his faithfull friend whom he held deere
(And whofe great worth was worthy fo to be)   390
How that he knew thofe hot difeafes were
Of that contagious force, as he did fee
That men were ouer-tumbled fudainly,
And therefore did defire to fet a courfe
And order t'his affaires as fpeedily ;
As might be, ere his ficknes fhould grow worfe :
And as for death, faid he, I do not wey,
I am refolu'd and ready in this cafe.
It cannot come t'affright me any way,
Let it looke neuer with fo grim a face :   400
And I will meete it fmiling, for I know,
How vaine a thing all this worlds glory is.
And herein did he keepe his word.   Did fhow
Indeede as he had promifed in this.
For fickneffe neuer heard him grone at all,
Nor with a figh confent to fhew his paine ;
Which howfoeuer being tirannicall,
He fweetly made it looke, and did retaine
A louely countenance of his being well,
And fo would euer make his tongue to tell.   410
    Although the feruour of extremity,
Which often doth throw thofe defences downe,
VVhich in our health, wall in infirmity,
Might open lay more then we would haue knowne:
Yet did no idle word in him bewray
Any one peece of nature ill fet in ;

1. 389—in 1607 edition here in margin ' Sir William Godolphin.'

Thofe lightneffes that any thing will fay
Could fay no ill of what they knew within ;
Such a fure locke of filent modefty
VVas fet in life vpon that noble heart   420
As that no anguifh, nor extremity
Could open it t'impaire that worthy part.
For hauing dedicated ftill the fame
Vnto deuotion, and to facred fkill,
That furnifh perfect held, that bleffed flame
Continued to the laft in feruour ftill.
And when his fpirit and tongue, no longer could
Do any certaine feruices befide,
Euen at the point of parting, they vnfold
VVith feruent zeale, how only he relide   430
Vpon the merits of the precious death
Of his redeemer ; and with rapt defires
H'appeales to grace, his foule deliuereth
Vnto the hand of mercy, and expires.
Thus did that worthy, who moft vertuoufly
And mildly liu'd, moft fweete, and mildly dy.
    And thus Great Patrone of my mufe haue I
Paid thee my vowes and fairely cleer'd the accounts
VVhich in my loue I owe thy memory.
And let me fay that herein there amounts   440
Something vnto thy fortune, that thou haft
This monument of thee, perhaps may laft.
Which doth not t'euery mighty man befall :
For loe how many when they die, die all.
And this doth argue too, thy great deferts,
For honour neuer brought vnworthineffe
Further then to the graue, and there it parts
And leaues mens greatnes to forgetfulnes.

And we do fee that nettles, thiftles, brakes
(The pooreft workes of nature) tread vpon   450
The proudeft frames that mans inuention makes,
To hold his memory when he is gone.
But *Deuonſhire* thou haft another Tombe
Made by thy vertues in a fafer roome.

SAMVEL DANIELL.

l. 455, 'Samuell.'

FINIS.

VII.

CERTAINE EPISTLES.
1601-3.

NOTE.

These 'Certaine Epiftles' are also found in the gift-folio of 1601, but probably like the 'Panegyrike' (which precedes them) were of later dates. They were described by the Author as 'after the manner of Horace.' A collation of the after-texts shows no various readings except slight orthographical changes. They appear in all the editions. See our Memorial-Introduction on the persons addressed. A. B. G.

TO
Sr. THOMAS EGERTON
Knight, Lord Keeper of the Great
feale of England.

Ell hath the pow'rfull hand of Maiefty,
Thy worthines, and *Englands* hap
befide,
Set thee in th'aidfull'ft roome of
dignity,
As th'*Ifthmus*, thefe two Oceans to
diuide,
Of *Rigor* and confuf'd *Vncerteinty*;
To keepe out th'entercourfe of wrong and pride,　　10
That they ingulph not vp vnfuccoured right
By the extreme current of licencious might.

Now when we fee the moft combining band,
The ftrongeft faftning of fociety,
Law ; whereon all this frame of men doth ftand,
Remaine concuffed with vncerteinty,
And feeme to fofter rather than withftand
Contention, and embrace obfcurity,
Only t'afflict, and not to fafhion vs,
Making her cure farre worfe than the difeafe ;　　20

l. 10—1601 'fafting' (error).

As if fhe had made couenant with Wrong,
To part the prey made on our weakneffes,
And fuffred Falfhood to be arm'd as ftrong
Vnto the combate, as is Righteoufneffe,
Or futed her, as if fhe did belong
Vnto our paffions, and did euen profeffe
Contention, as her only myftery,
Which fhe reftraines not, but doth multiply.

Was fhe the fame fh'is now in ages paft ?
Or was fhe leffe when fhe was vfed leffe :   30
And growes as malice growes, and fo comes caft
Iuft to the forme of our vnquietneffe ?
Or made more flow, the more that ftrife runs faft,
Staying t'vndo vs ere fhe will redreffe ?
That th'ill fhe checks feemes fuffred to be ill,
When it yeelds greater gaine than goodnes will.

Muft there be ftill fome difcord mixed among
The Harmony of men ? whofe mood accords
Beft with Contention, tun'd t'a note of wrong,
That when warre failes, peace muft make warre with
    words,   40
And b'arm'd vnto deftruction euen as ftrong,
As were in ages paft our ciuill fwords ;
Making as deepe, although vnbleeding wounds,
That whenas fury failes, wifdome confounds.

If it be wifdome, and not cunning, this
Which fo imbroiles the ftate of truth with brawles,
And wraps it vp in ftrange confufedneffe,
As if it liu'd immur'd within the walls

Of hideous termes, fram'd out of barbaroufneffe
And forren cuftomes, the memorialls   50
Of our fubiection, and could neuer be
Deliu'red but by wrangling fubtilty.

Whereas it dwells free in the open plaine,
Vncurious, Gentle, eafie of acceffe ;
Certaine vnto it felfe, of equall vaine,
One face, one colour, one affuredneffe :
It's falfhood that is intricate and vaine,
And needes thefe labyrinths of fubtleneffe :
For where the cunningft cou'rings moft appeare,
It argues ftill that all is not fincere.   60

Which thy cleere-ey'd experience well difcries
Great *Keeper* of the ftate of Equity,
Refuge of mercy, vpon whom relies
The fuccour of oppreffed mifery ;
Altar of fafegard, whereto affliction flies
From th'eage. purfuit of feuerity ;
Hauen of peace, that labour'ft to withdraw
Iuftice from out the tempefts of the Law.

And fet her in a calme and euen way,
Plaine, and directly leading to redreffe,   70
Barring thefe counter-courfes of delay,
Thefe wafting dilatory proceffes :
Ranging into their right and proper ray,
Errors, demurs, effoines, and trauerfes ;
The heads of *Hydra* fpringing out of death,
That giues this monfter, Malice, ftill new breath.

That what was made for the vtility
And good of man, might not be turn'd t'his hurt,
To make him worfer by his remedy,
And caft him downe, with what fhould him fupport: 80
Nor that the ftate of Law might lofe thereby
The due refpeƈt, and reu'rence of her port ;
And feeme a trap to catch our ignorance,
And to intangle our intemperance.

Since her interpretations and our deeds
Vnto a like infinity arife,
As being a Science, that by nature breeds
Contention, ftriefe, and ambiguities :
For altercation controuerfie feeds,
And in her agitation multiplies :   90
The field of *Cauill* lying all like wide,
Yeelds like aduantage vnto either fide.

Which made the graue Caftillian king deuife
   Ferdinand A prohibition, that no Aduocate
   king of Should be conuai'd to th'Indian Colonies,
  Castile (1601.)Left their new fetting, fhaken with debate,
Might take but flender root, and fo not rife
To any perfeƈt grow'th of firme eftate :
For hauing not this fkill, how to contend,
Th'vnnourifht ftrife wold quickly make an end.   100

So likewife did th'Hungarian, when he faw
  The king of Thefe great Italian Bartolifts, who were
  Hungarie. Call'd in of purpofe to explane the Law,
T'imbroile it more, and make it much leffe cleere ;

Cauf'd them from out his kingdom to withdraw
With this infeſtious ſkill, ſome other-where : *Difficultatem*
Whoſe learning, rather let men farther out, *facit doctrina.*
And opened wider paſſages of doubt.

Seeing euen Iniuſtice may be regulare,
And no proportion can there be betwixt   110
Our actions, which in endleſſe motion are,
And th'ordinances which are alwayes fixt;
Ten thouſand lawes more can not reach ſo far,
But malice goes beyond, or liues immixt
So cloſe with goodneſſe, as it euer will
Corrupt, diſguiſe, or counterfet it ſtill.

And therefore did thoſe glorious Monarchs, (who
Diuide with God the ſtile of Maieſty
For being good, and had a care to do
The world right, and ſuccour honeſty)   120
Ordaine this ſanctuary, whereunto
Th'oppreſt might flie, this feat of Equity ;
Whereon thy vertues ſit with faire renowne,
The greateſt grace and glory of the Gowne.

Which *Equity*, being the ſoule of law,
The life of iuſtice, and the ſpirit of right,
Dwell's not in written lines, or liues in awe
Of bookes : deafe powers, that haue nor eares nor ſight
But out of well-weigh'd circumſtance doth draw
The eſſence of a iudgement requiſit ;   130
And is that Leſbian ſquare, that building fit,
Plies to the worke, not forc'th the worke to it.

Maintaining ftill an equall paralell,
Iuft with th'occafions of humanity ;
Making her iudgement euer liable
To the refpeɛt of peace and amity ;
When furely *Law*, fterne, and vnaffable,
Cares only but it felfe to fatisfie :
And often innocencies fcarfe defends,
As that which on no circumftance depends.   140

But *Equity*, that beares an euen raine
Vpon the prefent courfes, holds in aw,
By giuing hand a little, and doth gaine
By a gentle relaxation of the law ;
And yet inuiolable doth maintaine
The end whereto all conftitutions draw ;
Which is the well-fare of fociety,
Confifting of an vpright policy :

Which firft being by neceffity compof'd,
Necessitas est Is by neceffity maintain'd in beft eftate ;   150
lex temporis. Where, whenas iuftice fhall be ill difpof'd,
It fickens the whole body of the State :
For if there be a paffage once difclof'd,
That Wrong may enter at the felfe-fame gate
Which ferues for Right, clad in a coate of Law,
What violent diftempers may it draw :

And therefore do'ft thou ftand to keepe the way,
And ftop the courfe that malice feekes to run,
And by thy prouident *Iniunɛtions* ftay
This neuer ending Altercation ;   160

Sending contention home, to the end men may
There make their peace whereas their ftrife begun,
And free thefe peftred ftreets they vainely weare,
Whom both the ftate, and theirs, do need elfewhere.

Left th'humor which doth thus predominate
Conuert vnto it felfe all that it takes ;
And that the law grow larger than debate,
And come t'exceede th'affaires it vndertakes :
As if the only Science of the State
That tooke vp all our wits for gaine it makes ;   170
Not for the good that thereby may be wrought,
Which is not good if it be dearely bought.

What fhall we thinke whenas ill caufes fhall
Inrich men more, and fhall be more defir'd
Than good, as farre more beneficiall ?
Who then defends the good ?   Who will be hir'd
To entertaine a right, whofe gaine is fmall ?   *A Remedie for*
Vnleffe the Aduocate that hath conspir'd   *defending ill*
To plead a wrong, be likewife made to runne   *caufes.*
His Clients chance, and with him be vndone.   180

So did the wifeft nations euer ftriue
To binde the hands of Iuftice vp fo hard,
That left fhe falling to proue Lucratiue
Might bafely reach them out to take reward :
Ordaining her prouifions fit to liue
Out of the publike, as a publike guard
That all preferues, and all doth entertaine,
Whofe end is only glory, and not gaine.

That eu'n the Scepter which might all command,
Seeing her s'vnpartiall, equall regular,   190
Was pleaf'd to put it felfe into her hand,
Whereby they both grew more admired far.
And this is that great bleffing of this land,
That both the Prince and people vfe one Barre ;
The Prince, whofe caufe (as not to be withftood)
Is neuer bad but where himfelfe is good.

This is that ballance which committed is
To thy moft euen and religious hand,
Great Minifter of Iuftice, who by this
Shalt haue thy name ftill gracious in this land :   200
This is that feale of pow'r which doth impreffe
Thy aꝏts of right, which fhall for euer ftand :
This is that traine of State, that pompoufly
Attends vpon thy reu'rent dignity.

All glory els befides ends with our breath,
And mens refpeꝏts, fcarfe brings vs to our graue :
But this of doing good, muft out liue Death,
And haue a right out of the right it gaue :
Though th'aꝏt but few, th'example profiteth
Thoufands, that fhall thereby a bleffing haue.   210
The worlds refpeꝏt growes not but on defarts,
Pow'r may haue knees, but iuftice hath our hearts.

TO

THE LORD HENRIE

HOWARD, one of his Maiefties

Priuy Councell.

Raife, if it be not choice, and layd aright,
Can yeeld no luftre where it is be-
ftow'd,
Nor any way can grace the giuers
Art,
(Tho'it be a pleafing colour to delight)
For that no ground whereon it can
be fhew'd
Will beare it well, but Vertue and Defart.   10
And though I might commend your learning, wit,
And happy vttrance ; and commend them right,
As that which decks you much, and giues you grace,
Yet your cleere iudgement beft deferueth it ;
Which in your courfe hath carried you vpright,
And made you to difcerne the trueft face,
     And beft complexion of the things that breed
The reputation and the loue of men ;
And held you in the tract of honefty,
Which euer in the end we fee fucceed ;   20

l 7, misprinted ' Not,' in all.

Though oft it may haue interrupted beene
Both by the times and mens iniquity.
    For fure thofe aćtions which do fairely runne
In the right line of honour, ftill are thofe
That get moft cleane and fafeft to their end,
And paffe the beft without confufion,
Either in thofe that act or els difpofe,
Hauing the fcope made cleere, whereto they tend.
    When this by-path of cunning doth s'imbroile
And intricate the paffage of affaires,   30
As that they feldome fairely can get out ;
But coft, with leffe fucceffe, more care and toyle,
Whil'ft doubt and the diftrufted caufe impaires
Their courage, who would els appeare more ftout.
    For though fome hearts are blinded fo, that they
Haue diuers doores whereby they may let out
Their wills abroad without difturbancy,
Int'any courfe, and into eu'ry way
Of humor that affećtion turnes about ;
Yet haue the beft but one t'haue paffage by,   40
    And that fo furely warded with the gard
Of confcience and refpećt, as nothing muft
Haue courfe that way, but with the certaine paffe
Of a perfwafiue right ; which being compar'd
With their conceit, muft thereto anfwere iuft,
And fo with due examination paffe.
    Which kind of men, raif'd of a better frame,
Are meere religious, conftant and vpright,
And bring the ableft hands for any effećt,
And beft beare vp the reputation, fame,   50
And good opinion, that the aćtion's right
When th'vndertakers are without fufpect :

But when the body of an enterprize
Shall go one way, the face another way,
As if it did but mocke a weaker truft,
The motion being monftrous, can not rife
To any good, but falls downe to bewray,
That all pretences ferue for things vniuft ;
    Efpecially where th'aótion will allow
Apparency, or that it hath a courfe   60
Concentrike with the vniuerfall frame
Of men combin'd ; whom it concerneth how
Thefe motions runne, and entertaine their force ;
Hauing their being refting on the fame.
    And be it, that the vulgar are but groffe,
Yet are they capable of truth, and fee,
And fometimes geffe the right, and do conceiue
The nature of that text that needs a gloffe,
And wholy neuer can deluded be :
All may a few, few cannot all deceiue.   70
    And thefe ftrange difproportions in the traine
And courfe of things doe euermore proceed
From th'ill-fet difpofition of their mindes,
Who in their aótions cannot but retaine
Th'incumbred formes which doe within them breed,
And which they cannot fhew but in their kindes.
    Whereas the wayes and counfels of the light
So fort with valour and with manlineffe,
As that they carry things affuredlie
Vndazling of their owne or others fight :   80
There being a bleffing that doth giue fucceffe
To worthineffe and vnto conftancie.
    And though fometimes th'euent may fall amiffe,
Yet fhall it ftill haue honour for th'attempt,

When craft begins with feare and ends with fhame,
And in the whole defigne perplexed is ;
Vertue, though luckleffe, yet fhall fcape contempt,
And though it hath not hap, it fhall haue fame.

TO

THE LADIE MARGARET

Counteſſe of Cumberland.

E that of ſuch a height hath built his
    minde,
And rear'd the dwelling of his
    thoughts ſo ſtrong,
As neither feare nor hope can ſhake
    the frame
Of his reſolued powr's, nor all the
    winde
Of vanitie or malice pierce to wrong
His ſetled peace, or to diſturbe the ſame ;
What a faire ſeate hath he, from whence he may   10
The boundleſſe waſtes and wildes of man ſuruay.

And with how free an eye doth he looke downe
Vpon theſe lower regions of turmoyle !
Where all the ſtormes of paſſions mainly beat
On fleſh and bloud ; where honour, pow'r, renowne
Are onely gay afflictions, golden toyle ;
Where greatneſſe ſtands vpon as feeble feet
As frailty doth, and onely great doth ſeeme
To little minds, who doe it ſo eſteeme.

He lookes vpon the mightieſt Monarchs warres   20
But onely as on ſtately robberies ;
Where euermore the fortune that preuailes
Muſt be the right ; the ill-ſucceeding marres

The faireſt and the beſt-fac't enterprize :
Great Pirat *Pompey* leſſer Pirats quailes ;
Iuſtice, he ſees, as if ſeduced, ſtill
Conſpires with pow'r, whoſe cauſe muſt not be ill.

He ſees the face of *Right* t'appeare as manifolde
As are the paſſions of vncertaine man ;
Who puts it in all colours, all attires,   30
To ſerue his ends and make his courſes holde :
He ſees, that let Deceit worke what it can,
Plot and contriue baſe wayes to high deſires ;
That the all-guiding Prouidence doth yet
All diſappoint, and mocks this ſmoake of wit.

Nor is he mou'd with all the thunder-cracks
Of Tyrants threats, or with the ſurly brow
Of power, that proudly ſits on others crimes,
Charg'd with more crying ſinnes then thoſe he checks ;
The ſtormes of ſad confuſion, that may grow   40
Vp in the preſent, for the comming times,
Appall not him, that hath no ſide at all
But of himſelfe, and knowes the worſt can fall.

Although his heart ſo neere allied to earth,
Cannot but pitty the perplexed State
Of troublous and diſtreſt mortalitie,
That thus make way vnto the ougly birth
Of their owne ſorrowes, and doe ſtill beget
Affliction vpon imbecillitie :
Yet ſeeing thus the courſe of things muſt runne,   50
He lookes thereon, not ſtrange, but as foredone.

And whilft diftraught Ambition compaffes
And is incompaft ; whil'ft as craft deceiues
And is deceiued ; whil'ft man doth ranfacke man,
And builds on bloud, and rifes by diftreffe ;
And th'inheritance of defolation leaues
To great expecting hopes ; he lookes thereon
As from the fhore of peace with vnwet eie,
And beares no venture in impietie.

Thus, Madam, fares that man that hath prepar'd   60
A reft for his defires, and fees all things
Beneath him, and hath learn'd this booke of man,
Full of the notes of frailty, and compar'd
The beft of glory with her fufferings:
By whom I fee you labour all you can
To plant your heart, and fet your thoughts as neare
His glorious manfion as your pow'rs can beare.

Which, Madam, are fo foundly fafhioned
By that cleere iudgement that hath carryed you
Beyond the feeble limits of your kinde,   70
As they can ftand againft the ftrongeft head
Paffion can make ; inur'd to any hue
The world can caft ; that cannot caft that minde
Out of her forme of goodneffe, that doth fee
Both what the beft and worft of earth can be.

Which makes, that whatfoeuer here befalles
You in the region of your felfe remaine ;
Where no vaine breath of th'impudent molefts,
That hath fecur'd within the brafen walles

Of a cleere confcience, that without all ftaine   80
Rifes in peace, in innocencie refts ;
Whilft all what malice from without procures,
Shewes her owne ougly heart, but hurts not yours.

And whereas none reioyce more in reuenge
Then women vfe to doe ; yet you well know,
That wrong is better checkt, by being contemn'd
Then being purfu'd : leauing to him t'auenge
To whom it appertaines ; wherein you fhow
How worthily your cleereneffe hath condemn'd
Bafe malediction, liuing in the darke,   90
That at the raies of goodneffe ftill doth barke.

Knowing the heart of man is fet to be
The centre of this world, about the which
Thefe reuolutions of difturbances
Still roule ; where all th'afpects of miferie
Predominate ; whofe ftrong effects are fuch
As he muft beare, being pow'rleffe to redreffe ;
And that vnleffe aboue himfelfe he can
Erect himfelfe, how poore a thing is man !

And how turmoyl'd they are, that leuell lie   100
With earth, and cannot lift themfelues from thence ;
That neuer are at peace with their defires,
But worke beyond their yeeres, and euen denie
Dotage her reft, and hardly will difpence
With death : that when ability expires,
Defire liues ftill : fo much delight they haue
To carry toyle and trauell to the graue.

Whofe ends you fee, and what can be the beft
They reach vnto, when they haue caft the fumme
And reckonings of their glory ; and you know   110
This floting life hath but this Port of reft,
A heart prepar'd, that feares no ill to come :
And that mans greatneffe refts but in his fhow ;
The beft of all whofe dayes confumed are
Either in warre, or peace conceiuing warre.

This concord, Madame, of a well-tun'd minde
Hath beene fo fet, by that all-working hand
Of heauen, that though the world hath done his worft
To put it out, by difcords moft vnkinde ;
Yet doth it ftill in perfe&t vnion ftand   120
With God and man, nor euer will be forc't
From that moft fweet accord, but ftill agree
Equall in Fortunes inequalitie.

And this note (Madame) of your worthineffe
Remaines recorded in fo many hearts,
As time nor malice cannot wrong your right
In th'inheritance of Fame you muft poffeffe ;
You that haue built you by your great deferts,
Out of fmall meanes, a farre more exquifit
And glorious dwelling for your honoured name   130
Then all the gold that leaden minds can frame.

S. D.

TO

THE LADIE LVCIE
Counteſſe of Bedford.

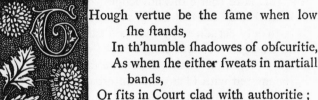Hough vertue be the fame when low
    ſhe ſtands,
  In th'humble ſhadowes of obſcuritie,
  As when ſhe either ſweats in martiall
    bands,
  Or ſits in Court clad with authoritie;
    Yet, Madam, doth the ſtrictneſſe of
    her roome
Greatly detract from her abilitie:
For as in-wall'd within a liuing tombe,   10
  Her hands and armes of action, labour ɳot;
  Her thoughts, as if abortiue from the wombe,
  Come neuer borne, though happily begot,
But where ſhe hath mounted in open ſight
  An eminent and ſpacious dwelling got.
  Where ſhee may ſtirre at will, and vſe her might,
There is ſhe more her ſelfe, and more her owne;
  There in the faire attire of honor dight,
  She ſits at eaſe and makes her glory knowne:
Applauſe attends her hands, her deeds haue grace, 20
  Her worth new-borne is ſtrait as if full growne.

With fuch a godly and refpected face
Doth vertue looke, that's fet to looke from hie ;
   And fuch a faire aduantage by her place
   Hath ftate and greatneffe to doe worthily.
And therefore well did your high fortunes meet
   With her, that gracing you, comes grac't thereby :
   And well was let into a houfe fo fweet,
So good, fo faire, fo faire fo good a gueft ;
   Who now remaines as bleffed in her feat,   30
   As you are with her refidencie bleft.
And this faire courfe of knowledge whereunto
   Your ftudies, learned Lady, are addreft,
   Is th'only certaine way that you can go
Vnto true glory, to true happineffe :
   All paffages on earth befides, are fo
   Incumbred with fuch vaine difturbances ;
As ftill we lofe our reft in feeking it,
   Being but deluded with apparances ;
   And no key had you elfe that was fo fit   40
T'vnlocke that prifon of your fex, as this,
   To let you out of weakneffe, and admit
   Your powers into the freedome of that bliffe
That fets you there where you may ouer-fee
   This rowling world, and view it as it is ;
   And apprehend how th'outfides doe agree
With th'inward, being of the things we deeme
   And hold in our ill-caft accounts, to be
   Of higheft value and of beft efteeme ;
Since all the good we haue refts in the minde,   50
   By whofe proportions onely we redeeme
   Our thoughts from out confufion, and doe finde
The meafure of our felues, and of our pow'rs ;

And that all happineſſe remaines confinde
Within the Kingdome of this breaſt of ours :
Without whoſe boundes all that we looke on lies
  In others iuriſdictions, others pow'rs,
  Out of the circuit of our liberties.
All glory, honor, fame, applauſe, renowne,
  Are not belonging to our royalties,   60
  But t'others wils, wherein th'are onely growne :
And that vnleſſe we find vs all within,
  We neuer can without vs be our owne,
  Nor call it right our life that we liue in :
But a poſſeſſion held for others vſe,
  That ſeeme to haue moſt int'reſt therein ;
  Which we doe ſo diſſeuer, part, traduce,
Let out to cuſtome, faſhion, and to ſhew,
  As we enioy but onely the abuſe,
  And haue no other deed at all to ſhew.   70
How oft are we conſtrained to appeare
  With other countenance then that we owe,
  And be our ſelues farre off, when we are neere !
How oft are we forc't on a cloudie hart
  To ſet a ſhining face, and make it cleere ;
  Seeming content to put our ſelues apart,
To beare a part of others weakeneſſes !
  As if we onely were compoſ'd by Art,
  Not Nature, and did all our deeds addreſſe
T'opinion, not t'a conſcience, what is right :   80
  As fram'd b'example, not aduiſedneſſe,
  Into thoſe formes that entertaine our fight.
And though books, Madam, cannot make this minde
  Which we muſt bring apt to be ſet aright,
  Yet doe they rectifie it in that kinde,

And touch it fo, as that it turnes that way
   Where iudgement lies : and though we cannot find
   The certaine place of truth, yet doe they ftay
And entertaine vs neere about the fame ;
   And giue the foule the beft delight that may   90
   Encheere it moft, and moft our fpirits inflame
To thoughts of glory, and to worthy ends :
   And therefore in a courfe that beft became
   The cleereneffe of your heart, and beft commends
Your worthy pow'rs, you run the righteft way
   That is on earth, that can true glory giue ;
   By which when all confumes, your fame fhal liue.

TO

THE LADIE ANNE
Clifford.

Nto the tender youth of thofe faire eies
The light of iudgement can arife but
new ;
And yong the world appeares t'a
yong conceit,
Whil'ft thorow the vnacquainted
faculties
The late inuefted foule doth rawly view
Thofe obiects which on that difcretion wait.

Yet you that fuch a faire aduantage haue   10
Both by your birth and happy pow'rs, t'out go,
And be before your yeeres, can fairely gueffe
What hue of life holdes fureft without ftaine ;
Hauing your well-wrought heart full furnifh't fo
With all the images of worthineffe,
As there is left no roome at all t'inueft
Figures of other forme but fanctitie :
Whilft yet thofe cleane-created thoughts, within
The Garden of your innocencies reft ;
Where are no motions of deformitie,   20
Nor any doore at all to let them in.

With fo great care doth fhe, that hath brought forth
That comely body, labour to adorne

That better part, the manſion of your minde,
With all the richeſt furniture of worth ;
To make y'as highly good as highly borne,
And ſet your vertues equall to your kinde.
    She tels you how that honour onely is
A goodly garment put on faire deſarts ;
Wherein the ſmalleſt ſtaine is greateſt ſeene,   30
And that it cannot grace vnworthineſſe ;
But more apparant ſhewes defeĉtiue parts,
How gay ſoeuer they are deckt therein.
    She tels you too, how that it bounded is,
And kept incloſed with ſo many eies,
As that it cannot ſtray and breake abroad
Into the priuate wayes of careleſneſſe ;
Nor euer may deſcend to vulgarize,
Or be below the ſphere of her abode.
    But like to thoſe ſupernall bodies ſet   40
Within their Orbs, muſt keepe the certaine courſe
Of order, deſtin'd to their proper place ;
Which onely doth their note of glory get.
Th'irregular apparances inforce
A ſhort reſpeĉt, and periſh without grace :
    Being Meteors ſeeming high, but yet low plac't,
    Blazing but while their dying matters laſt :
    Nor can we take the iuſt height of the minde,
But by that order which her courſe doth ſhew,
And which ſuch ſplendor to her aĉtions giues ;   50
And thereby men her eminencie finde,
And thereby onely doe attaine to know
The Region, and the Orbe wherein ſhe liues.
    For low in th'aire of groſſe vncertaintie
    Confuſion onely rowles, order ſits hie.

And therefore fince the deareft thinge on earth,
This honour, Madam, hath his ftately frame
From th'heau'nly order, which begets refpect ;
And that your Nature, vertue, happy birth,
Haue therein highly interplac'd your name,   60
You may not runne the leaft courfe of neglect,

 For where, not to obferue, is to prophane
Your dignity ; how carefull muft you be
To be your felfe ? And though you may to all
Shine faire afpects, yet muft the vertuous gaine
The beft effects of your benignitie :
Nor muft your common graces caufe to fall
The price of your efteeme t'a lower rate,
Then doth befit the pitch of your eftate.

 Nor may you build on your fufficiencie,   70
For in our ftrongeft parts we are but weake ;
Nor yet may ouermuch diftruft the fame :
Left that you come to checke it fo thereby,
As filence may become worfe then to fpeake ;
Though filence women neuer ill became.

 And none we fee were euer ouerthrowne
 By others flattery more then by their owne.
For though we liue amongft the tongues of praife,
And troopes of fmoothing people that collaud
All that we doe, yet 'tis within our harts   80
Th'ambufhment lies, that euermore betraies
Our iudgements, when our felues be come t'applaud
Our owne abilitie and our owne parts.

 So that we muft not onely fence this fort
Of ours, againft all others fraud, but moft
Againft our owne ; whofe danger is the moft,
Becaufe we lie the neereft to doe hurt,

And foon'ſt deceiue our felues, and foon'ſt are loſt
By our beſt pow'rs, that doe vs moſt tranſport.
    Such are your holy bounds, who muſt conuay   90
(If God ſo pleaſe) the honourable bloud
Of *Clifford,* and of *Ruſſell,* led aright
To many worthy ſtems ; whoſe ofspring may
Looke backe with comfort, to haue had that good
To ſpring from ſuch a branch that grew ſ'vpright ;
    Since nothing cheeres the heart of greatneſſe more
    Then th'Anceſtors faire glory gone before.   97

l. 89 misprinted 'tranſpord' in 1623 4to.

TO

HENRY VVRIOTHESLY

Earle of *Southamton.*

Non fert vllum ictum illæfa fœlicitas.

E who hath neuer warr'd with miferie,
Nor euer tugg'd with Fortune and
diftreffe,
Hath had n'occafion nor no field to
trie
The ftrength and forces of his worthi-
neffe :
Thofe parts of iudgement which felicitie
Keepes as conceal'd, affliction muft expreffe ;   10
And onely men fhew their abilities,
And what they are, in their extremities.

The world had neuer taken fo full note
Of what thou art, hadft thou not beene vndone ;
And onely thy affliction hath begot
More fame, then thy beft fortunes could haue done ;
For euer, by aduerfitie are wrought
The greateft workes of admiration.
And all the faire examples of renowne
Out of diftreffe and miferie are growne.   20

Mutius the fire, the tortures *Regulus,*
Did make the miracles of faith and zeale,
Exile renown'd, and grac'd *Rutilius* ;
Imprifonment and poyfon did reueale

The worth of *Socrates* ; *Fabritius'*
Pouertie did grace that Common-weale
More then all *Syllaes* riches, got with ſtrife ;
And *Catoes* death did vie with *Cæſars* life.

Not to b'vnhappy is vnhappyneſſe ;
And miſery not t'haue knowne miſerie :   30
For the beſt way vnto diſcretion, is
The way that leades vs by aduerſitie.
And men are better ſhew'd what is amiſſe,
By th'expert finger of calamitie,
Then they can be with all that Fortune brings ;
Who neuer ſhewes them the true face of things.

How could we know that thou could'ſt haue indur'd
With a repoſed cheere, wrong and diſgrace ;
And with a heart and countenance aſſur'd
Haue lookt ſterne death and horror in the face !   40
How ſhould we know thy ſoule had beene ſecur'd
In honeſt counſels and in way vnbaſe !
Hadſt thou not ſtood to ſhew vs what thou wert,
By thy affliction, that diſcri'd thy heart.

It is not but the Tempeſt that doth ſhow
The Sea-mans cunning ; but the field that tries
The Captaines courage : and we come to know
Beſt what men are, in their worſt ieoperdies :
For lo, how many haue we ſeene to grow
To high renowne from loweſt miſeries,   50
Out of the hands of death, and many a one
T'haue beene vndone, had they not beene vndone.

He that indures for what his confcience knowes
Not to be ill, doth from a patience hie
Looke onely on the caufe whereto he owes
Thofe fufferings, not on his miferie:
The more h'endures, the more his glory growes,
Which neuer growes from imbecillitie:
Onely the beft compof'd and worthieft harts
God fets to act the hardeft and conftant'ft parts.   60

S. D.

VIII

Muſophilus, or Defence of all Learning.

1602-3.

In the 1601 gift-folio, again, 'Mufophilus' is found with this title (undated) :—

A

Defence of Ryme

Againſt a Pamphlet enti-
tuled

Obferuations in the Art of
Englifh Poefie.

Wherein is demonſtratiuely pro-
ued, that Ryme is the fitteſt har-
monie of words that comportes
with our language.

By Sa. D.

At London
Printed by V. S. for *Edward Blount.*

As Dr. Thomas Campion's 'Obferuations' did not appear until 1602, the 'Defence' cannot have been printed sooner than 1602-3. A collation of the after-texts yields no various readings save slight orthographical changes. See our Memorial-Introduction on 'Mufophilus,' and Daniel's prose 'Defence' (in his Prose Works). The general title was thus altered later.

Mvſophilus :

Containing

A General Defence
of Learning.

In the 4to of 1623 and elsewhere the placing of the stanzas is irregular (from p. 248, l. 717) ; all have been made uniform, *i.e.*, 8 lines each, with first line projecting instead of a line projecting and two lines ; also l. 728 a misprint 'temp'ring' corrected by 'tamp'ring.' G.

To the right VVorthy and Iudicious

Fauorer of Vertue, Maſter
Fulke Greuill.

I Doe not here vpon this hum'rous Stage,
Bring my transformed Verſe, apparelled
With others paſſions, or with others
rage ;
With loues, with wounds, with factions
furniſhed :
But here preſent thee, onely modelled
In this poore frame, the forme of mine owne heart :
Where, to reuiue my ſelfe, my Muſe is led   10
With motions of her owne, t'act her owne part ;
Striuing to make her now contemned Art,
As faire t'her ſelfe as poſſibly ſhe can ;
Leſt, ſeeming of no force, of no deſert,
She might repent the courſe that ſhe began ;
And, with theſe times of diſſolution, fall
From Goodneſſe, Vertue, Glory, Fame and all.   17

MVSOPHILVS

Containing,

A generall Defence of all
Learning.

Philocofmus.

Ond man *Mufophilus*, that thus doft
    fpend,
    In an vngainefull Arte thy deereft
    dayes,
    Tyring thy wits, and toyling to no end,
    But to attaine that idle fmoake of
    Praife :
Now when this bufie world cannot attend   10
Th'vntimely Muficke of neglected layes.
  Other delights then thefe, other defires
  This wifer profit-feeking Age requires.

Mufophilus.

Riend *Philocofmus*, I confeffe indeede,
    I loue this facred Arte thou fett'ft fo light,
And though it neuer ftand my life in fteede,
It is enough, it giues my felfe delight ;
The whiles my vnafflicted minde doth feede
On no vnholy thoughts for benefit.   20

Be it, that my vnſeaſonable Song
    Come out of time ; that fault is in the Time,
    And I muſt not doe Vertue ſo much wrong,
    As loue her aught the worſe for others crime :
    And yet I finde ſome bleſſed ſpirits among,
    That cheriſh me, and like, and grace my Rime.
Againe, that I doe more in Soule eſteeme,
    Then all the gaine of duſt the world doth craue :
    And, if I may attaine, but to redeeme
    My name from Diſſolution and the Graue ;   30
    I ſhall haue done enough, and better deeme
    T'haue liu'd to be, then to haue dide to haue.
Short-breath'd Mortalitie would yet extend
    That ſpanne of life ſo farre forth as it may,
    And robbe her Fate ; ſeeke to beguile her end
    Of ſome few lingring dayes of after-ſtay,
    That all this little All, might not deſcend
    Into the darke, a vniuerſall pray.
    And giue our labours yet this poore delight,
    That when our daies doe end, they are not done : 40
    And though we die, we ſhall not periſh quite,
    But liue two liues, where other haue but one.

Philocoſmus.

S Illy deſires of ſelfe-abuſing man,
        Striuing to gaine th'inheritance of Aire,
That hauing done the vttermoſt he can,
Leaues yet, perhaps, but beggarie to his heire :
All that great purchaſe of the breath he wan,
Feedes not his race, or makes his houſe more faire.

                    l. 44, 'Seely' 1601.

And what art thou the better, thus to leaue   50
  A multitude of words to fmall effe&ct,
  Which other times may fcorne, and fo deceiue
  Thy promif'd name, of what thou doft expe&ct ?
  Befides, fome viperous Criticke may bereaue
  Th'opinion of thy worth for fome defe&ct ;
And get more reputation of his wit,
  By, but controlling of fome word or fence,
  Then thou fhalt honour for contriuing it,
  With all thy trauell, care and diligence ;
  Being Learning now enough to contradi&ct,   60
  And cenfure others with bold infolence.
Befides, fo many fo confufedly fing,
  Whofe diuerfe difcords haue the Muficke mar'd,
  And in contempt that myfterie doth bring,
  That he muft fing alowd that will be heard :
  And the receiu'd opinion of the thing,
  For fome vnhallowed ftring that vildely iar'd,
Hath fo vnfeafon'd now the eares of men,
  That who doth touch the tenour of that vaine,
  Is held but vaine ; and his vnreckned pen   70
  The title but of Leuitie doth gaine.
  A poore light gaine, to recompence their toyle,
  That thought to get Eternitie the while.
And therefore, leaue the left and out-worne courfe
  Of vnregarded wayes, and labour how
  To fit the times with what is moft in force ;
  Be new with mens affe&ctions that are new ;
  Striue not to runne an idle counter-courfe,
  Out from the fcent of humours, men allow.
For not difcreetly to compofe our partes   80
  Vnto the frame of men (which we muft be)

Is to put off our felues, and make our Artes
Rebels to Nature and Societie ;
Whereby we come to burie our defarts,
In th'obfcure graue of Singularitie.

Mufophilus.

DOe not prophane the worke of doing well,
    Seduced man, that canft not looke fo hie
From out that mift of earth, as thou canft tell
The wayes of Right, which Vertue doth defcrie ;   90
That ouer-lookes the bafe contemptibly,
And low-laid follies of Mortalitie :
Nor mete out Truth and right-difcerning Praife,
    By that wrong meafure of Confufion,
    The vulgar foote ; that neuer takes his wayes
    By Reafon, but by Imitation,
    Rowling on with the reft ; and neuer weighs
    The courfe which he fhould goe, but what is gone.
Well were it with Mankinde, if, what the moft
    Did like, were beft : But Ignorance will liue   100
    By others fquare, as by example loft :
    And man to man muft th'hand of Errour giue
    That none can fall alone, at their owne coft;
    And all, becaufe men iudge not, but beleeue.
For what poore bounds haue they, whom but th'earth
        bounds;
    What is their end whereto their care attaines,
    When the thing got, relieues not, but confounds,
    Hauing but trauell to fucceede their paines ?
    What ioy hath he of liuing, that propounds
    Affliction but his end, and Griefe his gaines ?   110

Gath'ring, incroching, wrefting, ioyning to,
   Deftroying, building, decking, furnifhing,
   Repayring, altring, and fo much adoe,
   To his foules toyle, and bodies trauelling :
   And all this doth he, little knowing who
   Fortune ordaines to haue th'inheriting.
And his faire houfe raif'd hie in Enuies eie ;
   Whofe Pillars rear'd (perhaps) on bloud and wrong,
   The fpoyles and pillage of Iniquitie :
   Who can affure it to continue long ?   120
   If Rage fpar'd not the walles of Pietie,
   Shall the prophaneft pyles of finne keepe ftrong ?
How many proud afpiring Pallaces
   Haue we knowne, made the prey of wrath and pride;
   Leuell'd with th'earth, left to forgetfulneffe ;
   Whilft titlers their pretended rights decide,
   Or ciuill tumults, or an orderleffe
   Order, pretending change of fome ftrong fide ?
Then where is that proud Title of thy name,
   Written in yce of melting vanitie ?   130
   Where is thine heire left to poffeffe the fame ?
   Perhaps, not fo well as in beggarie.
   Something may rife to be beyond the fhame
   Of vile and vnregarded Pouertie.
Which I confeffe, although I often ftriue
   To clothe in the beft habit of my fkill,
   In all the faireft colours I can giue :
   Yet for all that, me thinkes fhe lookes but ill.
   I cannot brooke that face, which dead-aliue
   Shewes a quicke body, but a buried will.   140
Yet oft we fee the barres of this reftraint
   Holdes goodneffe in, which loofe wealth would let flie;

And fruitleffe riches barriner then want,
Brings forth fmall worth from idle Libertie :
Which when Diforders fhall againe make fcant,
It muft refetch her ftate from Pouertie.
But yet in all this interchange of all,
   Vertue we fee, with her faire grace, ftands faft :
For what high races hath there come to fall,
   With low difgrace, quite vanifhed and paft,   150
Since *Chaucer* liu'd ; who yet liues, and yet fhall,
   Though (which I grieue to fay) but in his laft.
Yet what a time hath he wrefted from Time,
   And wonne vpon the mighty wafte of dayes,
Vnto th'immortall honour of our clime !
   That by his meanes came firft adorn'd·with Bayes ;
Vnto the facred Relickes of whofe rime,
   We yet are bound in zeale to offer praife ?
And, could our lines, begotten in this age,
   Obtaine but fuch a bleffed hand of yeares,   160
And fcape the fury of that threatning rage,
   Which in confufed cloudes gaftly appeares ;
Who would not ftraine his trauels to ingage,
   When fuch true glory fhould fucceede his cares?
But whereas he came planted in the Spring,
   And had the Sunne, before him, of Refpeft :
We, fet in th'Autumne, in the withering
   And fullen feafon of a cold defeft,
Muft tafte thofe fowre diftafts the times do bring
   Vpon the fulneffe of a cloy'd Negleft ;   170
Although the ftronger conftitutions fhall
   Weare out th'infeftion of diftempred dayes,
And come with glory to out-liue this fall :
   Recou'ring of another fpringing of Praife,

Cleer'd from th'opprefing humours wherewithall
The Idle multitude furcharge their laies.
Whenas (perhaps) the words thou fcorneft now
    May liue, the fpeaking picture of the minde ;
    The extract of the foule, that laboured, how
    To leaue the Image of herfelfe behinde ;   180
    Wherein Pofteritie, that loue to know
    The iuft proportion of our Spirits, may finde.
For thefe Lines are the veines, the arteries,
    And vndecaying life-ftrings of thofe harts
    That ftill fhall pant, and ftill fhall exercize
    The motion, fpirit and Nature both imparts ;
    And fhall, with thofe aliue fo fympathize,
    As, nourifht with their powers, inioy their parts.
O bleffed Letters, that combine in one,
    All Ages paft, and make one liue with all :   190
    By you, we doe conferre with who are gone,
    And, the dead-liuing vnto Councell call :
    By you, th'vnborne fhall haue communion
    Of what we feele, and what doth vs befall.
Soule of the world, Knowledge, without thee,
    What hath the Earth, that truly glorious is ?
    Why fhould our pride make fuch a ftirre to be,
    To be forgot ? What good is like to this,
    To doe worthy the writing, and to write
    Worthy the reading, and the worlds delight ?   200
And let th'vnnaturall and wayward Race,
    Borne of one wombe with vs, but to our fhame,
    That neuer read t'obferue, but to difgrace;
    Raife all the tempeft of their powre, to blame.
    That puffe of folly neuer can deface,
    The worke a happy *Genius* tooke to frame.

Yet why fhould ciuill Learning feeke to wound
   And mangle her owne members with defpight?
   Prodigious wits, that ftudy to confound
   The life of wit, to feeme to know aright,   210
   As if themfelues had fortunately found
   Some ftand from off the earth beyond our fight;
   Whence, ouer-looking all as from aboue,
   Their grace is not to worke, but to reproue.
But how came they plac'd in fo high degree
   Aboue the reach and compaffe of the reft?
   Who hath admitted them onely to be
   Free-denizons of fkill, to iudge the beft?
   From whom the world as yet could neuer fee
   The warrant of their wit foundly expreft.   220
T'acquaint our times with that perfection
   Of high conceipt, which onely they poffeffe;
   That we might haue things exquifitely done,
   Meafur'd with all their ftrict obferuances:
   Such would (I know) fcorne a Tranflation,
   Or bring but others labours to the Preffe:
   Yet, oft thefe monfter-breeding mountaines will
   Bring forth fmall Mice of great expected fkill.
Prefumption euer fulleft of defects,
   Failes, in the doing, to performe her part: 230
   And I haue knowne proude words and poore effects,
   Of fuch indeede as doe condemne this Arte:
   But let them reft, it euer hath beene knowne,
   They others vertues fcorne, that doubt their owne.
And for the diuers difagreeing cordes
   Of inter-iangling Ignorance, that fill
   The dainty eares, and leaue no roome for words,
   The worthier mindes neglect, or pardon will:

Knowing the beft he hath, he frankely foordes,
And fcornes to be a niggard of his fkill. 240
And that the rather, fince this fhort-liu'd race,
Being fatally the fonnes but of one day ;
That now with all their powre plie it apace,
To hold out with the greateft might they may,
Againft Confufion, that hath all in chace,
To make of all, an vniuerfall pray.
For now great Nature hath laid downe at laft
That mighty birth, wherewith fo long fhe went,
And ouer-went the times of ages paft,
Here to lye in, vpon our foft content : 250
Where fruitfull fhe, hath multiplyed fo faft,
That all fhe hath, on thefe times feem'd t'haue fpent.
All that which might haue many ages grac'd,
Is borne in one, to make one cloy'd with all;
Where Plenty hath impreft a deepe diftaft,
Of beft and worft, and all in generall :
That Goodneffe feemes Goodneffe to haue defac't,
And Vertue hath to Vertue giuen the fall.
For Emulation, that proude nurfe of Wit,
Scorning to ftay below or come behinde, 260
Labours vpon that narrow top to fit
Of fole Perfection in the higheft kinde :
Enuy and Wonder looking after it,
Thruft likewife, on the felfefame bliffe to finde :
And fo, long ftriuing, till they can no more,
Doe ftuffe the place, or others hopes fhut out ;
Who, doubting to ouertake thofe gone before,
Giue vp their care, and caft no more about :
And fo in fcorne, leaue all as fore poffeft,
And will be none, where they may not be beft. 270

Eu'n like fome empty Creeke, that long hath laine,
  Left or neglected of the Riuer by,
  Whofe fearching fides, pleaf'd with a wandring vaine,
  Finding fome little way that clofe did lie ;
  Steale in at firft, then other ftreames againe
  Second the firft, then more then all fupply ;
Till all the mighty maine hath borne, at laft,
  The glory of his chiefeft powre that way ;
  Plying this newfound pleafant roome fo faft,
  Till all be full, and all be at a ftay :   280
  And then about, and backe againe doth caft,
  Leauing that full to fall another way :
So fares this hum'rous world, that euermore
  Rapt with the current of a prefent courfe,
  Runnes into that which lay contemn'd before :
  Then glutted, leaues the fame, and falles t'a worfe :
  Now Zeale holdes all, no life but to adore,
  Then cold in fpirit, and faith is of no force.
Strait, all that holy was, vnhallowed lies,
  The fcattred carcaffes of ruin'd vowes :   290
  Then Truth is falfe, and now hath Blindneffe eies,
  Then Zeale trufts all, now fcarcely what it knowes :
  That euermore, to foolifh or to wife,
  It fatall is to be feduc'd with fhowes.
Sacred Religion, mother of Forme and Feare,
  How gorgeoufly fometimes doft thou fit deckt ?
  What pompous veftures doe we make thee weare ?
  What ftately piles we prodigall erect ?
  How fweet perfum'd thou art, how fhining cleare ?
  How folemnely obferu'd, with what refpect ?   300

l. 280, 'folempnly' 1601 ; l. 289, misprinted 'vnhollowed.'

Another time, all plaine, all quite thread-bare,
    Thou muſt haue all within, and nought without ;
    Sit poorely without light, difrob'd, no care
    Of outward grace, to amuze the poore deuout ;
    Powreleſſe, vnfollowed, fcarcely men can fpare
    The neceſſary rites to fet thee out.
Either Truth, Goodneſſe, Vertue are not ſtill
    The felfefame which they are, and alwayes one,
    But alter to the proieɕt of our will,
    Or we, our aɕtions make them waite vpon,   310
    Putting them in the liuery of our ſkill,
    And caſt them off againe when we haue done.
You mightie Lords, that with refpeɕted grace
    Doe at the ſterne of faire example ſtand,
    And all the body of this populace
    Guide with the turning of your hand ;
    Keepe a right courfe, beare vp from all difgrace,
    Obferue the poynt of glory to our land :
Hold vp difgraced knowledge from the ground,
    Keepe Vertue in requeſt, giue Worth her due,   320
    Let not Negleɕt with barbarous meanes confound
    So faire a good, to bring in night anew.
    Be not, O be not acceſſary found
    Vnto her death, that muſt giue life to you.
Where will you haue your vertuous name fafe laide ?
    In gorgeous Tombes, in facred Cels fecure ?
    Doe you not fee thofe proſtate heapes betraide
    Your fathers bones, and could not keep them fure ?
    And will you truſt deceitfull ſtones faire laide,
    And thinke they will be to your honour truer ?   330

l. 327,—' prostrate.'

No, no, vnſparing Time will proudly ſend
  A warrant vnto Wrath ; that with one frowne
  Will all theſe mock'ries of Vaine-glory rend,
  And make them, as before, vngrac'd, vnknowne ;
  Poore idle honours that can ill defend
  Your memories, that cannot keepe their owne.
And whereto ſerue that wondrous *Trophei* now,
  That on the goodly Plaine neere *Wilton* ſtands ?
  That huge dumbe heape, that cannot tell vs how,
  Nor what, nor whence it is, nor with whoſe hands, 340
  Nor for whoſe glory, it was ſet to ſhew
  How much our pride mocks that of other lands ?
Whereon, whenas the gazing paſſenger
  Hath greedy lookt with admiration,
  And faine would know his birth, and what he were,
  How there erected, and how long agone :
  Enquires, and aſkes his fellow traueller,
  What he hath heard, and his opinion :
And he knowes nothing.   Then he turnes againe,
  And lookes, and ſighs, and then admires afreſh, 350
  And in himſelfe with ſorrow doth complaine
  The miſery of darke Forgetfulneſſe :
  Angry with Time that nothing ſhould remaine
  Our greateſt wonders wonder, to expreſſe.
Then Ignorance, with fabulous diſcourſe,
  Robbing faire Arte and Cunning of their right,
  Tels, how thoſe ſtones, were by the Deuils force,
  From *Affrike* brought to *Ireland* in a night,
  And thence, to *Britannie*, by Magicke courſe,
  From Gyants hands redeem'd, by *Merlins* ſleight. 360
And then neere *Ambri* plac'd, in memorie
  Of all thoſe noble Britons murthered there,

By *Hengift* and his Saxon trecherie,
Comming to parlee in peace at vnaware.
With this old Legend then Credulitie
Holdes her content, and clofes vp her care :
But is Antiquitie fo great a liar ?
   Or, doe her yonger fonnes her age abufe,
   Seeing after-commers ftill, fo apt t'admire
   The graue authoritie that fhe doth vfe,   370
   That reuerence and Refpect dares not require
   Proofe of her deedes, or once her words refufe ?
Yet wrong they did vs, to prefume fo far,
   Vpon our eafie credit and delight :
   For, once found falfe, they ftrait became to mar
   Our faith, and their owne reputation quite,
   That now her truths hardly beleeued are :
   And though fh'auouch the right, fhe fcarce hath right.
And as for thee, thou huge and mighty frame,
   That ftands corrupted fo with times defpight,   380
   And giu'ft falfe euidence, againft their fame
   That fet thee there, to teftifie their right ;
   And art become a Traitour to their name
   That trufted thee with all the beft they might.
Thou fhalt ftand ftill belide, and flaundered,
   The onely gazing-ftocke of Ignorance ; ·
   And by thy guile, the wife admonifhed,
   Shall neuer more defire fuch heapes t'aduance ;
   Nor truft their liuing glory with the dead
   That cannot fpeake, but leaue their fame to Chance :
Confidering in how fmall a roome doe lie,   391
   And yet lie fafe, as frefh as if aliue,
   All thofe great worthies of antiquitie ;
   Which long foreliu'd thee, and fhall long furuiue ;

Who ftronger tombes found for Eternitie,
Then could the powres of all the earth contriue.
Where they remaine thefe trifles to obraid
    Out of the reach of Spoyle, and way of Rage ;
    Though Time with all his power of yeeres hath laid
    Long batterie, back'd with vndermining Age,   400
    Yet they make head, onely with their owne aide
    And warre, with his all-conquering forces, wage.
Pleading the Heau'ns prefcription to be free,
And t'haue a grant, t'indure as long as hee.

Philocofmus.

BEholde how euery man, drawne with delight
    Of what he doth, flatters him in his way ;
    Striuing to make his courfe feeme onely right
    Doth his owne reft, and his owne thoughts betray :
    Imagination bringing brauely dight,   410
    Her pleafing Images in beft aray.
With flattering glaffes that muft fhew him faire,
    And others foule : his fkill and wit beft,
    Others feduc'd, deceiu'd and wrong in their :
    His knowledge right, all ignorant the reft.
    Not feeing how thefe Minions in the aire
    Prefent a face of things falfely expreft,
    And that the glimmering of thefe errours fhowne,
    Are but a light, to let him fee his owne.
Alas poore Fame, in what a narrow roome,   420
    As an incaged Parrot art thou pent
    Here amongft vs, where, euen as good be dombe
    As fpeake, and to be heard with no attent ?
    How can you promife of the time to come,
    Whenas the prefent are fo negligent ?

Is this the walke of all your wide renowne,
    This litle Point, this fcarce difcerned Ile,
    Thruft from the world, with whom our fpeech vnknowne
    Made neuer any traffike of our Stile?
    And in this All, where all this care is fhowne,   430
    T'inchant your fame to laft fo long a while?
    And for that happier tongues haue wonne fo much,
    Thinke you to make your barbarous language fuch?
Poore narrow limits for fo mightie paines,
    That cannot promife any forraine vent :
    And yet, if here, to all, your wondrous vaines
    Were generally knowne, it might content :
    But loe, how many reades not, or difdaines
    The labour of the chiefe and excellent?
How many thoufands neuer heard the name   440
    Of *Sidney*, or of *Spencer*, or their Bookes?
    And yet braue fellowes, and prefume of Fame,
    And feeme to beare downe all the world with lookes?
    What then fhall they expeɛt of meaner frame,
    On whofe indeuours few or none fcarce lookes?
Doe you not fee thefe Pamphlets, Libels and Rymes,
    Thefe ftrange confufed tumults of the minde,
    Are growne to be the fickneffe of thefe times,
    The great difeafe inflicted on mankinde?
    Your Vertues by your Follies made your crimes, 450
    Haue iffue with your indifcretion ioyn'd.
Schooles, Artes, Profeffions, all in fo great ftore,
    Paffe the proportion of the prefent ftate ;
    Where, being as great a number as before,
    And fewer roomes them to accommodate :
    It cannot be but they muft throng the more,
    And kick, and thruft, and fhoulder with Debate.

For when the greater wits cannot attaine
   Th'expected good, which they account their right,
   And yet perceiue others to reape that gaine   460
   Of farre inferiour vertues in their fight :
   They prefent, with the fharpe of Enuie, ftraine
   To wound them with reproches and defpight :
   And for thefe cannot haue as well as they,
   They fcorne their faith fhould deigne to looke that way.
Hence, difcontented Sects and Schifmes arife,
   Hence interwounding Controuerfies fpring,
   That feede the Simple, and offend the Wife,
   Who know the confequence of cauelling
   Difgrace, that thefe to others doe deuife :   470
   Contempt and Scorne on all in th'end doth bring,
   Like fcolding wiues, reckning each others fault,
   Make ftanders-by imagine both are naught.
For when to thefe rare dainties, time admits
   All commers, all complexions, all that will,
   Where none fhould be let in but choifeft wits,
   Whofe milde difcretion could comport with fkill :
   For when the place their humour neither fits,
   Nor they the place, who can expect but ill ?
For being vnapt for what they tooke in hand,   480
   And for aught els whereto they fhall b'addreft,
   They eu'n become th'incumbrance of the land,
   As out of ranke, difordring all the reft :
   This grace of theirs, to feeme to vnderftand,
   Marres all their grace, to doe, without their reft.
Men finde, that action is another thing,
   Then what they in difcourfing papers reade :
   The worlds affaires require in managing,
   More Artes then thofe wherein you Clerkes proceede:

Whilſt timorous Knowledge ſtands conſidering, 490
Audacious Ignorance hath done the deede ;
For who knowes moſt, the more he knowes to doubt;
The leaſt diſcourſe is commonly moſt ſtout;
This ſweet inchaunting Knowledge turnes you cleene
Out from the fields of naturall delight,
And makes you hide, vnwilling to be ſeene
In th'open concourſe of a publike ſight :
This ſkill, wherewith you haue ſo cunning beene,
Vnſinues all your powres, vnmans you quite.
Publike ſocietie and commerce of men   500
Require another grace, another port :
This Eloquence, theſe Rymes, theſe Phraſes then,
Begot in ſhades, doe ſerue vs in no ſort ;
Th'vnmateriall ſwelling of your Pen
Touch not the ſpirit that action doth import :
A manly ſtile, fitted to manly eares
Beſt grees with wit ; not that which goes ſo gay,
And commonly the gawdy liu'ry weares
Of nice Corruptions, which the times doe ſway,
And waites on th'humour of his pulſe that beares 510
His paſſions ſet to ſuch a pleaſing kay :
Such dainties ſerue onely for ſtomackes weake;
For men doe fowleſt, when they fineſt ſpeake.
Yet doe I not diſlike that in ſome wiſe
Be ſung, the great heroicall deſerts,
Of braue renowned ſpirits; whoſe exerciſe
Of worthy deeds may call vp others hearts,
And ſerue a modell for poſterities,
To faſhion them fit for like glorious parts :
But ſo, that all our ſpirits may tend hereto,   520
To make it, not our grace, to ſay, but do.

Muſophilus.

MVch thou haſt ſaid, and willingly I heare,
  As one that am not ſo poſſeſt with Loue
Of what I doe, but that I rather beare
  An eare to learne, then a tongue to diſproue :
  I know men muſt, as carried in their ſpheare,
  According to their proper motions, moue.
  And that courſe likes them beſt which they are on,
  Yet Truth hath certaine bounds, but Falſhood none.
I doe confeſſe our limits are but ſmall,   531
  Compar'd with all the whole vaſte earth beſide;
  All which, againe, rated to that great All,
  Is likewiſe as a poynt, ſcarcely deſcride :
  So that in theſe reſpects, we may this call,
  A poynt but of a poynt, where we abide.
But if we ſhall deſcend from that high ſtand
  Of ouer-looking Contemplation,
  And caſt our thoughts, but to, and not beyond
  This ſpacious circuit which we tread vpon ;   540
  We then may eſtimate our mighty land,
  A world, within a world ſtanding alone.
Where, if our fame confind cannot get out,
  What, ſhall we imagine it is pen'd,
  That hath ſo great a world to walke about,
  Whoſe bounds with her reports haue both one end ?
  Why ſhall we not rather eſteeme her ſtout,
  That farther then her owne ſcorne to extend ?
Where being ſo large a roome, both to doe well,
  And eke to heare th'applauſe of things well done, 550
  That farther, if men ſhall our vertues tell,
  We haue more mouthes, but not more merit won ;

It doth not greater make that which is laudable,
The flame is bigger blowne, the fire all one.
And for the few that onely lend their eare,
    That few, is all the world ; which with a few
    Doe euer liue, and moue, and worke, and ftirre.
    This is the heart doth feele and onely know
    The reft of all, that onely bodies beare,
    Rowle vp and downe, and fill vp but the row.   560
And ferues as others members, not their owne,
    The inftruments of thofe that doe direct.
    Then what difgrace is this, not to be knowne
    To thofe know not to giue themfelues refpect ?
    And though they fwell with pompe of folly blowne,
    They liue vngrac'd, and die but in Neglect.
And for my part, if onely one allow
    The care my labouring fpirits take in this,
    He is to me a Theater large enow,
    And his applaufe onely fufficient is :   570
    All my refpect is bent but to his brow,
    That is my All ; and all I am, is his.
And if fome worthy fpirits be pleafed too,
    It fhall more comfort breede, but not more will.
    But what if none ? It cannot yet vndoo
    The loue I beare vnto this holy fkill :
    This is the thing that I was borne to doo,
    This is my Scene, this part muft I fulfill.
Let thofe that know not breath, efteeme of winde,
    And fet t'a vulgar ayre their feruile fong ;   580
    Rating their goodneffe by the praife they find,
    Making their worth on others fits belong;
    As Vertue were the hireling of the minde,
    And could not liue if Fame had ne'r a tong.

Hath that all-knowing powre that holdes within
  The goodly profpe&iue of all this frame,
  (Where, whatfoeuer is, or what hath bin,
  Refle&s a certaine image of the fame)
  No inward pleafures to delight her in,
  But fhe muft gad to feeke an almes of Fame?   590
Muft fhe, like to a wanton Curtezan,
  Open her brefts for fhew, to winne her praife ;
  And blaze her faire bright beauty vnto man
  As if fhe were enamour'd of his wayes,
  And knew not Weakeneffe, nor could rightly fcan
  To what defe&s his hum'rous breath obayes ?
She that can tell, how proud Ambition
  Is but a Beggar, and hath nought at all,
  But what is giu'n of meere Deuotion :
  For which, how much it fweats, how much it's thrall ?
  What toyle it takes, and yet, when all is done,   601
  Th'endes in expe&ation neuer fall ;
Shall fhe ioyne hands with fuch a feruile mate,
  And proftrate her faire body, to commit
  Folly with earth, and to defile that ftate
  Of cleereneffe, for fo groffe a benefit ?
  Hauing Reward dwelling within her gate,
  And Glory of her owne to furnifh it :
Her felfe, a recompence fufficient
  Vnto her felfe, to giue her owne content.   610
  I'ft not enough, that fhe hath raif'd fo hie,
  Thofe that be hers, that they may fit and fee
  The earth below them, and this All to lie
  Vnder their view, taking the true degree
  Of the iuft height of fwolne Mortalitie,
  Right as it is, not as it feemes to be ?

And vndeceiued with the Paralax
  Of a miftaking eye of paffion, know
  By thefe mafk'd outfides what the inward lackes ;
  Meaf'ring man by himfelfe, not by his fhow ;   620
  Wondering not at their rich and golden backes,
  That haue poore mindes and little elfe to fhew :
Nor taking that for them which well they fee
  Is not of them, but rather is their loade :
  The lies of Fortune, wherewithall men be
  Deemed within, when they be all abroade :   [knee,
  Whofe ground, whofe graffe, whofe earth haue cap and
  Which they fuppofe, is on themfelues beftow'd.
And thinke like *Ifis* Affe, all Honours are
  Giuen vnto them alone, the which are done   630
  Vnto the painted Idoll which they beare,
  That onely makes them to be gazed on :
  For take away their packe, and fhew them bare,
  And fee what beft this Honour rides vpon.
Hath Knowledge lent to hers the priuy kay,'
  To let them in vnto the higheft Stage
  Of Caufes, Secrets, Counfels, to furuay
  The wits of men, their hearts, their colds, their rage,
  That build, deftroy, praife, hate, fay and gainefay,
  Beleeue and vnbeleeue, all in one age.   640
And fhall we truft goodneffe as it proceedes
  From that vnconftant mouth, which with one breath
  Will make it bad againe vnleffe it feedes
  The prefent humour that it fauoureth ?
  Shall we efteeme and reckon how it heedes
  Our workes, that his owne vowes vnhalloweth ?
Then whereto ferues it to haue bin inlarg'd
  With this free manumiffion of the mind,

If for all that, we ftill continue charg'd
With thofe difcou'red errors which we finde ?　650
As if our knowledge onely were difcharg'd,
Yet we our felues ftaid in a feruile kinde.
That Vertue muft be out of countenance,
　If this groffe fpirit, or that weake fhallow braine,
　Or this nice wit, or that diftemperance,
　Neglect, diftafte, vncomprehend, difdaine ;
　When fuch ficke eyes can neuer caft a glance,
　But through the colours of their proper ftaine.
Though, I muft needes confeffe, the fmall refpect,
　That thefe great-feeming beft of men doe giue,　660
　(Whofe brow begets th'inferior forts neglect,)
　Might moue the weake irrefolute to grieue :
　But ftronger, fee how iuftly this defect
　Hath ouertooke the times wherein we liue :
That Learning needs muft runne the common fate
　Of all things elfe, thruft on by her owne weight,
　Comporting not her felfe in her eftate
　Vnder this burthen of a felfe conceit :
　Our owne diffentious hands opening the gate
　Vnto Contempt, that on our quarrels waite,　670
Difcou'red haue our inward gouernement,
　And let in hard opinion to Difgrace
　The generall, for fome weake impotent
　That beare out their difeafe with a ftolne face ;
　Who (filly foules) the more wit they haue fpent,
　The leffe they fhew'd, not bettring their bad cafe.
And fee how foone this rowling world can take
　Aduantage for her diffolution,
　Faine to get loofe from this withholding ftake
　Of ciuill Science and Difcretion :　　　680

How glad it would runne wilde, that it might make
One formeleffe forme of one confufion ?
Like tyrant *Ottomans* blindefolded ftate,
  Which muft know nothing more, but to obay :
  For this, feekes greedy Ignorance t'abate
  Our number, order, liuing, forme and fway :
  For this, it practifes to diffipate
  Th'vnfheltred troupes, till all be made away.
For, fince our Fathers finnes pull'd firft to ground
  The pale of their diffeuered dignitie,   690
  And ouerthrew that holy reuerent bound
  That parted learning and the Laiety,
  And laid all flat in common, to confound
  The honour and refpect of Pietie :
It did fo much invile the eftimate
  Of th'opened and inuulgar'd myfteries,
  Which now reduc'd vnto the bafeft rate,
  Muft waite vpon the *Norman* fubtilties,
  Who (being mounted vp into their ftate)
  Doe beft with wrangling rudeneffe fympathize.   700
And yet, though now fet quite behinde the traine
  Of vulgar fway (and light of powre weigh'd light)
  Yet would this giddy innouation faine
  Downe with it lower, to abafe it quite :
  And thofe poore remnants that doe yet remaine
  The fpoyled markes of their diuided right :
They wholly would deface to leaue no face
  Of reuerent Diftinction and Degree,
  As if they weigh'd no diffrence in this cafe,
  Betwixt Religions Age and Infancie :   710
  Where th'one muft creepe, th'other ftand with grace,
  Left turn'd to a child it ouerturned be.

Though to pull backe th'on-running ſtate of things,
  (Gath'ring corruption, as it gathers dayes)
  Vnto the forme of their firſt orderings,
  Is the beſt meanes that diſſolution ſtayes,
  And to goe forward, backward, right, men brings,
  T'obſerue the line from whence they tooke their wayes.
Yet being once gone wide, and the right way
  Not leuell to the times condition :   720
  To alter courſe, may bring men more aſtray,
  And leauing what was knowne to light on none ;
  Since eu'ry change the reuerence doth decay,
  Of that which alway ſhould continue one.
For this is that cloſe kept *Palladium*
  Which once remoou'd, brings ruine euermore :
  This ſtir'd, makes men fore-ſetled, to become
  Curious, to know what was beleeu'd before :
  Whilſt Faith diſputes that vſed to be dombe,
  And more men ſtriue to talke, then to adore.   730
For ſleuer head-ſtrong Reformation will
  Reſt, till to th'extreame oppoſite it runne,
  And ouer-runne the meane diſtruſted ſtill,
  As being too neare of kinne, to that men ſhunne :
  For good, and bad, and all, muſt be one ill,
  When once there is another truth begunne.
So hard it is an euen hand to beare,
  In tamp'ring with ſuch maladies as theſe ;
  Left that our forward paſſions launce too neare,
  And make the cure proue worſe then the diſeaſe: 740
  For with the worſt we will not ſpare the beſt,
  Becauſe it growes with that, which doth diſpleaſe :
And faults are eaſier lookt in, then redreſt :
  Men running with ſuch eager violence,

At the firſt view of errours freſh in queſt ;
As they, to rid an inconuenience,
Sticke not to raiſe a miſchiefe in the ſteed,
Which after mocks their weake improuidence :
And therefore doe make not your owne ſides bleed
To pricke at others : you that would amend   750
By pulling downe, and thinke you can proceed,
By going backe vnto the farther end,
Let ſtand that little Couert left behinde,
Whereon your ſuccours and reſpeéts depend.
And bring not downe the prizes of the minde,
With vnder-rating of your ſelues ſo baſe :
You that the mighties doores doe crooching find,
To ſell your ſelues to buy a little grace,
Or waite whole months to out-bid Symonie,
For that, which being got, is not your place :   760
For if it were, what needed you to buy
What was your due; your thirſting ſhewes your ſhift,
And little worth that ſeekes iniuriouſly
A worthier from his lawfull roome to lift ?
We cannot ſay, that you were then prefer'd,
But that your money was, or ſome worſe gift.
O ſcattring gath'rers, that without regard
Of times to come, will to be made, vndo
As if you were the laſt of men, prepar'd
To bury in your graues all other to.   770
Dare you prophane that holy portion
Which neuer ſacrilegious hand durſt do ?
Did forme-eſtabliſhing Deuotion,
To maintaine a reſpeétiue reuerence
Extend her bountifull prouiſion,
With ſuch a charitable prouidence,

For your deforming hands to diffipate,
And make Gods due, your impious expence?
No maruell then, though th'ouerpeſtred State
 Want roome for goodneſſe, if our little hold 780
 Be leſned vnto ſuch a narrow rate,
 That Reuerence cannot ſit, fit as it ſhould :
And yet what neede we thus for roomes complaine,
 That ſhall not want voyde roomes if this courſe hold?
And more then will be fill'd ; for who will ſtraine
 To get an empty title, to betray
 His hopes, and trauell for an honour vaine,
 And gaine a Port, without ſupport or ſtay?
 What neede hath Enuy to maligne their ſtate,
 That will themſelues, ſo kind, giue it away? 790
This makes indeede our number paſſe the rate
 Of our prouiſions : which, if dealt aright,
 Would yeeld ſufficient roome t'accommodate,
 More then we haue in places requiſite.
 The ill diſpoſing onely doth vs ſet
 In diſaray, and out of order quite.
Whiles other guifts then of the minde ſhall get
 Vnder our colours, that which is our dues,
 And to our trauels, neither benefit,
Nor grace, nor honour, nor reſpeƈt accrewes : 800
 The ſickneſſe of the States foule, Learning, then
 The bodies great diſtemprature inſues.
For if that Learnings roomes to learned men
 Were as their heretage diſtributed,
 All this diſordred thruſt would ceaſe : for when
 The fit were call'd, th'vnworthy fruſtrated,
 Theſe would b'aſham'd to ſeeke, thoſe to b'vnſought,
 And ſtay'ng their turne, were ſure they ſhould be ſped.

Then would our drooping Academies, brought
  Againe in heart, regaine that reuerend hand   810
  Of loft Opinion, and no more be thought,
  Th'vnneceffary furnifh of the land,
  Nor difcourag'd with their fmall efteeme,
  Confuf'd, irrefolute and wauering ftand :
Caring not to become profound, but feeme
  Contented with a fuperficiall fkill ;
  Which for a fleight reward enough they deeme,
  When th'one fucceedes as well as th'other will :
  Seeing fhorter wayes leade fooner to their end,
  And others longer trauels thriue fo ill.   820
Then would they onely labour to extend
  Their now vnfearching fpirit beyond thefe bounds
  Of others powres ; wherein they muft be pend,
  As if there were befides, no other grounds :
  And fet their bolde *Plus vltra* farre without
  The pillers of thofe Axioms Age propounds :
Difcou'ring daily more and more about,
  In that immenfe and boundleffe Ocean
  Of Natures riches ; neuer yet found out,
  Nor fore-clof'd, with the wit of any man.   830
  So farre beyond the ordinary courfe
  That other vninduftrious Ages ran,
That thefe more curious times, they might diuorce
  From the opinion they are linckt vnto
  Of our difable and vnactiue force,
  To fhew true knowledge can both fpeake and do :
  Arm'd for the fharpe, which in thefe dayes they finde,
  With all prouifions that belong thereto :
That their Experience may not come behinde
  The times conceipt, but leading in their place,   840

May make men fee the weapons of the minde
Are States beft ftrengths, and kingdomes chiefeft grace;
And roomes of charge, charg'd full with worth and
    praife,
Makes Maieftie appeare with her full face,
Shining with all her beames, with all her raies,
    Vnfcanted of her parts, vnfhadowed
    In any darkened poynt; which ftill bewrayes
    The wane of Powre, when powr's vnfurnifhed,
    And hath not all thofe intire complements
    Wherewith the State fhould for her ftate be fped. 850
And though the fortune of fome age confents
    Vnto a thoufand errours groffely wrought,
    Which flourifht ouer with their faire euents,
    Haue paft for currant, and good courfes thought :
    The leaft whereof, in other times againe
    Moft dang'rous inconueniences haue brought,
Whilft to the times, not to mens wits pertaine,
    The good fucceffes of ill manag'd deedes :
    Though th'ignorant deceiued with colours vaine,
    Miffe of the caufes whence this lucke proceedes. 860
    Forraine defeЄts giuing home-faults the way,
    Make eu'n that weakeneffe fometimes well fucceedes.
I grant, that fome vnlettred praЄtique may
    (Leauing beyond the *Alpes*, Faith and RefpeЄt
    To God and man) with impious cunning, fway
    The courfes fore-begunne with like effeЄt,
    And without ftop, maintaine the turning on,
    And haue his errours deem'd without defeЄt :
But when fome powerfull oppofition,
    Shall, with a found incountring fhocke, difioynt 870
    The fore-contriued frame, and thereupon,

Th'experience of the prefent difappoynt,
And other ftirring fpirits, and other hearts
Built-huge, for action, meeting in a poynt :
Shall driue the world to fommon all their Artes,
And all too little for fo reall might,
When no aduantages of weaker parts
Shall beare out fhallow councels from the light :
And this fence-opening action (which doth hate
Vnmanly craft) fhall looke to haue her right.   880
Who then holdes vp the glory of the State
(Which letred armes, and armed letters won)
Who fhall be fitteft to negotiate,
Contemn'd *Iuftinian*, or elfe *Littleton* ?
When it fhall not be held wifedome to be
Priuately made, and publikely vndone :
But found defignes that iudgement fhall decree
Out of a true difcerne, of the cleere wayes
That lie direct, with fafe-going Equitie ;
Imbroyling not their owne and others dayes.   890
Extending forth their prouidence, beyond
The circuit of their owne particular :
That eu'n the ignorant may vnderftand,
How that deceit is but a cauillar ;
And true vnto it felfe can neuer ftand,
But ftill muft with her owne conclufions warre.
Can Truth and Honeftie, wherein confifts
The right, repofe on earth ? the fureft ground
Of Truft, come weaker arm'd into the lifts,
Then Fraud or Vice, that doth it felfe confound ?   900
Or fhall Prefumption that doth what it lifts,
Not what it ought, carry her courfes found ?
Then, what fafe place out of confufion

Hath plaine proceeding Honeſtie to dwell?
What ſute of grace hath Vertue to put on,
   If Vice ſhall weare as good, and doe as well?
   If Wrong, if Craft, if Indiſcretion,
   Act as faire parts, with ends as laudable?
   Which all this mighty volume of euents,
   The world, the vniuerſall map of deedes   910
Strongly controwles, and proues from all diſcents,
   That the directeſt courſes beſt ſucceedes
   When Craft, wrapt ſtill in many comberments
   With all her cunning thriues not, though it ſpeedes.
   For, ſhould not graue and learn'd Experience
   That lookes with th'eyes of all the world beſide,
And with all ages holdes intelligence,
   Goe ſafer then Deceit without a guide?
   Which in the by-paths of her diffidence
   Croſſing the waies of Right, ſtill runs more wide: 920
   Who will not grant? and therefore this obſerue,
   No ſtate ſtands ſure, but on the grounds of Right,
Of Vertue, Knowledge, Iudgement to preſerue,
   And all the powres of Learning requiſite:
   Though other ſhifts a preſent turne may ſerue,
   Yet in the tryall they will weigh too light.
   And doe not thou contemne this ſwelling tide
   And ſtreame of words, that now doth riſe ſo hie
Aboue the vſuall bankes, and ſpreads ſo wide
   Ouer the borders of Antiquitie: 930
   Which I confeſſe comes euer amplifide
   With th'abounding humours that doe multiplie:
   And is with that ſame hand of happineſſe
   Inlarg'd, as vices are out of their bands:
Yet ſo, as if let out but to redreſſe,

And calme, and fway th'affeċtions it commands :
Which as it ftirres, it doth againe repreffe
And brings in, th'out-gone malice that withftands.
Powre aboue powres, O heauenly Eloquence,
That with the ftrong reine of commanding words, 940
Doft manage, guide, and mafter th'eminence
Of mens affeċtions, more then all their fwords :
Shall we not offer to thy Excellence,
The richeft treafure that our wit affords ?
Thou that canft doe much more with one poore pen
Then all the powres of Princes can effeċt :
And draw, diuert, difpofe and fafhion men
Better then force or rigour can direċt :
Should we this ornament of Glory then
As th'vnmateriall fruits of fhades, negleċt ? 950
Or fhould we careleffe, come behinde the reft
In powre of words, that goe before in worth,
Whenas our accents equall to the beft,
Is able greater wonders to bring forth :
When all that euer hotter fpirits expreft,
Comes bettred by the patience of the North.
And who, in time, knowes whither we may vent
The treafure of our tongue, to what ftrange fhores
This gaine of our beft glory fhall be fent,
T'inrich vnknowing Nations with our ftores ? 960
What worlds in th'yet vnformed Occident
May come refin'd with th'accents that are ours ?
Or, who can tell for what great worke in hand
The greatneffe of our ftile is now ordain'd ?
What powrs it fhall bring in, what fpirits command,
What thoughts let out, what humours keepe reftrain'd,
What mifchiefe it may powrefully withftand,

And what faire ends may thereby be attain'd.
And as for Poefie (mother of this force)
That breedes, brings forth, and nourifhes this might,
Teaching it in a loofe, yet meafured courfe,　　　　971
　　With comely motions how to goe vpright :
　　And foftring it with bountifull difcourfe,
　　Adornes it thus in fafhions of delight,
　　What fhould I fay ? fince it is well approu'd
　　The fpeech of heauen, with whom they haue commerce;
That onely feeme out of themfelues remou'd,
　　And doe with more then humane fkills conuerfe :
　　Thofe numbers wherewith heau'n and earth are mou'd,
　　Shew, weakeneffe fpeakes in Profe, but powre in Verfe.
　　Wherein thou likewife feemeft to allow,　　　　981
　　That th'acts of worthy men fhould be preferu'd :
As in the holieft Tombes we can beftow
　　Vpon their glory that haue well deferu'd,
　　Wherein thou doft no other Vertue fhow,
　　Then what moft barbrous Countries haue obferu'd :
　　When all the happieft Nations hitherto
　　Did with no leffer glory fpeake, then do.
Now to what elfe thy malice fhall obiect,
　　For Schooles, and Artes, and their neceffitie :　　990
　　When from my Lord, whofe iudgement muft direct,
　　And forme, and fafhion my abilitie,
　　I fhall haue got more ftrength ; thou fhalt expect
　　Out of my better leafure, my reply.

FINIS.

IX.

OCCASIONAL POEMS

FROM

VARIOUS SOURCES.

1593—1607.

NOTE.

The sources of these scattered Poems are recorded in their places. See on them our 'Memorial-Introduction II.—Critical' in closing volume.

A. B. G.

OCCASIONAL POEMS.

An Ode.[1]

OW each creature ioyes the other,
    paſſing happy dayes and howers ;
One Bird reports vnto another,
    in the fall of ſiluer ſhowers ;
Whilſt the earth (our common mother)
    hath her boſome deckt with flowers.

Whilſt the greateſt Torch of heauen,
    with bright rayes warmes FLORAS lap,   10
Making nights and dayes both euen,
    chearing plants with freſher ſap :
My field of flowers quite bereuen,
    wants refreſh of better hap.

ECCHO, daughter of the Aire,
    (babling gueſt of Rocks and hils,)
Knows the name of my fierce Faire,
    and ſounds the accents of my ils.
Each thing pitties my diſpaire,
    whilſt that ſhe her Louer kils.   20

[1] Appeared originally in 1592 'Delia,' [1], [2].

Whilſt that ſhe (O cruell Mayd)
　　doth me and my true loue deſpiſe ;
My liues floriſh is decayed,
　　that depended on her eyes :
But her will muſt be obeyed,
　　and well he ends for loue who dies.

A Paſtorall.[1]

O Happy golden Age,
　　Not for that Riuers ranne
With ſtreames of milke, and hunny dropt from trees ;
Not that the earth did gage　　　　　　　　　31
Vnto the huſband-man
Her voluntary fruites, free without fees :
Not for no cold did freeze,
Nor any cloud beguile,
Th'eternall flowring Spring
Wherein liu'd euery thing,
And whereon th'heauens perpetually did ſmile ;
Not for no ſhip had brought
From forraine ſhores, or warres or wares ill ſought. 40
But onely for that name,
That Idle name of wind :
That Idoll of deceit, that empty found
Call'd HONOR, which became
The tyran of the minde,
And ſo torments our Nature without ground ;
Was not yet vainly found :
Nor yet ſad griefes imparts

---

[1] Appeared originally in 1592 'Delia,' [1] [2],

Amidſt the ſweet delights
Of ioyfull amorous wights.   50
Nor were his hard lawes knowne to free-borne
    hearts.
But golden lawes like theſe
Which nature wrote. *That's lawfull which doth pleaſe.*
Then amongſt flowres and ſprings
    Making delightfull ſport,
Sate Louers without conflict, without flame ;
And Nymphs and ſhepheards ſings,
    Mixing in wanton ſort
Whiſp'rings with Songs, then kiſſes with the ſame
Which from affection came :   60
    The naked virgin then
    Her Roſes freſh reueales,
Which now her vaile conceales :
    The tender Apples in her boſome ſeene.
    And oft in Riuers cleere
The Louers with their Loues conſorting were.
HONOR, thou firſt didſt cloſe
    The ſpring of all delight :
Denying water to the amorous thirſt
Thou taught'ſt faire eyes to loſe   70
    The glory of their light ;
Reſtrain'd from men, and on themſelues reuerſt.
Thou in a lawne didſt firſt
    Thoſe golden haires incaſe,
    Late ſpred vnto the wind ;
Thou mad'ſt looſe grace vnkind,
Gau'ſt bridle to their words, art to their pace.
    O Honour it is thou
That mak'ſt that ſtealth, which loue doth free allow.

It is thy worke that brings 80
  Our griefes, and torments thus :
  But thou fierce Lord of Nature and of Loue,
  The quallifier of Kings,
  What doeſt thou here with vs
  That are below thy power, ſhut from aboue ?
  Goe and from vs remoue,
  Trouble the mighties ſleepe,
  Let vs negleéted, baſe,
  Liue ſtill without thy grace,
  And th'vſe of th'ancient happy ages keepe : 90
  Let's loue : this life of ours
  Can make no truce with time that all deuours.

    Let's loue : the ſun doth ſet, and riſe againe,
    But whenas our ſhort light
    Comes once to ſet, it makes eternall night.

A Defcription of Beauty, tranflated out of Marino.[1]

1

Beauty (beames, nay flame
  Of that great lampe of light)
That fhines a while, with fame,
  But prefently makes night :
  Like Winters fhort-liu'd bright,
  Or Summers fuddaine gleames,
  How much more deare, fo much
    loffe-lafting beames.

2

Wing'd Loue away doth flye,
  And with it time doth beare ;
And both take fuddainly
  The fweate, the faine, the deare :
  A fhining day, and cleare,
  Succeedes an obfcene night,
  And forrow is the hewe of fweet delight.

3

With what then doft thou fwell,
  O youth of new-borne day ?
Wherein doth thy pride dwell
  O beauty made of clay ?

[1] First appeared in 4to of 1623.

Not with to fwift away
The headlong corrant flyes,
As do the fparkling rayes of two faire eyes.

4

Do not thy felfe betray
VVith wantonizing yeares :
O beauty, traytors gay,
Thy melting life that weares,
Appearing, difappeares,
And with thy flying dayes,
Ends all thy good of price, thy faire of prayfe.

5

Truft not, vaine creditor
Thy apt deceiued view,
In thy falfe counfellor,
That neuer tels thee true :
Thy forme, and flattred hew,
Which fhall fo foone tranfpaffe,
Is farre more faire, then is thy looking-glaffe.

6

Inioy thy Aprill now,
Whilft it doth freely fhine ;
This lightning flafh and fhow,
With that cleare fpirit of thine,
Will fuddainly decline ;
And thou faire murthering eyes
Shalbe loues tombes, where now his cradle lyes.

7

Old trembling age will come,
   With wrinkled cheekes, and ftaines,
   With motion troublefome,
   With fkinne and bloodleffe veines,
   That liuely vifage reauen,
   And made deform'd and old,
Hates fight of glaffe, it lou'd fo to behold.

8

Thy gold, and fcarlet fhall
   Pale filuer colour bee,
   Thy rowe of pearles fhall fall
   Like withred leaues from tree ;
   And thou fhalt fhortly fee
   Thy face and haire to grow
All plough'd with furrowes, ouer-fowne with fnow.

9

That which on *Flora's* breft,
   All frefh and flourifhing,
   Aurora newly dreft,
   Saw in her dawning fpring ;
   Quite dry and languifhing
   Depriu'd of honour quite,
Day-clofing *Hefperus* beholds at night.

10

Faire is the Lilly, faire
   The Rofe, of flowers the eye ;
   Both wither in the ayre,

Their beautious colours die ;
And fo at length fhall lye
Depriu'd of former grace,
The lillies of thy brefts, the rofes of thy face.

I I

What then wilt it auaile,
O youth aduifed ill,
In lap of beauty fraile
To nurfe a way-ward will ;
Like fnake in funne-warme hill?
Plucke, plucke, betime thy flower,
That fprings, and parcheth in one fhort howre.

To the *Angell Spirit* of the *moſt* ex-
cellent, Sʳ. Phillip Sidney.[1]

O the pure Spirit, to thee alone addreſt
Is this ioynt worke, by double intriſt
 thine ;
Thine by his owne, and what is done
 of mine
Infpir'd by thee, thy fecret powre
 impreſt.   [combine
My Muſe with thine, it ſelfe dar'd to
As mortall ſtaffe with that which is diuine :
Let thy faire beames giue luſter to the reſt.

That Iſraels King may daygne his owne transform'd
In ſubſtance no, but ſuperficiall tire :   11
And Engliſh guiſ'd in ſome ſort may afpire
To better grace thee what the vulgar form'd :
His ſacred Tones, age after age admire.
Nations grow great in pride, and pure deſire
So to excell in holy rites perform'd.

O had that ſoule which honour brought to reſt
To ſoone not leaft, and reaft the world of all
What man could ſhew, which we perfeċtion call ;
This precious peece had ſorted with the beſt.   20
But ah ! wide feſtred wounds that neuer ſhall
Nor muſt be cloſ'd, vnto freſh bleeding fall :
Ah memory, what needs this new arriſt.

¹ First appeared in 4to of 1623—query for Sidney's ' Pſalmes.' See
' Memorial-Introduction II.—Critical ' in closing volume.

Yet bleſſed griefe, that ſweetnes can impart
Since thou art bleſt.   Wrongly do I complaine ;
What euer weights my heauy thoughts ſuſtaine
Deere feeles my ſoule for thee.   I know my part,
Nor be my weaknes to thy rites a ſtaine ;
Rites to aright, life bloud would not refraine :
Aſſiſt me then, that life what thine did part.   30

Time may bring forth, what time hath yet ſuppreſt,
In whom, thy loſſe hath layd to vtter waſt
The wracke of time, vntimely all defac't,
Remayning as the tombe of life diſceaſt :
VVhere, in my heart the higheſt roome thou haſt ;
There, truly there, thy earthly being is plac't :
Triumph of death, in life how more then bleſt.

Behold ! O that thou were now to behold,
This finiſht long perfections part begun ;
The reſt but peic'd, as leaſt by thee vndone ;   40
Pardon bleſt ſoule, preſumption ouerbold :
If loue and zeale hath to this error run
Tis zealous loue, loue that hath neuer dun,
Nor can enough, though iuſtly here contrould.

But ſince it hath no other ſcope to go,
Nor other purpoſe but to honour thee,
That thine may ſhine, where all the graces be ;
And that my thoughts (like ſmalleſt ſtreames that flow,
Pay to their ſea, their tributary fee)
Do ſtriue, yet haue no meanes to quit nor free,   50
That mighty debt of infinits I owe.

To thy great worth which time to times inroule
VVonder of men, fole borne, foule of thy kind
Compleat in all, but heauenly was thy mind,
For wifdome, goodnes, fweetnes, faireft foule :
To good to wifh, to faire for earth, refin'd
For Heauen, where all true glory refts confin'd :
And where but there no life without controule.

O when from this accompt, this caft-vp fomme,
This reckning made the Audit of my woe,   60
Some time of rafe my fwelling paffions know,
How work my thoughts, my fenfe, is ftriken dombe
That would the more then words could euer fhew ;
Which all fall fhort.   Who knew thee beft do know
There liues no wit that may thy prayer become.

And reft faire monuments of thy faire fame,
Though not complete.   Nor can we reach, in thought,
What on that goodly peece, time would haue wrought.
Had diuers fo fpar'd that life (but life) to frame
The reft : alas fuch loffe the world hath nought   70
Can equall it, nor O more grieuance brought,
Yet what remaines muft euer crowne thy name.

    Receiue thefe Hims, thefe obfequies receiue,
    (If any marke of thy fecret fpirit thou beare)
    Made only thine, and no name els muft weare.
    I can no more deare foule, I take my leaue,
    My forrow ftriues to mount the higheft Sphere.

Vliſſes and the Syren.[1]

Syren.   Come worthy Greeke, *Vliſſes* come
　　　　Poſſeſſe theſe ſhores with me :
　　　　The windes and Seas are troubleſome,
　　　　And heere we may be free.
　　　　　　Here may we ſit, and view their toile
　　　　That trauaile on the deepe,
　　　　And ioy the day in mirth the while,
　　　　And ſpend the night in ſleepe.

Vlis.　Faire Nimph, if fame, or honor were　　　10
　　　　To be atteynd with eaſe,
　　　　Then would I come and reſt with thee,
　　　　And leaue ſuch toyles as theſe.
　　　　　　But here it dwels, and here muſt I
　　　　With danger ſeeke it forth :
　　　　To ſpend the time luxuriouſly
　　　　Becomes not men of worth.

Syr.　*Vliſſes*, O be not deceiu'd
　　　　With that vnreall name :
　　　　This honour is a thing conceiu'd,　　　　20
　　　　And reſts on others fame.
　　　　　　Begotten onely to moleſt
　　　　Our peace, and to beguile
　　　　(The beſt thing of our life) our reſt,
　　　　And giue vs vp to toile.

[1] From " Certaine Small Poems Lately Printed : with the
　　Tragedie of Philotas.　Written by Samvel Daniel.
　　　At London.　Printed by *G. Eld* for *Simon Waterſon* 1605 (12mo),"
also in 1607, 1611, etc., but not in 4to of 1623.　　　G.

Vlis. Delicious Nimph, fuppofe there were
Nor honour, nor report,
Yet manlines would fcorne to weare
The time in idle fport.
    For toyle doth giue a better touch,   30
To make vs feele our ioy :
And eafe finds tedioufneffe as much
As labour yeelds annoy.

Syr. Then pleafure likewife feemes the fhore
Whereto tends all your toyle,
Which you forgo to make it more,
And perifh oft the while.
    Who may difporte them diuerfly,
Finde neuer tedious day,
And eafe may haue varietie,   40
As well as action may.

Vlis. But natures of the nobleft frame,
Thefe toyles, and dangers pleafe,
And they take comfort in the fame,
As much as you in eafe.
    And with the thoughts of actions paft
Are . . . . reuealed ftill ;
When pleafure leaues a touch at laft,
To fhew that it was ill.

Syr. That doth opinion onely caufe,   50
That's out of cuftome bred,
Which makes vs many other lawes
Then euer Nature did.
    No widdowes waile for our delights,
Our fportes are without bloud,
The world we fee by warlike wights,
Receiues more hurt then goud.

Vlis.   But yet the ftate of things require
          Thefe motions of vnreft,
          And thefe great Sports of high defire,   60
          Seeme borne to turne them beft.
                To purge the mifchiefes that increafe
          And all good order mar :
          For oft we fee a wicked peace,
          To be well chang'd for war.

Syr.   Well, well *Vliffes* then I fee
          I fhall not haue thee heare,
          And therefore I will come to thee,
          And take my fortunes there.
                I muft be wonne that cannot win,   70
          Yet loft were I not wonne :
          For beauty hath created bin,
          T'vndoo, or be vndonne.

⁂ " *The paſſion of a diſtreſſed man, who being in a tempeſt on the Sea, and hauing in his Boate two Women, of whom, he loued the one that diſdained him, and ſcorned the other who affeſted him, was by commandement from* Neptune, *to caſt out one of them, to appeaſe the rage of the tempeſt, but which, was referred to his owne choice.*"—Prefixed to this poem in the folio of 1602 is the following short letter :—

" To Edward Seymour   10
Earle of Hertford :

Concerning his queſtion of a diſtreſſed
man in a Boate vpon the Seas.

Noble Lord, the iudgements of
men, as euer according to the
ſet of their affeſtions, and as
the images of their paſſions are
drawn within, ſo they ſend forth the
forme of their opinions : and accordingly
muſt I iudge of this caſe (which your 20
Honour hath moued vnto me) as my ſelfe
do ſtand looking thorow the proſpeſtiue
of min owne imagination, that onely
takes meaſure of other mens paſſions by
that itſelfe feeles. Referring the ſame to
the better cenſure of your honour,
Who ſhall euer commaund me,
     Samvel Daniel." 28

Y vnkinde Loue, or fhe that loues me
     deare,
Neptune will haue caft forth to calme
     the Seas.
One of thefe two, or all muft perifh
     here :
And therefore now, which fhall I
     faue of thefe ?
  Ah ! doe I make a queftion which to faue,
When my defires fhare but one onely part !
Who fhould it be but fhe to whom I haue
Refign'd my life, and facrific'd my hart ?
She, fhe muft liue, the tempefts of whofe brow
Confound me more then all thefe ftormes can doo,   10
And but for whom I liue :   And therefore how
Can any life be life, leffe fhe liue too ?
For by that meanes I both may pacifie
The rigour of thefe waues, and her hard heart,
Who muft faue him who would not let her die :
Nor can fhe but reward fo great defert.
     She cannot, but in mercy needes muft giue
     Comfort to him, by whom her felfe doth liue.

Pars altera.

B Vt fhall the bloud of her that loues me then   20
     Be facrifiz'd to her difdainefulneffe
That fcornes my loue ? and fhall I hope to win
Mercie from her, by being mercileffe ?

Will not her fafety being thus attain'd,
Raife her proude heart t'a higher fet of fcorne,
When fhe fhall fee my paffions are diftain'd
With bloud, although it were to ferue her turne ?
Since th'act of ill, though it fall good to vs,
Makes vs yet hate the doer of the fame :
And though my hand fhould haue preferu'd her thus, 30
Yet being by cruèll meanes, it is my fhame ;
Which fhe will but afcribe to my defects,
And th'imperfections of my paffions ; which
She knowes the influence of her eyes effects,
And therein ioyes t'haue vanquifht me fo much.
And when defert fhall feeme t'exact reward,
It breedes a loathing in the heart of Grace ;
That muft worke free out of her owne regard,
And haue no dues t'obraid her to her face.
So fhall I then haue bent againft my foule   40
Both her difdaine, and th'horror of that deed ;
Which euer muft my crueltie controule,
And checke the wrong that neuer can fucceed.
And though it be requir'd that one muft go,
By meffage fent me from the powrs Diuine,
Yet will I not redeeme my fafety fo ;
Though life be in their hand, death is in mine.
    And therefore fince compaffion cannot be
    Cruell to either, *Neptune* take all three.

Refumptio.   50

BVt that were to be cruell to all three,
    Rebell to Nature, and the gods arreft,
Whofe ordinances muft obferued be ;
Nor may our frailty with the heauens conteft.

Why then that muſt be done that's leaſt vniuſt,
And my affeꞔtions may not beare a part
With crueltie and wrong.   But here I muſt
Be of a ſide, to goe againſt my hart,
   And her diſdaine her due reward muſt haue :
   She muſt be caſt away that would not ſaue.   60

S. D.

Of William Jones, his "Nennio 1595."

*H Ere doſt thou bring (my friend) a ſtranger borne
        To be indenized with vs, and made our owne,*
Nobilitie ; *whoſe name indeed is worne
By manie that are great, or mightie growne :
    But yet to him moſt natural, beſt knowne,
To whom thou dooſt thy labours ſacrifize,
And in whom al thoſe vertues beſt are ſhowne
Which here this little volume doth comprize.*
    Wheron when he ſhall caſt his worthie eies,   10
*He here ſhal glaſſe himſelfe, himſelfe ſhal reed :
The modell of his owne perfeĉtions lies
Here plaine deſcrib'd, which he preſents indeed :
    So that if men can not true worth diſcerne
    By this diſcourſe, looke they on him and learne.*

Sa. Danyel.

l. 6, the person meant is " Robert Devreux [*sic*], Earle of Essex and Ewe, Vicount of Hereford, Lord Ferrer of Chartley," etc., to whom Wm. Jones dedicates *Nennio*. This Sonnet follows Ed. Spenser's "Who ſo wil feeke by right deferts t'attaine," etc., and precedes George Chapman's Sonnet, "Accept thrice Noble *Nennio* at his hand," etc.   G.

From "Penelopes Complaint : Or, A Mirrour
for wanton Minions. Taken out of Homer's
'Odiſſea,' and written in English Verſe. By
Peter Colfe, 1596" appended to "Willobie's Auiſa"
(Dr. Grosart's "OCCASIONAL ISSUES," 1880).

Amico ſuo chariſſimo P. C.—S. D.

O Vid quærit titulos, quid dotes iaɛ̃tat Auiſa.
  Anne ea Penelope eſt æquiparanda tuæ ?
Penelope clara eſt, veneranda, fidelis : Auiſa
  obſcura, obſcuro fœmina nata loco.   10
Penelope ſatrapæ eſt coniux illuſtris : Auiſa
  coniux cauponis, filia pandochei.
Penelope caſta eſt cum ſponſus abeſſet : Auiſa
  caſta ſuo ſponſo noɛ̃te diéque domi.
Penelopeia annos bis denos manſit : Auiſa
  tot (vix credo) dies intemerata foret.
Penelopeia procos centum neglexit : Auiſa
  Vix ſeptem pretium ſuſtinuit precem,
Penelope neuit, penſum confecit : Auiſæ
  laſſauit nunquam pendula tela manus.   20
Penelope Graijs, Latijs celebratur : Auiſæ
  vnus homo laudes, nomen, & aɛ̃ta canit.
Ergo Penelope vigeat, cantetur : Auiſa
  nullo Penelope eſt æquiualenda modo.

TRANSLATION (from Introduction to Willobie's *Avisa*, pp. xxv-vi).

To his most dear friend P. C.—S. D.[1]

WHy seeks she titles, boasts she riches, why—
Avisa ?
Is she with thy Penelope to vie ?
The one renowned, revered, true to her own : Avisa
An unknown woman from a place unknown.
The one spouse of a prince of glorious name : Avisa
Child of an innkeeper, wife of the same.   10
The one is chaste, her husband being away : Avisa
Chaste when he is at home, by night and day.
The one through twice ten years strong to endure :
Avisa
Through scarce as many days could be kept pure.
The one to a hundred lords refused her hand : Avisa
The force and prayers of seven could scarce withstand.
The one would spin until her task was done : Avisa
Ne'er tired the spinning-wheel with what she spun.
The one to the Greeks and Romans praise : Avisa
Has but one man her name and fame to raise.   20
Long live Penelope and flourish fair : Avisa
May never with Penelope compare.

[1] As in Introduction *supra*, I doubt if the S. D. represent our Daniel ; still others think so, and it isn't impossible.

From " Il Paſtor Fido ; or The Faithfull
Shepheard." Translated out of Italian into
English. 1602.

To the right worthy and
learned Knight, ... Syr *Edward
Dymock,* Champion to her Maieſtie, concerning
this tranſlation of *Paſtor Fido.*

I Do reioyce learned and worthy Knight,
That by the hand of thy kinde Country-man
(This painfull and induſtrious Gentleman)   10
Thy deare eſteem'd Guarini *comes to light :*
Who in thy loue I know tooke great delight
As thou in his, who now in England can
Speake as good Engliſh as Italian,
And here enioyes the grace of his owne right.
Though I remember he hath oft imbaſ'd
Vnto us both the vertues of the North,
Saying, our coſtes were with no meaſures grac'd,
Nor barbarous tongues could any verſe bring forth.
I would he ſawe his owne, or knew our ſtore,   20
Whoſe ſpirits can yeeld as much, and if not more.

                                        Sam. Daniell.

From "BARTAS his Deuine WEEKES & Workes." Tranflated by Iofuah Syluester, 1605.

To my good friend,
M. Syluefter, *in honour of this
facred Worke.*

THus to aduenture forth, and re-conuay
　　The beft of treafures, from a Forraine Coaft,
And take that wealth wherin they gloriɇd moft,
And make it Ours by fuch a gallant pray,
And that without in-iuftice ; doth bewray　　　　　10
　　The glory of the Worke, that we may boaft
　　Much to haue wonne, and others nothing loft
By taking fuch a famous prize away.
As thou induftrious SYLVESTER haft wrought,
　　And heere enritch'd vs with th'immortall ftore
　　Of others facred lines : which from them brought
Comes by thy taking greater then before :
　　So haft thou lighted from a flame deuout,
　　As great a flame, that neuer fhall goe out.

Samuel Daniel. 20

From Clement Edmundes (Remembrancer of the Cittie of London): his "Obferuations vpon Cæfars Comentaries, 1609."

To my friend, Maifter Clement Edmonds.

WHo thus extraſts, with more then Chymique Art,
　　The fpirit of Bookes, fhewes the true way to
　　finde
Th'Elixer that our leaden Parts conuart
Into the golden Metall of the Minde.
　Who thus obferues in fuch materiall kinde
The certaine Motions of hie Practifes,　　　　　　10
Knowes on what Center th'Aſtions of Mankinde
Turne in their courfe, and fees their fatalnes.
　And hee that can make thefe obferuances,
Muſt be aboue his Booke, more then his Pen.
For, wee may be affur'd, hee men can gheffe,
That thus doth Cæsar knowe ; the Man of men.
　Whofe Work, improu'd here to our greater gaine,
　Makes Cæsar more then Cæsar to containe.

Sam. Danyell. 19

From " Queen Anna's New World of Words,"
etc. Collected by John Florio. 1611.

To my deare friend and brother *M. Iohn Florio,*
one of the Gentlemen of hir Maiefties Royall
Priuy-chamber.

I Stand not to giue praife before the face
    Of this great worke, that doth it felfe commend:
But to congratulate the good and grace
    That England com's thereby to apprehend:
And in hir name to thanke your induftry   10
    Laborius Flório, *who haue fo much wrought*
To honour hir in bringing Italy
    To fpeake hir language, and to giue hir note
Of all the treafure that rich tongue containes:
    Wherein I cannot but admire your paines
In gathering vp this vniuerfall ftore,
    And furniture of words for euery arte,
And fkill of man: So that there feem's no more
    Beyond this fearch, that knowledge can impart.
Which being a worke which would take vp the powers 20
    Of more then one whole man, I wonder how
You could fubtract fo many ferious howres
    From that great fumme of feruice that you owe.
But that it feemes the beaming Gracefulneffe
    That lightens from the moft refulgent QVEENE
Our facred Miftris, work's that ableneffe
    As mak's you more, then els you could haue beene.
Wherein the power of Princes well is feene
    That can infufe fuch force, and make age greene.

And it were well, if in this feafon, when 　　　30
　　They leaue erecting Churches, Colledges,
And pious monuments, they would build men
　　Who of their glory may be witneffes,
And what they doe be theirs : As Mazons raife
　　Work's not jor them, but for their mafters praife.
For, would they but be plef'd to know, how fmall
　　A portion of that ouer-flowing wafte
Which run's from them, would turne the wheeles and all
　　The frame of wit, to make their glory laft :
I thinke they would doe fomething : but the ftirre 　　40
　　Still about greatneffe, giues it not the fpace
To looke out from it felfe, or to conferre
　　Grace but by chance, and as men are in place.
But that concern's not me, It is ynow
　　I doe applaud your worke.　Thus from my Plow.

Samuel Daniel.

From John Florio's 1613 edition of his " Done into Englifh " Essayes written in French by Michael Lord of Montaigne.

To my deare brother and friend M. IOHN FLORIO,
one of the Gentlemen of hir Maiefties moft
Royall Priuie Chamber.

B Ooks, like *fuperfluous humors bred with eafe*
   So ftuffe the world, as it becomes oppreft
With taking more than it can well digeft ;
And now are turn'd to be a great difeafe.   10
For by this ouercharging we confound
The appetite of fkill they had before :
There be'ng no end of words, nor any bound
Set to conceit the Ocean without fhore.
As if man laboured with himfelfe to be
As infinite in writing, as intents ;
And draw his manifold vncertaintie
In any fhape that paffion reprefents :
That thefe innumerable images
And figures of opinion and difcourfe   20
Draw'n out in leaues, may be the witneffes
Of our defeCts much rather than our force.
And this proud frame of our prefumption,
This Babel *of our fkill, this* Towre *of wit,*
Seemes only checkt with the confufion
Of our miftakings that diffolueth it.

And well may make vs of our knowledge doubt,
Seeing what vncertainties wee build vpon,
To be as weake within booke as without ;
Or els that truth hath other ſhapes then one.   30
    But yet although wee labor with this ſtore
And with the preſſe of writings ſeeme oppreſt,
And haue to many bookes, yet want wee more,
Feeling great dearth and ſcarceneſſe of the beſt ;
Which caſt in choiſer ſhapes haue bin produc'd,
To giue the beſt proportions to the minde
Of our confuſion, and haue introduc'd
The likelieſt images frailtie can finde.
And wherein moſt the ſkill-deſiring ſoule
Takes her delight, the beſt of all delight ;   40
And where her motions eueneſt come to rowle
About this doubtfull center of the right.
    Which to diſcouer this great Potentate,
This Prince Montaigne *(if he be not more)*
Hath more aduentur'd of his owne eſtate
Than euer man did of himſelfe before :
And hath made ſuch bold ſallies out vpon
Cuſtome : *the mightie tyrant of the earth,*
In whoſe Seraglio *of ſubiection*
Wee all ſeeme bred-vp, from our tender birth ;   50
As I admire his powres, and out of loue,
Here at his gate do ſtand, and glad I ſtand
So neere to him whom I do ſo much loue,
T'applaude his happie ſetling in our land :
And ſafe tranſpaſſage by his ſtudious care
Who both of him and vs doth merit much,
Hauing as ſumptuouſly, as he is rare
Plac'd him in the beſt lodging of our ſpeach.

And made him now as free, as if borne here,
And as well ours as theirs, who may be proud 60
That he is theirs, though he be euery where
To haue the franchife of his worth allow'd.
  It be'ing the proportion of a happie Pen,
Not to b'inuaffal'd to one Monarchie,
But dwell with all the better world of men,
Whofe fpirits all are of one communitie ;
Whom neither Ocean, Defarts, Rockes *nor* Sands
Can keepe from th'intertraffique of the minde,
But that it vents her treafure in all lands,
And doth a moft fecure commercement finde. 70
  Wrap Excellencie *vp neuer fo much,*
In Hierogliphicques, Ciphers, Caraƈters,
And let her fpeake neuer fo ftrange a fpeach,
Her Genius *yet finds apt difcipherers :*
And neuer was fhe borne to dye obfcure,
But guided by the ftarres of her owne grace,
Makes her owne fortune, and is euer fure
In mans beft hold, to hold the ftrongeft place.
  And let the Critick *fay the worft he can,* 80
He cannot fay but that Montaigne *yet,*
Yeeldes moft rich pieces and extraƈts of man ;
Though in a troubled frame confuf'dly fet.
Which yet h'is bleft that he hath euer feene,
And therefore as a gueft in gratefulneffe,
For the great good the houfe yeelds him within,
Might fpare to taxe th'vnapt conuayances.
But this breath hurts not, for both worke and frame,
Whilft England English *fpeakes, is of that ftore*
And that choyfe ftuffe, as that without the fame 90
The richeft librarie can be but poore.

And they vnbleſt who letters doe profeſſe
And haue him not : whoſe owne fate beates their want
With more ſound blowes, then Alcibiades
Did his Pedante that did Homer *want.*

By Sam. Daniel one of the Gentlemen
extraordinarie of hir Maiefties moſt
royall priuie Chamber.   98

Concerning the honor of bookes.[1]

S Ince Honor from the Honorer proceeds,
How well do they deſerue that memorie
And leaue in bookes for all poſterities
The names of worthyes, and their vertuous deedes
When all their glorie els, like water weedes
Without their element, preſently dyes,
And all their greatnes quite forgotten lyes :
And when, and how they floriſht no man heedes.
How poore remembrances, are ſtatutes, Toomes 10
And other monuments that men erect
To Princes, which remaine in cloſed roomes
Where but a few behold them ; in reſpect
Of Bookes, that to the vniuerſall eye
Shew how they liu'd, the other where they lye.

[1] This Sonnet in 1613 edn. (not 1603) immediately follows the preceding poem, and though it has no signature, seems to belong to Daniel. G.

From "The Effayes, of Morall Politike and
Millitarie Difcourfes of Lo: Michaell de Montaigne,
Kn*, 1603 edition."[1]

To my deere friend M. *Iohn Florio*, concerning
his tranflation of Montaigne.

B Ookes the amaffe of humors, fwolne with eafe,
　　The Griefe of peace, the maladie of reft ;
So ftuffe the world, falne into this difeafe,
As it receiues more then it can digeft :
And doe fo ouercharge, as they confound　　　　　10
The apetite of fkill with idle ftore :
There being no end of words, nor any bound
Set to conceipt, the Ocean *without fhore.*
　　As if man labor'd with himfelfe to be
As infinite in words, as in intents,
And drawe his manifold incertaintie
In eu'ry figure, paffion reprefents ;
That thefe inuumerable vifages
And ftrange fhapes of opinions and difcourfe
Shadowed in leaues, may be the witneffes　　　　　20
Rather of our defeets, then of our force.
And this proud frame of our prefumption,
This Babel *of our fkill, this* Towre *of wit,*
Seemes onely checkt with the confufion
Of our miftakings, that diffolueth it.

---

[1] The re-casting of this poem for 1613 edn., or ten years later, seems to
call for the reproduction separately of its original form.　　　　　G

And well may make vs of our knowledge doubt,
Seeing what vncertainties we build vpon,
To be as weake within booke as without ;
Or els that truth hath other ſhapes then one.
  But yet although we labor with this ſtore   30
And with the preſſe of writings ſeeme oppreſt,
And haue too many bookes, yet want we more,
Feeling great dearth and ſcarſeneſſe of the beſt ;
Which caſt in choiſer ſhapes haue bin produc'd,
To giue the beſt proportions to the minde
Of our confuſion, and haue introduc'd
The likelieſt images frailtie can finde.
And wherein moſt the ſkill-deſiring ſoule
Takes her delight, the beſt of all delight ;
And where her motions eueneſt come to rowle   40
About this doubtfull center of the right.
  Which to diſcouer this great Potentate,
This Prince Montaigne *(if he be not more)*
Hath more aduentur'd of his owne eſtate
Then euer man did of himſelfe before :
And hath made ſuch bolde ſallies out vpon
Cuſtome : *the mightie tyrant of the earth,*
In whoſe Seraglio *of ſubiection*
We all ſeeme bred-vp, from our tender birth ;
As I admire his powres, and out of loue,   50
Here at his gate do ſtand ; and glad I ſtand,
So neere to him whom I do ſo much loue,
T'applaude his happie ſetling in our land :
And ſafe tranſpaſſage by his ſtudious care,
Who both of him and vs doth merit much ;
Hauing as ſumptuouſly, as he is rare
Plac'd him in the beſt lodging of our ſpeach,

And made him now as free, as if borne here,
And as well ours as theirs, who may be proud
That he is theirs ; though he be euery where   60
To haue the franchife of his worth allow'd.
   It being the portion of a happie Pen,
Not to b'inuaffal'd to one Monarchie,
But dwell with all the better world of men
Whofe fpirits are all of one communitie.
Whom neither Ocean, *Defarts,* Rockes *nor* Sands
Can keepe from th'intertraffique of the minde,
But that it vents her treafure in all lands,
And doth a moft fecure commercement finde.
   Wrap Excellencie *vp neuer fo much,*   70
In Hierogliphicques, Ciphers, Caracters,
And let her fpeake neuer fo ftrange a fpeach,
Her Genius *yet finds apt difcipherers :*
And neuer was fhe borne to dye obfcure,
But guided by the Starres of her owne grace,
Makes her owne fortune, and is euer fure
In mans beft hold, to hold the ftrongeft place.
   And let the Critic *fay the worft he can,*
He cannot fay but that Montaigne *yet,*
Yeeldes moft rich pieces and extracts of man ;   80
Though in a troubled frame confuf'dly fet.
Which yet t'is bleft that he hath euer feene,
And therefore as a gueft in gratefulneffe,
For the great good the houfe yeelds him within
Might fpare to taxe th'vnapt conuayances.
But this breath hurts not, for both worke and frame,
Whilft England Englifh *fpeakes, is of that ftore*
And that choyfe ftuffe, as that without the fame
The richeft librarie can be but poore.

And they vnbleſt who letters do profeſſe   90
And haue him not : whoſe owne fate beates their want
With more ſound blowes, then Alcibiades
Did his Pedante that did Homer *want.*

SAM. DANYEL.

To the Right Reuerend Father in God,

Iames Montague, Lord Bifhop of *Winchefter*,
Deane of the Chapell, and one of his Maiefties
moft Honorable Priuy Councell.[1]

Lthough you haue out of your proper
ftore
The beft munition that may fortifie
A Noble heart as no man may haue
more,
Againft the batteries of mortality :
Yet reuerend Lord voutfafe me leaue
to bring
One weapon more vnto your furnifhment ;   10
That you the Affaults of this clofe vanquifhing,
And fecret wafting fickneffe may preuent :
For that my felfe haue ftruggled with it too,
And know the worft of all that it can do ;
And let me tell you this you neuer could
Haue found a gentler warring enemy,
And one that with more faire proceeding would
Encounter you without extremity,
Nor giue more time to make refiftances
And to repair your breaches, then will this.   20
For whereas other fickneffes furprize,
Our fpirits at vnawares difweopning fodainely,

All fenfe of vnderftanding in fuch wife,
As that they lay vs dead before we die,
Or fire vs out of our inflamed fort,
With rauing Phrenfies in a fearefull fort ;
 This comes and fteales vs by degrees away ;
And yet not that without our priuity
They rap vs hence, as Vultures do their pray ;
Confounding vs with tortures inftantly.   30
This fairely kills, they fowly murther vs,
Trippe vp our heeles before we can difcerne ;
This giues vs time of treaty to difcus
Our fuffring, and the caufe thereof to learne.
 Befides therewith we oftentimes haue truce
For many months, fometimes for many yeares,
And are permitted to inioy the vfe
Of ftudy, and although our body weares
Our wit remaines ; our fpeach, our memory
Faile not, or come before our felues to die :   40
We part together and we take our leaue
Of friends, of kindred ; we difpofe our ftate,
And yeeld vp fairely what we did receiue
And all our bufineffes accomodate :
So that we cannot fay we were thruft out,
But we depart from hence in quiet fort :
The foe with whom we haue the battaile fought,
Hath not fubdu'd vs but got our Fort,
And this difeafe is held moft incident
To the beft natures and moft innocent.   50
 And therefore reuerend Lord, there cannot be
A gentler paffage then there is hereby,
Vnto that port wherein we fhall be free
From all the ftormes of worldly mifery.

And though it fhow vs dayly in our glaffe,
Our fading leafe turn'd to a yellow hue,
And how it withers as the fap doth paffe,
And what we may exfpect is to infue.
   Yet that I know difquiets not your mind,
Who knowes the brittle mettaile of mankind,   60
And haue all comforts vertue can beget,
And moft the confcience of well acted dayes ;
Which all thofe monuments which you haue fet
On holy ground to your perpetuall praife,
(As things beft fet) muft euer teftifie ;
And fhew the worth of Noble *Montague.*
And fo long as the Walls of Piety
Stand, fo long fhall ftand the memory of you ;
And Bath, and Wells, and Winchefter fhall fhow
Their faire repaires to all Pofterity ;   70
And how much bleft and fortunate they were
That euer Gracious hand did plant you there ;
Befides, you haue not only built vp walls
But alfo (worthier edifices) men ;
By whom you fhall haue the memorialls
And euerlafting honor of the pen
That whenfoeuer you fhall come to make
Your Exit from this Scene wherein you haue
Perform'd fo noble parts, you then fhall take
Your leaue with honor, haue a glorious graue.   80
  " For when can men go better to their reft
  " Then when they are efteem'd and loued beft ? "

SAM. DANIEL.

END OF VOL. I.